NULLIUS

THE ANTHROPOLOGY OF OWNERSHIP, SOVEREIGNTY, AND THE LAW IN INDIA

T0345743

Hau
Books

Director
Anne-Christine Taylor

Editorial Collective
Deborah Durham
Catherine V. Howard
Vita Peacock
Nora Scott
Hylton White

Managing Editor
Nanette Norris

Editorial Officer
Jane Sabherwal

Hau Books are published by the
Society for Ethnographic Theory (SET)

www.haubooks.org

NULLIUS

THE ANTHROPOLOGY OF OWNERSHIP, SOVEREIGNTY, AND THE LAW IN INDIA

Kriti Kapila

Hau Books
Chicago

Cover: Cellular Jail Museum, Port Blair, Andaman and Nicobar Islands, 2007
Photograph: Kriti Kapila

Cover design: Ania Zayco
Layout design: Deepak Sharma, Prepress Plus
Typesetting: Prepress Plus (www.prepressplus.in)

ISBN: 978-1-912808-47-2 (Paperback)
ISBN: 978-1-912808-48-9 (PDF)
ISBN: 978-1-912808-83-0 (eBook)
LCCN: 2021931195

Hau Books
Chicago Distribution Center
11030 S. Langley Ave.
Chicago, Il 60628
www.haubooks.org

Hau Books publications are printed, marketed, and distributed by The University
of Chicago Press.
www.press.uchicago.edu

Printed in the United States of America on acid-free paper.

Contents

Acknowledgements   vii

CHAPTER 1

Nullius: An Introduction   1

CHAPTER 2

The Promise of Law   25

CHAPTER 3

The Truths of Dispossession   49

CHAPTER 4

Terra Nullius: The Territory of Sovereignty   77

CHAPTER 5

Res Nullius: The Properties of Culture   107

CHAPTER 6

Corpus Nullius: The Labor of Sovereignty   129

CHAPTER 7

Coda: The Illusion of Property   155

References   159

Index   185

Acknowledgements

Debts that have made me rich.

For a book that has been so many years in the making, I have ac-cumulated more debts than I will ever be able to repay in this lifetime. Acknowledging these goes a small way to salute those whose presence has deeply enriched my life.

Like all anthropologists, I cannot but acknowledge at the very outset my debt to individuals and families in the village I call Meghla, who welcomed me, tolerated my ignorance, indulged my questions, and gave me love and warmth over these years. You have taught me everything that is contained within these pages and even more beyond. I especially thank Anu Kapur, Baldev Bharsain, Jalandhari Ranaut, Milap Ranaut, Ammaji (*in memoriam*), and all generations of the Kapur-Bharsain clan spread across Chandpur, Kandi, and Gadhiara for so generously sharing copious quantities of time, food, and insight.

The research that makes its way into this book was funded by grants from the Morris Finer Trust (London School of Economics), the Emslie Horniman Anthropological Scholarship Fund (Royal Anthropological Institute), the Charles Wallace India Trust, London School of Econom-ics Staff Research Fund, a British Academy Postdoctoral Fellowship and a British Academy Small Grant, the UK India Education and Research Initiative, and Faculty Personal Research Allowance (King's College London). I duly acknowledge their support.

I also thank staff at several libraries and archives who helped me find my way with recalcitrant catalogues and obscure classifications. These include the National Archives of India and Nehru Memorial Library in New Delhi, the Punjab State Archives in Patiala and Chandigarh, the Himachal Pradesh State Archives in Shimla, the Royal Anthropological Institute, the India Office collections at the British Library in London, and the Anthropological Survey of India in Kolkata and in Port Blair.

Vaidya Ji, Kapil Mandyal, and Rajni Singh made the sub-divisional magistrate's court one of the best and most instructive classrooms I have ever sat in. It is not often that a judge stops mid-sentence while delivering a judgement and opens a separate explanatory conversation on jurisprudence or judicial process, as if in square brackets and mainly for the pedagogical benefit of a visitor. My sincerest thanks to all three for walking a non-lawyer through various legal hoops with immense patience and staggering generosity.

Sunita and Rajesh Nag gave me a roof and lasting ties. But those two years in a picture-postcard village would have been decidedly unidimensional had I not found the friendship of Ashwini Chhatre, Shomona Khanna, and Bambam. A lifelong bond was formed, always ready to come back to life after any number of years in hibernation and pick up seamlessly from where the last conversation was left off. Thank you for the endless rounds of *chai-samosa* and *kadhi-chawal*, and for the precious dial-up internet connection while debating all the mundanity and every one of the excitements with equal fervor.

Conversations, and now long-distance but still long-running WhatsApp chats, with Angus Bowers, Bharati Chaturvedi, Rohit De, Kaveri Gill, Annu Jalais, and Mareike Junge have been life-affirming through the years, as has been having Rosie Gosling, Sridhar Venkatapuram, Anjli Kapoor, Kapil Kapoor, Roahan Kapoor, and Vijay Sawhney in my corner.

Conversations and comradeship with Gregory Delaplace, Stefan Ecks, Rebecca Empson, Tatiana Flessas, Elizabeth Kolsky, Javed Majeed, Andrew Moutu, Lucia Michelutti, Elinor Payne, Norbert Peabody, Alain Pottage, Benedetta Rossi, Mitra Sharafi, Edward Simpson, Bhrigupati Singh, and Stelios Tofaris over the years have made their way into the book in obvious and not-so-obvious ways. My very special thanks are reserved for Nilanjan Sarkar for his magnanimous support and sage advice.

I have been very fortunate to have had wonderful students over the years. I especially thank Abin Thomas, Rahul Advani, Nilanjana Sen, Vignesh Karthik, Nikita Simpson, Helena Fallstrom, Rachel Douglas-Jones, and Sonia Raheja for keeping me on my toes and for providing much joy with your ideas and intellect.

For their collegiality and support at the LSE, Cambridge, and King's, I thank Mauricio Avendano-Pabon, Maurice Bloch, Rudra Chaudhuri, Trudi Darby, Harri Englund, James Gagen, Jonathan Grant, Caroline Humphrey, Archita Jha, Ann Kelly, Sunil Khilnani, Thibaud Marcesse, Sunil Mitra Kumar, Martha Mundy, Yael Navaro, Bree Neale, Jahnavi Phalkey, Srinath Raghavan, Nikolas Rose, Michael Scott, Sarah Somers, and Lyanne Wilde.

Christopher Bayly (*in memoriam*), Anthony Costello, Veena Das, Peter Fitzpatrick (*in memoriam*), Akhil Gupta, Dipankar Gupta, Elizabeth Povinelli, Deborah Swallow, and Patricia Uberoi gave encouragement and support beyond their call of duty. My thanks are also due to Jonathan Parry and Chris Fuller for their engagement with my doctoral research.

Anne-Christine Taylor, John Borneman, Carlos Londono-Sulkin, Michael Lambek, Maria Luisa Nodari, and Enrique Martino became unexpected colleagues and comrades, and it has been an utter joy to work with them. I admire their quiet strength and thank each one of them for coming through these momentous times with patience and dignity. None of it, nor indeed this book, would have been possible without Giovanni da Col. For this unexpected gift of HAU, and for your belief in this book, my gratitude and solidarity.

Luiz Costa, Veena Das, the late Peter Fitzpatrick, Ian Jack, Surinder Jodhka, and Stewart Motha read unpolished versions of these ideas over the years with characteristic generosity. Luiz Costa, Jonathan Parry and Christopher Pinney solved bibliographic puzzles at high speed. My generous thanks to all. Earlier versions of these ideas were presented at conferences and workshops over the years, and I am particularly thankful to the late Chris Bayly, Mario Biagioli, Faisal Devji, Marc Galanter, Javier Lauzan, Lynn Meskell, Rajani Palariwala, Mitra Sharafi, and Anton Schutz for invitations, engagements, and feedback.

The manuscript has hugely benefitted from the sharp but generous reading of the two anonymous reviewers. I thank both of them for their input, which has improved the manuscript immensely. I thank Nanette Norris for creating the index. Catherine Howard's eagle eye ensured a sharper prose. Rustum Kozain's engagement with the text smoothened the rough edges and carefully culled the gremlins. But my biggest thanks are reserved for Hylton White. He has been a great colleague and an even more brilliant editor, with saintly patience and integrity. The book owes much to his close reading, and engaged and generous interventions, which have resulted in a much-improved manuscript. All remaining shortcomings are mine and mine alone.

I offer my most profound thanks to Vincent Dachy, without whose help this book may yet have stayed where it started. Isabelle de Rehyer is a rare energy in this world, and I am very fortunate to have been its beneficiary. A very special thanks go to Catelijne Coopmans for her help with reaching the finishing line.

No citational practice can ever capture all that I have learned and borrowed from Marilyn Strathern, whose intellect and magnanimity remain a constant inspiration and the gold standard. For all that she has shared through her work and for her unwavering support, I owe her the greatest of debts.

For my very own stellar constellation dispersed across continents, that shines bright even when it is a distant flicker: Geetan Batra, Sanjeev Bikhchandani, Maurice Biriotti, Marie-Laure Davenport, Marinos Diamentides, Catherine Fieschi, Ian Jack, Nina Lath, Henrietta Moore, Stewart Motha, Nadira Naipaul, Maja Petrovic-Steger, and Suparna Singh—thank you for your friendship and love.

And finally, the debt of love for which no words, no thanks could ever be commensurate:
To Shruti and Ashish, for being there in the very beginnings of my world.
To Mama, for your incomparable singularity, with immeasurable admiration.
This is for you Papa. For everything, but especially for your love. In *pitrirhinh*.

How terrible it would have been . . . to have lived without even attempting to lay claim to one's portion of the earth; to have lived and died as one had been born, unnecessary and unaccommodated.

– V. S. Naipaul, *A House for Mr Biswas*, 1961

CHAPTER I

Nullius: An Introduction

What is left when something is taken away?

Anthropologists since Marcel Mauss have been fascinated by the *hau* of the gift, by the excess generated in giving, by that which exceeds the actual thing given in gift. This excess is generative of lingering relationality, of amplification or diminution of status, and of prompts that propel movement and exchange. But relatively little attention has been paid to the opposite of the gift—to what happens in the event of taking away. This book explores this obverse, the other excess that is produced in and through dispossession, and the relationality generated in its wake. Specifically, it presents an anthropological account of the dispossessing instincts of the Indian state as sovereignty-making and describes the relations that are created and cast anew in acts of erasure. At the heart of dispossession lies the question of ownership and any understanding of its erasure requires an understanding of owning, having, and holding, as well as what can and cannot be taken away. Who can take one's possessions away? And, when one's possessions are taken away, what indeed is left?

***

"The local vegetable-seller's wife ran away with someone from Kullu two days ago," Ramana announces in a less than hushed tone as she walks up the stairs to my room. This was the first I have heard anything of it

1

and I am somewhat puzzled as to how little interest this development has provoked in this otherwise gossipy corner of the village. It is 1999 and early days in my doctoral research. I naively put the general lack of interest in the elopement as a sign of difference in sexual mores in the village, compared to other places I was more familiar with. "The ideology of marital permanence is not as universally shared in India as it is sometimes assumed to be," I write in my field notes of the day, and then later in a paper that challenges the prevailing understandings of conjugal modernity in scholarship (Kapila 2004). And yet, just a few months later, widespread censure and intrigue—and not indifference—greet Ramana's own sister-in-law's temporary elopement with a lover from a nearby village. My puzzlement from a few months before returns, if now recast. It is not until later that winter, while attending a wedding in the village, that the first pieces of a jigsaw began to take the form of a pattern. But this pattern itself was to become apparent to me only much later.

It was now the first spring of the new millennium, and it was the day Simi was getting married. Her mother, Buglo, was a woman in her forties, and a mother of four. Simi was her first-born. Bursting with kin and neighbors of all ages, the house had a characteristic festive, yet hectic air of a *shadi wala ghar* (a household which had a wedding going on) about it. On the ground floor, some men were arranging things in the courtyard for the evening, while others were catching up with their kin and mates they had not seen in some time. Children of different ages ran about from room to room, their shrill voices colliding with the melodious singing of the women on the first floor. The festivities of the preceding days were reaching a crescendo. It was early afternoon and time to start dressing up for the evening's ceremonies. As the day wore on, the mundane attire of *salwar-kameez* (loose trousers worn with a long shirt) was beginning to give way to the more elaborate *luancharee* (a long, kimono-like skirt). The transformation of appearances was immediate and immense. In keeping with ritual requirements, the only unanointed person left in the house was the bride (Simi) herself. The singing was picking up volume. Suddenly, the bride's mother, Buglo, emerged from the kitchen, dressed in a heavily embellished *luancharee*, carrying what looked like a reasonably heavy sack. She sat down in the middle of the room, with all seven meters of her skirt's chintz flared around her and in one single gesture emptied the contents of the sack onto the freshly painted mud floor. With some jingle-jangle, a few kilos of silver jewelry made its way to the floor. Picking up one ornament at a time, she went through her jewelry, allocating each item a place as she went along: her own body, for her younger daughters, something even for her non-Gaddi sister-in-law, so that she too might "look" adequately Gaddi. At first, the whole process of distribution looked entirely spontaneous and part of the excess that usually marks weddings, largely in those forms of exchange that appear as outside the purview of rigid rules and governed mostly by affective and material extravagance.

"My *bhabhi* (brother's wife) looks excluded from us without her *chirhi* (a distinctive and ornate forehead ornament worn by Gaddi women), so why don't I give her my spare one?" Buglo asked. "These earrings, I think my younger one will look nice in these, or should I give them to her older sister? But this necklace I must keep for myself, well at least till my daughter-in-law arrives..." In the end, there was just a handful of ornaments left on the floor: mainly of a few silver bangles, earrings, and small hair ornaments. This was Simi's share, Buglo's alienated wealth, the mother's gift to her daughter on her wedding day.

As I watched Buglo redistribute her jewelry, I saw clearly what numerous ethnographies had already made abundantly clear: one needed to have things to make relations, and one needed to have relations for things to pass between one and another. Ownership and relations were constitutive of each other. This vignette from the earliest days of my fieldwork among the Gaddis of Kangra, north India sowed the first seeds of my interest in the property question, the puzzle of ownership in contemporary India, and its relationship to different scales at which ordinary life is lived and experienced (Kapila 2003). The Kangra Gaddis, among whom I have conducted my research since 1999, are a pastoralist community who live on either side of the Dhauladhar mountain range in the western Himalaya. Like other communities in India, Gaddis hold a view of property that is as much a product of their own history as it is of the society they are embedded in, as I discuss in detail in the next chapter. Some of their notions, especially of what counts as their *jaid-aad* ("wealth" and "property", used interchangeably) are always explicitly held, even though these do not always coincide with what counts for property under dominant understandings or even within its formal codification under the law. For example, "children"—along with animals— feature easily, early, and prominently in any Gaddi's list of possessions and property, while they are certainly not regarded as property in the law. On the other hand, things such as herding permits or clan goddesses are held in a fundamentally proprietary relation and carry the powerful charge that ownership bestows on the possessor. What one owns allows one to make or amend relations with others, like Buglo's gift of her *chirhi* to her sister-in-law. These exchange relations in turn confirm or bolster one's social viability. What was not clear to me then was the common thread with the two elopements, and the underlying question of the kind of relationality that is forged in the absence of possessions and in the condition of dispossession. The absence or a deficit of these relations could potentially render one invisible or socially irrelevant. Ramana's sister-in-law's elopement was as much a disambiguation from her conjugal ties as it was an abandonment of several cycles of exchange that were threatened with their incompleteness as a result of her having gone missing. What has been readily understood as censure or conservative sexual morality was equally an articulation of this threat and the potential indignity inflicted by this abandonment of relations.

The vegetable seller and his wife on the other hand were already marginal. They were non-Gaddis in a predominantly Gaddi village; they had moved relatively recently from a neighboring valley and had little entanglement other than their small-scale commerce in local relations of exchange. Hence the disappearance of a marginal outsider's wife produced minimal sucking of teeth on the day (if at all), nor any lasting disapproval in any real sense. Cycles of exchange depended on both the things and the relations one had and not having them or being dispossessed (of them) rendered one socially irrelevant, if not altogether invisible.

The Residue of Dispossession

In commonsensical understanding, the capacity to possess or own something is understood primarily in economic terms. The capacity to dispossess, on the other hand, is political. To rupture relationality and cast it anew is a possibility made by power. While bestowing or giving things accrues relational density, dispossessing someone of their possessions creates distance, separation, and accrues power for the dispossessor. This book is about practices of dispossession and the troubled status of ownership in India. Specifically, it is about the dispossession enacted by and as a specific form of power, that of the state, and its consequences for contemporary notions of ownership. This book aims to provide an anthropological reading of the place of property in structuring different scales of relatedness: from kinship-making to a signature of sovereignty-making state practices in India. I approach the question of property not from the vantage point of ownership, but from its other side and so subject dispossession to anthropological scrutiny. I read sovereignty-making dispossession in three different realms—land, persons, and things—against a theological suspicion of accumulation. The book proposes that, although avowedly secular, Indian legal doctrine on property and ownership repeats the theological suspicion and ambivalence around possession and accumulation, making for unique problems that link issues as diverse as indigenous title, museum objects, and contemporary biometrics. What follows is an exploration of proprietary practices in contemporary India that ostensibly lie at the margins of everyday life and at the center of state sovereignty. My aim is to demonstrate, through these marginal exemplifications, the fundamentally constitutive nature of property in state power.

Based on long-term ethnographic fieldwork on the legal question in contemporary India, my objective is to present an *anthropological* reading of property and sovereignty. Instead of taking any of these as a given or as self-evident, in other words, and following Marilyn Strathern (2014: 24), I intend to describe property, sovereignty and state power with and within anthropological terms. For this book it has meant not taking state power and sovereignty as either self-evident or explicable only though categories of political theory. I rely instead on the discipline's conceptual archive to restore to anthropology the state as a "proper object of study" (see Abrams 1988). This is not to wish away the concept of the state, nor then to deem it as lying outside the purview of the discipline. But I listen to an older critique of the anthropology of the state with a new pair of ears, if only to make an even more vigorous case for it. I hope to show that it is possible to study the state within the terms of the discipline. And instead of posing difficulties (Abrams ibid.), such an anthropology proves to be fecund and, *pace* Singh and Guyer (2016), even joyful.

To begin, I read state power and sovereignty not as self-explanatory givens either in their unfolding or in their effects. I step away from the more familiar framework and language of rights and liberty, or then emergency, even as I ask familiar questions about the configuration of asymmetric relationality in daily life in the context of the colonial and postcolonial Indian state. The material presented in this book exemplifies what Navaro has recently described as "negative methodology" (Navaro 2020), since I try to explicate a series of erasures, denials, and nullifications. I do so while not relying on the terms borrowed from liberal political theory that are more routinely deployed by anthropologists studying the state and state power. Even as they present rich ethnographic and sophisticated theoretical accounts, *pace* Akhil Gupta's field-defining paper (1995), of the "blurred boundaries" between the society and the state, many of these works are cast within a Foucauldian mold. This is true of the anthropology of the cognate concept of sovereignty as well, whose career and terms in anthropology have been defined by the wider ascendance and influence of Giorgio Agamben's resurrection of Carl Schmitt's notion of exception. I read these accounts carefully and learn much from them, but part ways with both of these frameworks to work instead with and within the gifts of the discipline.

I provide an anthropology of sovereignty as the foundational and potent expression of state power by bringing to it the disciplinary corpus on predation, gift, and hospitality. These concepts from structural anthropology are usually deployed in the study of Amazonian or Melanesian societies, and more recently to sequester the problem of scale as a question of "ontology".[1] In fact, some of the most trenchant critiques of anthropology in the wake of the "postcolonial turn" were precisely driven by the scalar problem, where scale was seen to have served as a motor for colonial enterprise and sovereignty (modern vs. pre-modern::complex vs. simple). My redescription of state power in India within this conceptual framework brings to the forefront an older discussion on scale within the discipline. My concern here is not comparison (see Candea 2019), and therefore the question of scale does not feature as a question of cultural relativism (see Carrithers et al. 2010). Rather, my reliance on the anthropology of the gift, hospitality, predation, debt, and slavery serves my primary aim, which is to study the relationality transformed by dispossession enacted by the state, and to understand sovereignty-making in and through these transformed relations. After all, sovereignty is also a particular relation between the ruler and the ruled, and the specific mode I study here is the one that is made not in the wake of the capacity of the state to bestow or to give, but in its instinct for dispossessing.

Using analytical frames from "elsewhere" helps to circumvent the risk of what at first may look like a flattening of scale (Strathern 1988b; 1989) and, additionally, to sidestep what Arjun Appadurai (1986) called "gatekeeping concepts" in anthropological theory, where certain regions and concepts become metaphorically and permanently cathected to each

---

1.   There is a growing body of scholarship on the "ontological turn" in anthropology (see, for example, Holbraad and Pedersen 2017; Holbraad, Pedersen and Vivieros de Castro 2014. See also Candea 2019 and Carrithers et al. 2010).

other. To study erasure, denial, and misappropriation through the wider disposition of the Indian state towards ownership allows us to examine the work of property beyond land and territory, and to explore the property in persons and in things. By bringing into view new archives of socio-legal history, I discuss how, at different times, the Indian state has de facto adopted the doctrines of *terra nullius*, *res nullius*, and, finally and controversially, *corpus nullius*. I take up these three doctrinal paradigms of erasure respectively affecting place, persons, and things through which proprietary title has been effaced, denied, or misappropriated by the state. My aim here is to understand how and why the colonial and the postcolonial Indian state may have been able to act thus, not so much to finesse the political theory of sovereignty or then even the socio-legal history of India, but rather to ask: what can anthropological insights on ownership and dispossession illuminate, not only about contemporary Indian society, but also about the anthropology of law and state power more generally?

Property, Law, Freedom

Ownership and property are at the very heart of liberal political theories of the modern state and modern law, as these form the scaffolding and the source of rights and liberty. The state via the order-producing law is seen as the realm of freedom in contradistinction to the state of nature, which is either chaotic or at war, or both. One of the most influential readings of the relationship between freedom, rights, and property is that of G.W.F. Hegel. The chaotic state of nature is central to Hegel's conception of nature as inherently unfree. The state for Hegel is the state of universal freedom (1967: 20). For him, the work of the modern state is to move away from a state of unfreedom to freedom, where the creation of property and ownership become fundamental steps in creating any antithesis to nature (Hegel 1967: 15). He conceptualizes right as the immediate embodiment of freedom as it originates in the will, and the will, he says, is free (1967: 22). Property, including property in oneself, is for Hegel the first *substantive* embodiment of freedom (1967: 38). For Hegel, property can be occupancy (1967: 45), taking possession (1967: 46), and imposing form on something (1967: 47). A final, fourth form of property lies in "merely making as [one's] own" (1967: 48). The idea of property as freedom in Hegel is thus intimately linked to the idea of enclosure (via occupation, or usurpation).

However, from Mauss onwards, anthropologists have been all too aware of the specificity of the Hegelian possessive individual and, instead, through a focus on exchange, the discipline has shown other conceptual and ontological constellations within which notions of ownership cohere. Epistemologically rooted in relationality, anthropology's interest in the property question comes via its mainstay: exchange. Hence the anthropological adage: property is the relationship between persons in relation to things, where neither persons nor things are stable categories, and their stability is won through exchange (Strathern 1989; Pottage 2001; Henare, et al. 2007). It is therefore no surprise that the anthropological corpus on ownership is able to side-step the particularly Hegelian or liberal anchoring of property in freedom and vice versa, which is the dominant way of understanding property in modern law and the statecraft embedded within it. Yet, the anthropology of the state, or even the "everyday state" (see Das 2006; Gupta 1995), remains trapped within liberal political categories of rights, duties, and power as universal *explicantia*. In this book I move away from these categories to ask a different set of questions. I approach the question of ownership and property in and through its nullification: *terra nullius*, or occupation (of other people's land); *res nullius*, or taking possession of (other people's) things; and, *corpus nullius*, the uncompensated and forcible capture of the citizen's laboring body. I do this not to ask what ownership brings with it and what kind of relationality it forges or disrupts, but rather to explore the relationality in forcible dispossession and involuntary loss. If *hau* is the excess produced in giving, what is the excess produced in and through taking? Is sovereignty the obverse of *hau*? Unravelling the puzzle of dispossession in the Indian context reveals that the route to freedom does not lie in ownership, but rather in knowledge and truth. Far from guaranteeing freedom, property and possessions in fact pose as obstacles for the ultimate liberation of the soul.

Indian Apparitions

Ravana asked Siva to give Parvati to him and Siva was forced to grant this wish to Ravana, who was a powerful devotee of his. But as Ravana was carrying Parvati south to Lanka, Visnu took the form of a sage standing by a grove of upside-down trees, their roots in the air. When Ravana stopped to inquire about this strange sight, the sage asked him who he and the lady were. Upon hearing Ravana's answer, the sage said, "Siva gave you *maya* [Illusion] and told you she was his wife." Ravana believed him and went off to a river to meditate in order to get the "real" Parvati, leaving the "false" one behind in the sage's care. As soon as Ravana was gone, Visnu raced away with Parvati, bringing her to Siva.

When Ravana returned to the grove, to find the sage and the goddess missing, he followed the footprints but could not find Parvati, for she was with Siva, who had rendered her invisible to Ravana by a wall of sacred ash. Siva then appeared and gave Ravana a woman that he called the Mayasakti [Illusion of Power, Sakti being a name for the wife of Siva]. Ravana, believing that he now had the real Sakti, Siva's wife, put Maya in his chariot and went to Lanka. On the way, he saw the sage again, this time beside a grove of trees right side up. The sage said, "All this was *maya*. Now you have received a real boon of a beautiful woman; there is no doubt of that." Ravana was content and went to Lanka with the Mayasakti." (O'Flaherty 1984: 93)

In her discussion on the varieties of illusion in Indian mythical thinking, Wendy O'Flaherty defines the specific doctrine of *maya* as "a kind of artistic power [. . .] which indicates a trick, the making of something that is not really there" (1984: 118). For O'Flaherty, *maya* is best translated as "transformation" (ibid). Derived from the same root word in Sanskrit as "mother" (*matr*), *maya* means making something that was not there before and also making something that was there into something that was not really there. O'Flaherty continues: "*Maya* not only deceives people about the things they think they know; more basically, it limits their knowledge to things that are epistemologically and ontologically second-rate." (1984: 119).

One of the significant aspects of *maya* is that, like in the story above, the capacity to create transformations and illusory tricks is vested only in the gods and cannot be earned by either merit or, indeed, knowledge. Thus, even the most devout and the wisest (e.g. Ravana) find themselves unable to discern the state they are in or the truth of their context, thereby inhabiting permanently with and within a second-rate ontology and epistemology. The second-rate epistemology—i.e. the inability to discern between *maya* and reality, as is the case with Ravana in the story above—is aided by the undisputed access and authority to "real" knowledge by the gods, which can itself be misleading (e.g. Vishnu duping Ravana into giving up the real Parvati by making him believe that she is not the real one). The divine ability to trick lesser beings into believing authorized truths therefore works in both directions: it makes the real look unreal or apparitional, and the apparition or the illusion real. This illusory double becomes important to us in unveiling the parallel with the contemporary Indian state.

As the basis for ontology, *maya* is also associated with the (second-rate) worldly or *samsaric* existence, as opposed to the (first-rate) ascetic or *mokshic* life (O'Flaherty 1984). In Hindu mythical thinking then, the householder and the ascetic are staged in opposition to each other. The world as experienced by humans is no more than an illusion, a play created by the divine. The second-rate nature of worldliness is embedded in attachments to things and to fellow beings. The normative cycle of human life moves from a life of kinship and the accumulation of relations to successively abjuring all attachments as it progresses from the stage of the householder to the ascetic. Relations and attachments are obstacles in the way of true knowledge and only in shedding and severing these can one move from *samsaric* to *mokshic* life. The companion concept to the doctrine of *maya* is that of *moh*, or attachment. Often the two come as a pair—*moh-maya*, or sometimes *maya-moh*—whereby the worldly life is characterized by its embeddedness in attachments or relations. While there is a relationship between *moh* (attachment) and knowledge, in that *moh* is seen to be borne from ignorance and therefore carries qualities of delusion, infatuation, and incommensurability with reality, unlike *maya*, one can emerge from it with better or more knowledge.[2] Therefore, relinquishing *moh* is what is prescribed for an individual's progression from the householder stage to that of the renouncer and, finally, the ascetic.[3]

Importantly, these relations of attachment are not just with persons (kin, friends); the concept of *moh-maya* is often used for attachment to accumulation of both relations (kin, persons) and possessions (things). The use of *moh-maya* to describe anyone's state carries a tacit opprobrium or is used pejoratively to signal the underlying assumption that the world of attachments is essentially an illusion (*maya*) and any attachment to either people, things, or indeed wealth embeds one in a life guided by illusion and away from one in pursuit of the truth. *Moh-maya*

---

2. This obfuscation of truth produced by attachment is not simply a problem of "objectivity" in scientific knowledge as outlined by Candea, et al. (2015), not least in terms of the scale of the truth pursued in ascetic and scientific thought.

3. See Veena Das (2014) for an illuminating discussion on the relationship between attachment, everyday ethics and the "problem of reality."

thus connotes a state of disorientation or moral delusion that accompanies the attachment to worldly goods and relations. The *Bhagwad Gita*, for example, famously teaches abandoning the prism of attachment when deciding on the right course of action, among other things. Attachment to persons and accumulation of things are in this sense problematic in the Hindu worldview, in that they impede the progression to knowledge and truth in the ascetic ideal. Thus, truth drives anti-accumulation, which redefines relationality to kin and other persons, to objects and wealth, and the world of action more generally. In this theological framing, anti-accumulation is aimed at producing at first a desired distance and eventually a non-relation between the person and their attachments and possessions.

This normative staging of life has rarely received anthropological attention via a consideration of possessions and ownership. In the literature, *samsaric* life, or the life of relatedness, is usually read through the prism of kinship, whereas the life of the ascetic, or *mokshic* life, is explored through and within the conceptual framework of the anthropology of religious life.[4] Laidlaw (1995), for example, examines the mutually constitutive nature of the pursuit of wealth and renunciation among the Jains, but does not dwell on the *nature* of the danger in possession and attachment. This danger is not like the danger of accumulation discussed in the context of "harnessing fortune"—where too much fortune can ensure misfortune (Empson 2012)—or the danger of excess consumption that spills over as waste (Gygi 2018). Rather, like for the hoarders of domestic objects and things (Newell 2019), accumulation carries a charge that endows a host with a worldly flourishing, while simultaneously posing the necessity to ward off the threat of parasitic excess.[5]

It is my proposition that modern Indian law, especially of property, repeats and replicates this ambivalence towards accumulation, at once safeguarding it and also making it suspect. Denying ownership or possession (coercive anti-accumulation) becomes the mode of accumulation of sovereignty by the state. But the coerced anti-accumulation pursued

---

4. While the literature on Hindu kinship is too vast to cite, on attachment in kinship, see Trawick (1990); on ascetics and asceticism in India, see Kasturi (2009), and Sinha and Saraswati (1978); on warrior ascetics, see Pinch (2006); on the relationship between wealth and renunciation as twin pursuits among the Jains, see Laidlaw (1995).

5. On parasitic hospitality, see Da Col (2012). See also Serres (2007).

by the state and the voluntary anti-accumulation sought by people in ordinary life produce distinctly different results. While the anti-accumulationist ideology underpinning *mokshic* life and directed at relational attachment to persons and things produces distance and detachment, the dispossession instigated by the state is aimed instead at the incorporation of the citizen-subject with ever greater attachment to the polity (Appadurai 1998). Mimicking the submission to the divine truth, anti-accumulation visited by the sovereign state therefore produces coerced proximity and (aggressive) incorporation with itself, rather than voluntary distance and detachment. While the motivation for anti-accumulation of relations and possessions may be to liberate one's soul from the exhausting and never-ending cycle of birth and rebirth into the world of illusion and delusions, what could possibly explain the coercive anti-accumulation instincts of the sovereign?

According to Georges Bataille, "we may call sovereign the enjoyment of possibilities that utility doesn't justify (utility being that whose end is productive activity). Life *beyond utility* is the domain of sovereignty" (1991: 198; emphasis added). Bataille's discussion of sovereignty is particularly illuminating as it rests on the notion of surplus, of excess, as luxurious "nothingness" and non-utility (1991: 207). In many ways, such an understanding runs counter to the Agambenian-Schmittian complex of emergency and bare life, where exception is purposive, and is explicitly aimed at producing order (Agamben 2005; Schmitt 2008). The complex of exception-emergency, like the Foucauldian paradigm of incarceration-discipline, elaborates order-producing curtailment from the perspective of the governed (e.g. killing, incarceration, camp, regulation). Anthropologists have found this framework productive to work with as it can afford the exploration of both state violence and state order, as well as the neighboring Foucauldian concept of disciplinary power (see for example, Bonilla 2017; Das and Poole 2004; Hansen and Stepputat 2005, 2006; Singh 2015). For Bataille, though, sovereignty is rooted not in exception but in excess, and not in curtailment, but in surplus. Sovereignty for Bataille lies in the ability to experience non-purposiveness (1991: 204). He illustrates his notion of sovereignty in the experience of laughter, tears, and miracles, as things that "cannot be the anticipated result of a calculated effort. What is sovereign can only come from the arbitrary, from chance. There ought not exist any *means* by which man might *become* sovereign: it is better for him to *be* sovereign, in which case sovereignty cannot be taken away" (1991: 226; emphases in original). Bataille's focus is the subjective experience of sovereignty. Yet, it is extremely helpful in thinking about sovereignty not as a one-swoop production of an austere condition as in the Agambenian-Schmittian formulation, but rather as an ongoing condition, and one that is rooted in the notions of surplus and excess. It also helps to understand what motors expansive instincts of sovereignty into ever-more realms and its amplification or intensification at different times.

In the chapters that follow, I explore annihilation, erasure, and nullification premised on the creation of a surplus – *extra* territory, *unclaimed* things, *excess* labor. In the realms of *terra*, *res*, and *corpus*, property is swallowed, appropriated, or accumulated by the state from prior, rightful owners not, or not just, as the primal moment of sovereignty, but also through iterative repetition and expansion into ever more realms.[6] This is sovereignty plus-plus, and in the Bataillian sense, beyond utility. The material presented highlights that sovereignty is neither a one-off event, nor finite and indivisible but, rather, that which can be accreted, intensified, and accumulated over time. It acts in time and on it. Under *terra nullius*, the usurpation of territory by the sovereign is accompanied by an erasure of time. The present is made to appear as an "as-if" (*pace* Motha 2018), which extends infinitely into the past as it does into the future, of always having been that way, despite material and symbolic evidence to the contrary. By contrast, the sovereignty-making erasure in the title of goods under *res nullius* is a one-off action on time, an act of severance of all connection from origins, thereby making origins untraceable, if not irrelevant. Finally, the erasure of title in one's person, or *corpus nullius*, is achieved in the production of a permanently unachievable future, as permanent debt-trap.

It is therefore no surprise that the temporality of sovereignty in India is best folded into the promissory structure of the constitution itself, which heralds a new temporality (of freedom) but where real freedom is "yet-to-be" (Mehta 2010). The constitution is based in a radical rupture with the past, and as such it cannot address issues that pre-exist it. This is as much an expression of its reformative ethos in which it bases its legitimacy, as it is it a feature of its sovereign force, to which I now turn.

---

6. This point is powerfully argued from different theoretical orientations and time periods in two remarkable works: the first by Ranganathan on ocean-floor grab (2019), and the second by Bhattacharyya (2018) on the drainage of land to create the urban landscape for building colonial Calcutta.

Constitutional Suspicions

One of the main concerns of this book is the different scales of ownership in relation to the law, sovereignty-making, and freedom made available ethnographically. It is a central argument of the book that, despite being a state of law and order like many other liberal democracies, the work of law in India is unique and this abides in the relation between the promissory nature of the Indian Constitution and other normative orders. The Indian Constitution, sometimes called the "People's Constitution" (De 2018), was adopted at the end of colonial rule and the establishment of the republic in 1950, thereby marking a firm break with the past and an equally firm commitment to a radically different future. One of the longest constitutions in the world, it is written in the vein of a promissory note (Kapila 2003; Mehta 2016) whereby the people deliver themselves from the tyranny and the squalor of the past to a just, equal, and equitable future for all.[7] Equality and equity were to be achieved in economic, political, and social life, and in the same measure across strata. Guaranteeing equality in law had to be substantialized by upholding principles of equity and redistributive justice. Although equality, equity, and justice as goals may sound banal today, blunted as they are from their meaning-free overuse in public discourse, during the time the constitution was drafted and adopted, these were certainly nothing less than revolutionary for a society configured around and by hierarchy, inequity, and inhumanity (Ambedkar 1935).[8]

As discussed earlier, all modern legal systems are liberal conceptualizations of the rights-bearing individual where the legal framework exists to safeguard freedom and liberty. This rights-bearing subject of modern law is constituted as a possessive individual on whom the law bestows rights. Group rights too are bestowed with an analogous unitary and possessive entity in view, whose liberty and freedom needs guaranteeing or safeguarding. Notions of liberty and equality which are fundamental to modern legal subjectivity cannot be substantialized without the bestowing of the right to life, which in turn depends on a prior right to property. For India, on the verge of becoming not just sovereign, but

---

7. There is a growing and exciting body of work on the Indian Constitution, starting with Granville Austin (1999), to the more recent scholarship on constitutional history (notably Bhatia 2018; De 2018; Khosla 2020).

8. On the genealogy of this liberal turn, see Bayly (2012). On the architect of the constitution, B. R. Ambedkar, see Kumar (2015).

also a republic, enshrining and guaranteeing freedom in and through its own constitution gained all the more significance. Its Constituent Assembly was formed in 1946 with the purpose of deliberating on each article of the draft constitution for independent India before its formal adoption on January 26, 1950, when India became a Republic.[9] The Constitutional Drafting Committee underpinned citizenship in India with fundamental rights to life (Article 21), freedom, and property.[10] The discussion on Article 19 (the fundamental right to property) was focused almost exclusively on the capacity of the right to protect against forcible confiscation of land without adequate compensation, rather than on the legal institutionalization of the possessive individual more broadly conceived. As a fundamental right, it was more redistributive (hence negative), rather than a positive liberty in its own right. There were two immediate and long-term consequences of such a framing of the right to property under Article 19. The first was the incarceration of the property question in its landed form, and the second was that it was framed almost exclusively to address land reform, and land redistribution in particular.[11] The latter was aimed at providing the legal and institutional scaffolding for the proposed abolition of zamindari—the feudal system of agrarian land relations—in independent India and the redistribution of surplus land to the landless.

The fundamental right to property was thus enshrined to ensure the recognition of prior title (hence contra *terra nullius*) and protection against forcible confiscation of anyone's land by the state or its agencies. As we will see in Chapter 4, unlike a number of other rights and

---

9. The Assembly sat from 1946 to 1949. On the Constituent Assembly Debates, see Bhatia (2017). See also Bajpai (2011) and Kapila (2014).

10. The fundamental rights guaranteed in the constitution are: Right to Equality (Articles 14–18), Right to Freedom (Articles 19–22), Right against Exploitation (Articles 23–24), Right to Freedom of Religion (Articles 25–28), Cultural and Educational Rights (Articles 29–30), Right to Constitutional Remedies (Article 32). For the basic structure of the constitution, see Austin (1999); see also Bajpai (2011); Bhatia (2019); De (2018); and Khosla (2020).

11. Land reform and land redistribution had been a key aspect of the anti-colonial politics in India because land revenue regimes introduced by the British colonial state (especially Permanent Settlement) had bolstered and fostered feudal landlordism and vast agricultural holdings, resulting in large-scale rural indebtedness and, in places, practices such as debt bondage (see Guha 1996 and Wahi 2015; also Prakash 1990 and Wilson 2010).

freedoms, because the right to property was conceived as an individual rather than a group right, any prior claim to title of a group could not and did not find room in either the Constituent Assembly Debates or afterwards in public debate. The constitution does recognize and bestow group rights, but these are recognized largely with a compensatory or redistributive intent for the rights of a "minority." Even when they are for a group, such as the ownership of *waqf* property (Muslim sacred property), the owner is a unitary entity in the form of the Waqf Board of India (Fazal 2019; Menon 2011).[12] In any case, it remains the prerogative of the constitution and the state to recognize "groups" with defined and protective rights. Redistribution of title under the fundamental right to property too was at an individual level and the redistributive function of Article 19 became limited to a tort or compensatory logic, which has had significant long term consequences.

Critics of this particular formulation of the property right in the Constituent Assembly and since were mainly free-marketeers and/or of deregulatory persuasion, and in the high moment of nationalist future-making on the eve of Independence, they remained marginal voices. But their limited influence on the final shape of Article 19 came as much from the force of the utopian spirit guiding the constitution, as it did from the narrowness of their own vision. Certainly in the Constituent Assembly comprising several barristers and lawyers, there was no strident Hegelian in the mix who made clear the link between the hard-won freedom and liberty that the constitution was to guarantee and what a non-redistributive property right might look like. Thus, a constitution with a very strong vision of freedom, and an equally well-defined and elaborate infrastructure of guaranteed fundamental rights, was promulgated with a very weak conception of the possessive citizen, which was weakened further by its eventual abolition in 1976, as I discuss below. It is the unfolding of this central contradiction that I explore in the rest of this book—not through legal doctrine or historical or political commentary, but anthropologically, and therefore in terms of its constitutive relationality.

A key feature of the Indian constitution under Article 32 is the power vested in parliament to amend it. To date, the constitution has been amended 104 times since it came into force in 1950.[13] The vast majority

---

12. On the global history of Islamic property regimes and charitable endowments, including *waqf,* see Moumtaz (2020).

13. In fact, the very first amendment came in 1950 itself and was brought in to safeguard the political and social vision enshrined in the constitution

of these amendments are piecemeal and have rarely touched the core or the "basic structure" of the constitution.[14] The 1970s were a turbulent decade in the history of the contemporary state in India, especially in relation to its constitution. The 42nd Amendment passed in 1976 was called a mini-constitution as it consolidated a particular direction for the future of the country, chief of which was adding two crucial words to the preamble: "socialist" and "secular." The 1970s began with an expressly leftward swing in government policy and legislation under Indira Gandhi.[15] At the core of this politically populist "leftward" swing was legislation and policy aimed at countering prevalent strategies of accumulation. The first of these moves was the nationalization of fourteen banks in 1969 (S. Sen 2017). As the decade progressed, Indira Gandhi continued to pursue left-populist politics and policies and consolidated the redistributive ethos of the constitution enshrined in the Directive Principles of State Policy, despite dissent in influential quarters (Khaitan 2018). But it was the subsequent government that was formed after Gandhi's defeat following the Emergency that sought to do away with the fundamental right to property altogether, spurred by the tailwind of the anti-accumulation mood of the nation. When the new government introduced the 44th Amendment in parliament, there was scarcely any opposition to it. The anti-accumulation and pro-redistributive political mood ensured the abrogation of the fundamental right to property without too much of a fuss. In fact, at the time, the main objection that was raised was that the government did not keep its manifesto promise of replacing the right to property with a fundamental right to employment.[16] Given that the recently concluded period of Emergency (1975-77) had

---

from legalistically minded advocates of a competing idea of India (T. Singh 2020).

14. A notable early exception was the 7th Amendment which was necessary for the linguistic reorganization of the states in 1956. An unamendable core spirit, or the "basic structure doctrine," itself emerged in a Supreme Court judgement of a landmark case (*Keshavananda Bharati v. the State of Kerala*, 1972) in the wake of the 25th amendment. On the Keshavananda Bharati case, see Krishnaswamy (2010).

15. On the politics of the 1970s and especially the Emergency, see Guha (2007); Jaffrelot and Anil (2020); Prakash (2019); Tarlo (2003).

16. The fundamental right to work eventually came about in 2004 to 2005, as part of a suit of rights created as a constitutional elaboration of the Right to Life (Article 15)

been until then the clearest threat to personal and civil liberties posed by the state, the steadfastness with which the property question remained legally and constitutionally sealed off from that of freedom remains a puzzle. Furthermore, to date, its analysis in otherwise insightful scholarship remains synonymous with the land question and its rightful acquisition (e.g. Wahi 2015).

The concept of freedom has largely remained outside of the anthropological canon and has only recently found itself a home in the scholarship on ethics (Heywood 2015; Laidlaw 2013). However, for the Indian state and its people, the register of freedom is different. Freedom is crucial to the foundation of the postcolonial state and therefore it is at once a political question for the people, and a jural obligation for the postcolonial state. The Indian state jurally and constitutionally guarantees "freedom" through its set of fundamental rights. To avail of these freedoms and enjoy the rights, the citizen-individual needs to have a prior right in themselves, or "own" themselves. In the absence of a fundamental right to property, (self-)ownership comes close to being illusory, which makes the work of the law in India and the relationality it engenders unique. While the constitutional and legal debates on the implications of the abrogated right to property are beyond the scope of this discussion, what they allude to is the mismatch between the formal and substantive freedoms via an ambiguity towards (self-)ownership. Far from being piecemeal, the repercussions of the absence of a fundamental right to property I argue are structural, omnipresent, and constantly acquire new life forms. The most recent of these comes in the garb of privacy concerns raised by the fast-proliferating data economy and the rise of state-enabled surveillance technologies in India, which I deal with in Chapter 6.

I open up the property question in modern India from the vantage point of the three doctrines: *terra nullius*, *res nullius*, and *corpus nullius*. None of these is part of commonsensical narratives or indeed canonical understandings of either state-making or property relations in India. Yet, as I show, these nullifications have been fundamental to the relationship between the state, people, territory, and property at key moments in history—under colonialism (*res nullius*), in the transition to Independence (*terra nullius*), and post-liberalization India (*corpus nullius*). Legal doctrine may be at the heart of this book, but the book is not an elaboration of doctrine. Rather, it is concerned with showing the absorption of doctrinal law in everyday life. The book takes up these three articulations of negation in modern Indian legal history in order to understand the particular formatting of state sovereignty in colonial and post-Independence India. But my object here is neither to delineate Indian legal history, nor to finesse the political theory of sovereignty. Instead, the aim is to explore what might the anthropological scrutiny of sovereignty reveal about sovereignty and, equally, what that might do for anthropology itself. Many of these concepts—and indeed doctrines—have their genesis in colonial expansion and conquest. Most often these are derived from settler-colonial contexts (such as *terra nullius*), and their applicability is seen to be restricted to them. However, legacy frameworks such as much of legal anthropology often disregard their genesis and insights from settler-colonial contexts are often applied to understand contexts that have had very different histories of colonial rule, all of which seem to be flattened in the reading of the contemporary moment. This has made for stilted and sometimes formulaic descriptions and analysis that run into dead ends before long. I step away from these frameworks and reopen the debate on the inseparability of ownership and sovereignty in non-settler-colonial contexts.

Furthermore, and as a result of the above, an anthropological approach to property relations in India helps to redescribe the limits of law and the relationship between law and society in unexpected ways. As discussed earlier, one of the aims here is to restore to anthropology the state as a proper object of study (Graeber and Sahlins 2017: 22; see Abrams 1988). This means bringing cognate anthropological paradigms to bear on the state-concept. For me, this has meant understanding, *pace* Weiner (1992) the kind of possession state power is, *pace* Da Col (2019) and Newell (2019) what is accumulated or hoarded in sovereignty, and *pace* Gamble (2014) and Gygi 2018), what is incorporated in dispossession. More specifically, what can the anthropology of predation tell us about the relational modes of settler-colonialism (*pace* Descola 2013; Costa and Fausto 2019)? What do Gaddi notions of labor tell us about biometric identification in India? Once dispossessed from their original owners, how does the state write its own ownership into objects? I set about answering these questions in view of the relationality that is constituted through these acts of dispossession. I bear in mind Bataille's characterization of sovereignty as based in the experience of non-purposive excess, which helps explain the iterative, repetitive, and ongoing nullification.

But first, a bit of context.

Outline

In the chapters that follow I examine ownership, erasure of title, and sovereignty-making in three domains—land, things, and people— through a set of three nullifications: via *terra nullius*—in land, the denial of indigenous title and the incorporation of new territories within the boundaries of the state, such as the Andaman Islands; in things, or in *res nullius*—through the study of ownership disputes of objects that today form the foundation for the South Asian collection at the Victoria and Albert Museum in London; and, finally, the erasure of personhood, or *corpus nullius*, achieved through the mandatory biometric identification card, "Aadhaar." I stay close to concepts and frameworks that emerge from the discipline itself, which, for my ethnographic context of India, is neither usual nor easy. Moving through different scales, locations, and histories in exploring the dynamic relationship between ownership and dispossession, it becomes possible to provide a new description of the relationality engendered through sovereignty-making, but it also helps to describe more fully the multiple scales and planes at which everyday life is lived, fought for, and experienced.

I begin in Chapter 2 with setting out the unique work of law in India and the far-reaching consequences of the reforms around ownership and property that were set forth in its constitution. To understand the legitimacy and the force of the law in India requires paying attention to its uniquely promissory work. In this chapter I elaborate on the dense normative ecology within which the law operates, but make an argument against the received understandings of the relationship between law and culture in the social and human sciences. Ethnographically based in the analysis of caste-killings, I challenge the reading of the normative landscape as "legal pluralism," and the complexity of "legal conscious-ness" in India simply as instrumental "forum shopping." The work of the constitution is fundamentally transformative in the relationality and the temporality it sought to produce. I argue that the recent caste-based killings can be traced to the rewriting of the relational grammar, which was aimed at unsettling the force of ritual hierarchy and substantializing formal legal equality. At the core of this relational rewriting were property and ownership structures within kinship. But, as I show, not all intentions went to plan, chief among which was the promissory hope in gender equality through the change in kinship laws. Though the Hindu Marriage Act and the Hindu Succession Act were radical and have brought about significant structural changes to Hindu kinship, their role in bringing about substantive gender equality will remain extremely limited, if always incomplete.

Chapter 3 is an ethnographic examination of the multiple scales at which ownership and property relations are lived and experienced. I explore what ownership means to the Gaddis in their everyday relations and their relations with others. I explore in particular the pluriverse of *jaidaad*, which can stand for possessions, wealth, and estate, and ranges from animals to children, and from pastures and biogenetic substance to clan goddesses through woolen blankets. Far from being a Borgesian catalogue, elements of Gaddi *jaidaad* signify temporal and spatial relations with each other as well as with the divine. It is the relationship forged through notions of *jaidaad* with the divine that forms the blueprint for their fundamental dispositions in the world, including that with the sovereign. Examining Gaddi women's wealth shows the limits of the law in incorporating social life, but also the sovereignty inherent in women's property. If possessions and ownership are the bedrock of Gaddi society, then dispossession too is foundationally rupturing. I show how the Gaddis have with regularity used dispossession as the idiom through which to negotiate with the state, thereby revealing the state's monopoly over it.

Chapter 4 examines dispossession of title in land and territory. Using Descola's schema of relational and identificatory modes (2013), I explore the relationality of settler-colonialism in the Andamans, not under the British in the eighteenth century, but in the transition from the colonial to the postcolonial state in the mid-twentieth century. I take up the key relational category that emerges from settler-colonialism, that of indigeneity. I examine the early history of this category in the transition from colonial to postcolonial India, specifically in light of the voided claims to indigenous title. Through an examination of the interventions made by the sole "tribal" representative in India's Constituent Assembly, the chapter outlines the disaggregation of the absolute claim to title into a more fragmentary and elemental form of usury rights in forests and forest produce. It compares this permanently ongoing fragmentation of indigenous communities' claims to absolute title with the more explicit deployment of the doctrine of *terra nullius* in the annexation of the territory and people of the Andaman Islands into the Union of India. Reading this material with Descola's relational schema allows me to investigate the category of indigeneity in historically diverse societies with a non-settler-colonial past, as well as a way to cast this history away from developmentalist or identitarian frameworks of coercive incorporation.

Chapter 5 shifts attention to the expansion of sovereignty in the realm of things. It examines the disputes surrounding the ownership of objects that were sent from India to London for the Great Exhibition of 1851 and the International Exhibition of 1862, some of which eventually ended up as the original South Asia collection of the Victoria and Albert Museum in London. Disputes around ownership and dispositional control emerged between colonial officials and the original owners as to whether these objects were a loan or gift to the colonial state, a consignment for international trade, or a contribution to the exhibitions. Eventually these objects were designated *res nullius* through elaborate mechanisms of theft and misappropriation. I follow their contested journeys with an anthropological lens, revealing the numerous exchange strategies though which ownership was erased and re-inscribed, thereby providing the colonial state a domain made of "*res*" or things through which it could consolidate its sovereignty. This chapter critically engages with the anthropology of things, on the one hand, and with the work of Callon et al. (2002) on the other hand, to show the salience of the work of the state (and not just the market) in the creation and re-inscription of value.

Chapter 6 takes as its starting point a controversial remark made in 2015 by the then Attorney General of India that Indian citizens did not have absolute rights over their bodies (*corpus nullius*). The Attorney General made this argument in *Puttuswamy v. Union of India* (2016), the landmark case challenging the inadequate privacy safeguards under Aadhaar, the largest biometric identification scheme ever launched by any government to date. Instead of dismissing this statement in outrage, I take it seriously and ask who does own the citizen's body, if not the citizen, and under what conditions. This allows me to shift the debate on Aadhaar, but also on data more generally beyond surveillance and privacy concerns examine the prior questions of ownership and the related question of labor. Drawing on Gaddi notions of the transformative potential of different forms of labor and their relation to servitude allows me to explore the relationship between labor, personhood, and sovereignty under the new biometric state. Outlining a genealogy of state intervention in relations of servitude, I argue that Aadhaar fundamentally transforms the state-citizen relationship to a debt relation and, the usurpation of the citizen's biometric labor as tantamount to slavery (*corpus nullius*).

The coda brings these diverse strands together to ask if and how one can propose an anthropology of sovereignty in its own (anthropological) terms. How else to understand the hollow center at the heart of India's liberal legal framework—the absent fundamental right to property? Mimicking the divine, the state deploys the illusion of ownership in land, persons, and things, while hoarding ever greater authority for itself.

CHAPTER 2

The Promise of Law

[T]he people when they grew accustomed to new laws and new procedures did not retain their love for the panchayat. . . . Courts of conciliation were no longer popular in the Punjab as soon as there were tribunals of another nature to which men could turn, and they are not likely to be successful again in the future as they do not appear . . . to be suited to the character of the people. A suitor does not wish to agree with his adversary, but to get the better of him if he can.

– Sir Robert Egerton, Secretary to the Government of India, September 17, 1880

The lacuna in anthropology is due not to any oversight of primitive legality, but on the contrary its overemphasis. Paradoxical as it sounds, it is yet true that present-day anthropology neglects primitive law just because it has an exaggerated, and I will add at once, a mistaken idea of its perfection.

– Bronislaw Malinowski, *Crime and Custom in Primitive Societies.* 1926.

Those who want to perpetuate their power, do so through the courts.

– M. K. Gandhi, *Hind Swaraj*, 1908

One of the questions that preoccupied early anthropologists was that of order in what were termed "acephalous", or stateless, societies.[1] Malinowski suggested that the omission of the study of the law on the part of anthropologists was not because they did not find any existence of rules and order, but the opposite—that there was complete identification with social norms in the societies they studied. Nothing could be further from the truth, he said. This mistake had arisen because these were seen as societies of control and not of law, whereas these were societies actually based in reciprocity and mutual obligation (Malinowski 1926). In the decades that followed, dispute resolution came to be the mainstay of legal anthropology, but the anthropological inquiry into modern liberal law remained at the edges of the canon, partly because of the ongoing suspicion of the state as an anthropological object proper.

The history of the career of law in anthropology is beyond the scope of this discussion. Nevertheless, this particular framing of Malinowski's invitation to anthropologists has cast a long shadow. In this chapter, I attend to what Malinowski described as the existing imperfection, the dissonance between norms and social life, or between law and "culture," as a way of framing the different scalarities in which property and ownership operate. The study of the relationship between law and culture has endured as a study of degrees of non-congruence between these two orders, which have been differently characterized as conflictual or hierarchical. My interest in studying this relationship is to describe the different scales and orders in which ordinary life is lived, on the one hand, and the role the state via its emissary, the law, plays in hierarchizing the orders and setting the scale, on the other hand.

The relationship between the law and other normative orders comes up over and again in the chapters that follow, most pertinently with reference to locally held ideas of ownership and those recognized in law. I want to suggest that the relationship between law and other normative orders goes beyond conflict or asymmetry. I resist describing the scalar and normative multiplicity as "legal pluralism" to allow myself to attend to the specificity of the force of law, but also to understand its unique work in contemporary India. How then to understand this crucial relationship? In this chapter, I provide an alternative reading of the work of law, and of the relationship between law and society in contemporary India. I focus on its work in everyday relationality as a way of opening

---

1. For an overview of the history of law and anthropology see Goodale (2017); Merry (2006); Moore (2002); Pottage and Mundy (2004).

up the space for understanding notions of ownership within and outside it. I show the inadequacy of legacy readings in the anthropology of law to understand historically diverse societies and to show the limits of understanding its work in India simply in terms of equality-inequality. By providing a longer frame account of this conflict in post-Independence India, my aim here is to uncover the underpinnings of why there remains the abiding, if now growing, imperfection between the work of society and culture and that of the law. The purpose of this chapter then is to set the stage for the chapters that follow on why the force of law in India lies in its promissory nature generally, but especially in relation to sovereignty.

I trace the recent violent turn in the relationship between legal and cultural norms in India—such as in the case of caste violence which I discuss below—in the moment of the legal restructuring of property relations and principles of ownership within the household. I argue that the reconfiguration of the structures of ownership within kinship was a key principle of social reform that was unleashed by the constitution, and especially in and through personal codes. Examining the recent surge in violence perpetrated at the behest of caste councils and aimed at cross-caste marriages, I show the structural unfolding of the logic of ownership and caste violence as an outcome of social reform.

At the End of the Constitution

"Jahaan Gurgaon ka border khatam hota hai, vahaan law khatam, madam," declares one of the characters in the 2015 Hindi film, *NH10*, territorialising the limit of the law, in this case, to just a few miles outside the national capital region ("Where the border of Gurgaon [now a suburb of New Delhi] ends, is where the law ends").[2] In recent years, India has seen a renewed, escalating conflict between its new laws and its older forms and forums of justice, sometimes resulting in acts of gross violence and inhumanity. One of the most spectacular of these conflicts has been the challenge posed by the rise of violence perpetrated at the behest of caste councils, or *khap panchayats*, as a form of blood justice. In recent years, these caste councils have focused almost entirely on policing the boundaries of matrimonial alliances and have violently retributed those marrying across the caste/dalit divide or within proscribed degrees of

---

2. *NH10* (2015, Dir. Navdeep Singh). NH stands for "national highway."

lineal separation. *Khap panchayats* are local councils comprising caste elders that have served as traditional forums of justice in north India, adjudicating local and domestic disputes. Each major sublineal exogamous group has a *khap* (a representative body formed of its elder males). In many ways, *khaps* can be seen as a "technology" that makes visible the cartography of alliances among middle castes in the region.

Khap panchayats appeared in the national consciousness a decade ago when, in March 2010, a sessions court in Karnal, Haryana, handed down the death penalty to five people for the murder of Manoj (a twenty-three-year-old man) and Babli (a nineteen-year-old woman) in 2007. Manoj and Babli had been brutally killed by their kin at the orders of a *khap panchayat* for marrying within the same *gotra* (lineal subcaste).[3] The Karnal court passed the death sentence for five members of Babli's family for carrying out the murders and a life sentence for the head of the *khap panchayat* who had ordered the killings (Sharma 2010). The court judgment and the ensuing meeting of the *khaps* in Kurukshetra in protest were new salvos from two old foes in a bid to break out of a deadlock that had been festering for more than two years. During this time, a growing number of young men and women had been killed by their kin at the behest of similar diktats issued by caste elders as retribution against mismarriages between men and women either of the same *gotra* or village or else across the *savarna* (twice-born caste Hindus) and dalit (erstwhile untouchable castes) divide. Through the Karnal court judgment, the state finally showed categorical disapprobation for what it held as runaway justice. The Kurukshetra meeting proved to be so popular, in the next few months several such congregations were convened. Thousands of ordinary and not-so-ordinary men and women from across the north Indian plains gathered as members or supporters of caste councils, giving further evidence to the growing unassailability of these *khaps*.

Both the killings of young men and women and the supporting congregations (or *khap-mahapanchayats*) attracted a fair amount of media frenzy and became the subject of scholarly attention (e.g. Baxi et al. 2006; Chowdhry 2007; Kaur 2010). The spate of murders swiftly led to the importing of the appellation "honor killings" in media and popular representations. This was perhaps a nod to the global imaginary in which India exists not only as a dominant economic player, but also as a country plagued by the same irritants as its global comrades—that

---

3. http://www.thehindu.com/news/national/article396373.ece. Accessed November 9, 2019.

is, by certain lumpy bits of culture; that ostensibly lead to clashes of civilizational proportions.

"Culture," in this instance, was identified with caste. Scholarly, journalistic, and civil society attention elaborated on the underlying caste and gender dynamics that informed this violent form of popular justice in north India (Baxi, et al. 2006; Dogra 2010; Kaur 2010; Reddy 2010). In most of these accounts, the persistence of an older jurisprudence was seen as an epiphenomenon of underlying obduracy in a region set against becoming "progressive" and unable to inculcate desired social reforms (Reddy 2010). Commenting in the national press on the situation, historian Prem Chowdhry said: "You cannot do away with [*khaps*] because they are old institutions, but I would suggest that they take the reformist agenda . . . *khaps have to reform*," highlighting at once the reading of the situation even by a regional expert through a premium of change (Reddy 2010; emphasis added). This was particularly curious given that Chowdhry has herself noted the shifting interests of the *khaps* in the course of the last century, including their once patently reformist concerns, such as their opprobrium against lavish expenditures at weddings and demands for exorbitant dowry.

Elsewhere she notes:

> After independence, different cases and *got panchayats* held in different villages and several *khap* and *sarv-khap panchayats* of different caste groups have been making similar attempts to curb [dowries and lavish weddings]. Several resolutions have been passed imposing heavy fines (as high as Rs 11,000) on all those breaking traditional norms and excommunicating them. All these have proved fruitless. The so-called biradari leaders, who think it a matter of pride and status to spend lavishly at marriages, have not observed such decisions. (Chowdhry 2007: 260)

Chowdhry observes: "It is significant that in the colonial period these . . . leaders had activated caste reform movement[s] in their move towards upward mobility. In the postcolonial period, the same affluent groups are apparently still theoretically committed to purging the worst social abuses" (2007: 260–61). For Chowdhry then, reform is merely a matter of political expediency. In a 2010 interview, she argues that *khap* leaders have abandoned the reformist agenda because it no longer brings any political purchase for them. She reads their stricter observance of caste strictures as an expeditious route to influencing popular sentiment "because it's an emotive issue on which they can mobilise" (in Reddy 2010). However, no explanation is needed by the interviewer nor was one offered by Chowdhry as to how or why stricture has come to entail an emotional appeal for some in north India.

As evident from the trajectory of the concerns Chowdhry outlines, the rise of *khaps* in the last few years is not due to an obduracy of a culture that refuses to change—were that true for any culture. Rather, the recent ascendance of *khaps* and their efficacious violence is precisely the result of tectonic shifts in local society and culture, none of which was either cognized or anticipated. The clue to these shifts lies in the choice of the adversary singled out by the *khaps*. Caste patriarchs had not identified romantic love or, indeed, individual choice as the root cause of their outrage, as has been hastily surmised by commentators and critics. In specifying the Hindu Marriage Act (1955; hereafter HMA), specifically the subclause pertaining to intra-*gotra* (sublineage) marriage, these councils have declared *substantive state law* as their direct adversary, indicting it for imposing new possibilities that were not scripted within their culture. The state, for its part, made it amply clear that it was not going to entertain any demand for amending the HMA, not least because of the state's unwillingness to share its juridical authority, even if it occasioned political discomfort. Mirroring the actions of the *khaps*, the state too handed death sentences to those who disputed its juridical supremacy, in this case Manoj and Babli's killers.

Thus, an old battle between law and culture had been stoked once again. Despite its recent vintage, the current debate has remained trapped within familiar and rehearsed domains, both from within (for example, like the battle between tradition and modernity in colonial law) and from without (as exemplified in labeling the murders as "honor killings"). These inferences are not wrong in themselves; however, to enable a reframing of the relationship between law and culture that does not repeat older epistemological disadvantages, it is imperative to move away from these legacy understandings.

Law's Culture

The contest between cultural and legal norms is not unique to India; in fact, it forms the bedrock of identity politics that scholars from divergent traditions and persuasions have written about extensively. While the inseparability of law from culture is undisputed, there remain significant differences in how the relationship is understood and explained in different contexts. Euro-Americanist social-legal scholarship tends to subsume the two into one on the grounds of a purported consensus between law and culture, based on the notion that law is but a codification and reinscription of everyday values, life-ways, or, in other words, culture (Merry 1990: 62; Ewick and Silbey 1998: 43; Mezey 2001: 36; Sarat and Simon 2003; Silbey 2005: 332). The tension between the two domains is acknowledged and understood by some to originate in the force of state power behind law (Derrida 1990; Peletz 2002; Supiot 2007). This tension gains new life every now and then, with its most recent manifestations being expressed in debates about making Muslim women's headscarves illegal in France (Scott 2008; Sunder 2003) or in the conflict between notions of human rights and certain cultural practices, such as female circumcision among certain African communities living in Europe (Benhabib 2004; Merry 2006). In these accounts, the gap between law and culture in the Euro-American context is sourced to the cultural heterogeneity that has arisen from immigration. That is to say, normative difference is understood to emerge from, if not lie outside of, society.

The scholarship on the relationship between law and culture in Euro-America, while valuable and insightful, is ultimately of limited use in understanding the relationship between culture and law in India for two main reasons. First, unlike Euro-American law, it is arguable to what extent state law in India draws on everyday social values. In fact, it may be more accurate to say that in India, legal and cultural norms are far from coinciding. Therefore, the subject of law and that of culture broadly defined often appear in contradistinction to each other. The relationship between the two is not necessarily or always one of hostility; rather, the public aspirations of law in India are aimed at attaining the eventual coincidence of the two in the future. Second, the source of divergence between cultural and legal norms in most multicultural states in Euro-America is seen to be located in an externality or a separation introduced either through settler-colonialism (e.g. Aboriginal rights in Australia, First Nations theory in North America) or through immigration (as viewed by most work on Islamic radicalism, ranging from the Salman Rushdie fatwa to the illegality of headscarves in France).[4] Therefore, it is plausible in these contexts to constitute "culture" as a problem, when

---

4. On First Nations, see Borrows (2010); on Australian Aborigine rights, see Povinelli (2002); on veiling, see Scott (2008) and Sunder (2003); on the fatwa, see Asad (1993).

"culture" stands in as shorthand for normative heterogeneity. In India, however, cultural difference is seen as intrinsic to the self-image of society. "Unity in Diversity" is the most oft-repeated state slogan and is seen as a law having the position of the émigré, as the outsider living in a foreign land.[5]

This distinctive nature of the relationship between law and culture in India has so far been inadequately explored. Situations such as the current standoff between the *khaps* and the state judiciary tend to become natural citizens of "analytical subcultures" (Strathern 1981: 670) such as legal pluralism, often falling prey to our habits of thinking about these domains.[6] Through a counterfactual reading of the relationship between law and culture in contemporary India, I want to explore the constitution of culture as a problem, an impediment in the work of law, in two distinct moments in north India, and bring out the salience of the property question in defining the relationship between cultural and legal subjectivity in India today.

Recognition

The current conflict between state law and popular justice in India bears an uncanny resemblance to a contest the region witnessed through the second half of the nineteenth century. The north Indian plains posed a special problem to the colonial state with respect to the question of law, both in terms of the rules by which people lived their lives and of the processes and particular institutions through which disputes were settled. For the best part of fifty years following the annexation of Punjab in 1846, the then-colonial state vacillated on how to contain the influence

---

5. As one of the earliest commentaries on the new constitution remarks: "The democratic features of the Constitution were as risk-taking as the unity features were cautious. Representative government with adult suffrage, a bill of rights providing for equality and personal liberty, were to become the spiritual and institutional bases of a new society—one replacing the traditional hierarchies and its repressions" (Austin 1999 [1966]: x).

6. With the new ruling dispensation in India and a fast changing relationship between law, society, and the state, these standoffs have taken a different dimension, and the "culture-concept" gaining ever more force to be mobilised (though differently) by the state as a legitimation device. Analysing this new direction is beyond the scope of this book.

of local councils and custom, and how to increase the force and authority behind its own laws (Kapila 2003). From 1846 to 1899, the colonial government in Punjab went back and forth on the legal recognition of local juridical institutions, the village *panchayats*. These councils of village elders adjudicated on local disputes, but in some places, the role of the *panchayats* was more varied and they were also responsible for collecting and keeping important records not related to revenue. In the hill districts of Kangra and Kulu, for example, specialist councils maintained records of marriage payments, which required approval in cases involving the annulment of marriages, records of transfer payments (*harjana*) in cases of the remarriage of women, and similar situations.[7] The colonial state viewed the *panchayats* with great skepticism but, as I explain below, for a host of reasons the state found it difficult to either ignore them or get rid of them altogether.

The process of instituting any credible form of colonial legal government in the region was a drawn out affair, one that both tested *and* helped to articulate the state's disposition towards the question of culture. When Punjab was first annexed in 1846, all *panchayats* were summarily made illegal across the province—a move meant to signal the advent of the new regime—and people were encouraged to take their disputes to the newly instituted state courts. But this was not as straightforward as the colonial state might have initially anticipated. In the first decade of colonial rule in Punjab, the new laws and institutions proved either too unpopular (as in the case of the North West Frontier Province [NWFP], where *jirgah* or tribal councils held sway) or too popular, thereby becoming inundated by the volume of litigation, especially in the Cis-Sutlej areas. These areas were the first to witness a surge in the value of land as a result of the spread of irrigation. At the same time, growing and unprecedented levels of rural indebtedness gave rise to large-scale unregulated transfers of land, resulting in high numbers of cases for litigation (Bhattacharya 1985; Islam 1995; Kapila 2003). While there was complete nonrecognition of the juridical authority of the state by the people in the NWFP, in the case of the Cis-Sutlej area, the state's inadequacies to deal with the consequences of its own policies and interventions were first revealed at the level of institutions. To tide over the crises of legitimacy as well as growing litigiousness, *panchayats* were made legal in 1869 and given the responsibility of adjudicating on local disputes.[8] But the challenge posed

---

7. NAI/ Home/ Judicial/ A Proceedings/ 25 March 1871/no. 40.

8. NAI/ Home/ Judicial/ A Proceedings/ October 1901/ no. 5.

by shared juridical authority did not go amiss and so, once again, in 1899, the colonial state derecognized the judicial capacities and capabilities of all such councils on the grounds of their processual opacity and lack of moral integrity, deepening the gulf between the domains of state law and prevailing cultural norms.[9]

The government tried to address this gulf through a two-pronged solution. It first put in place resources to extend the state judicature to every locality. More entry-level courts in towns and *qasbahs* (old walled towns) were created in order to increase the reach of and access to the state judiciary. The expansion of the judiciary was accompanied by the appropriation of local jurisprudence within the state juridical regime. It also resulted in the recognition of *panchayats* as and where they existed, allocating to them jurisdiction over certain kinds of affairs that were deemed "customary." This required clarifying and codifying what was meant by "customary." The incorporation of local jurisprudence within the colonial state led to the inscription and codification of local norms and practices in compendia of rules and regulations to be used by the state courts for jurisprudential reference (e.g. Ellis 1917; Middleton 1919; Roe and Rattigan 1895; Tupper 1881).

In other parts of British India, such matters were the subject of personal law (i.e., governed by religious tenets). But the area that stretched from the North West Frontier Province to Delhi was regarded by the colonial state as a region where religious codes did not necessarily find resonance in people's daily habits. A senior judge advised the administration: "The Punjab is unique in one particular respect.... The primary rule of Civil Judicature as to all the important personal relations and as to rights of property in land among the rural classes (who form the bulk of the population) is Customary Law, and not, as elsewhere in India, the Hindu and the Muhammadan Laws, which here are of secondary importance, though these also have to be administered."[10]

Since tribal, community, and local rules were considered to have greater influence, the state found it necessary to systematize these local laws. Great debates took place on whether the axis of variability of custom lay at the level of group or at the level of territory. In keeping with

---

9. NAI/ Home/ Judicial/ A Proceedings/ October 1901/ no. 5.

10. Memorandum by Sir Meredith Plowden, Senior Judge of the Chief Court of the Punjab, to the Chief Secretary to the Government of Punjab. Letter no. 1334, dated October 24, 1893, Lahore. NAI/Home/Judicial/A Proceedings/ March 1895/no. 385.

the ethnological imagination of the time, the locus of culture was seen as rooted in territory and, therefore, district-based manuals of customary law were compiled for jurisprudential reference when adjudicating disputes in courts (Bhattacharya 1996; Kapila 2003). These manuals remained in use until the constitution came into force in 1950, following Independence.

In collecting and publishing several compendia of local customary law in Punjab, the state at once signaled the discrepancy and the distance between legal and cultural norms. Even more significantly, it abjured its responsibility in resolving this dissonance by separating two distinct realms of influence. While the colonial state would hold juridical sway over matters of general interest and criminal activity, other matters deemed as "ordinary occurrence" (such as marriage or inheritance) were to be governed by people's own rules—a convention that continued until Independence.[11] The existence of parallel jurisdictions of state, religious, and customary law made for Punjab litigants to opportunistically assume variable subject positions. Typically in colonial Punjab, people would litigate on the basis of the most expedient jurisdiction for their case. Due to the fact that custom was never formally codified, only "legally recognized" for reference in courts, it was never a stable category. In fact, it became ossified over time not as a consequence of its inscription but, rather, through repeated litigation and the subsequent emergence of regional case law (see Kapila 2003: 86–115). The colonial state thus addressed the question of culture in the region by first recognizing it as custom and contained its realm of influence by incorporating it within state law.

Nonrecognition

The relationship between law and culture changed once again when the constitution came into force after Independence, particularly with the promulgation of the Hindu Marriage Act (HMA) and the Hindu Succession Act (HSA) in 1955 and 1956, respectively. All matters hitherto regarded as being of "ordinary occurrence, or customary" were brought under the single jurisdiction of an all-India law, in stark contrast not just

---

11. Partha Chatterjee (1993), among others, has read this separation of the realm of culture from law as a fine example of the annexation by nationalists of the domestic or the internal world as sovereign, a view that has since become refined (Birla 2009; Kapila 2004).

with the prevailing norms, but also with prevailing jurisprudence. This move towards achieving legal universalism as a key strategy for nation-making has been examined to some extent in relation to the debates surrounding the incommensurability of India's Uniform, Civil, and Personal Codes (see Das 1997; Mody 2008). However, its effects on the structuring principles in north Indian society has yet to receive any systematic attention, a topic to which I now turn.

The HMA and the HSA were fragmentary and watered-down versions of a more radical, comprehensive Hindu Code Bill, the promulgation of which had caused much political and social upheaval.[12] The bill emerged out of the recommendations of the Rau Committee, set up in 1941 to review the Women's Rights to Property Act of 1937, a controversial statute in its own day (Uberoi 2002). Political leaders of all hues, including, famously, Rajendra Prasad (India's first president), feared the rupture the two Acts of the 1950s might cause within Hindu society. Most notably, while some people came to oppose the HSA for its potential to alter the bond between brothers and sisters once the sister became a holder of rights in her natal property (Naziruddin 1949: 21), others saw the HMA as merely a license for indiscriminate sexual activity, therefore as a threat to existing moral values (Chatterjee 1954). These and other capacities of the Acts to reform, reshape, and reorder Hindu society have been scrutinized by scholars for their role in the changed household composition (Uberoi 2002), the project of nationalism and developmentalism (Majumdar 2009: 206–38), and gender relations in postcolonial India (Kishwar 1994; Majumdar 2009; Parashar 1992). Although these studies are diverse in emphasis and persuasion, they all use a sociological or sociohistorical reading of the Acts and their effects on Hindu society. They illuminate the changed nature of the Hindu household and the gendered character of nationalism and postcolonial development, but they are unable to throw light on the structural features of the effects of these Acts.[13] I suggest that shifting the vantage point from the sociological underpinnings and manifestations of these Acts to the anthropology of kinship and personhood they entail will provide an

---

12. They were only passed once the demand for B. R. Ambedkar's resignation, the architect of the Indian Constitution, had been met. Among those who vehemently opposed the Code was the first President of India, Rajendra Prasad.

13. Uberoi (2002) is an exception in examining the status of Dravidian kinship rules in the two Acts.

aperture on the unexamined aspects of the relationship between law and culture in contemporary India.

As observed earlier, when the colonial state marked out a legally distinct sphere labeled "customary," it at once signaled the gap between cultural and legal norms, as well as its inability or disinclination to resolve the tension arising from this gap. This was a crucial step through which the colonial state continued to rule, and call it a rule-of-law, but through a regime of "indirect rule" (see Mamdani 2012). The life and status of this gap have been of a different order in the postcolonial era, given that the gap has remained mostly unacknowledged. It is noteworthy that the Constituent Assembly (the body responsible for drafting the constitution of postcolonial India) did not include a single member who was either mandated or who advocated the recognition of customary or local laws, or even of the *Dharmashastras*, the classical legal texts (Galanter 1972: 55). In staying close to the motto of "Unity in Diversity," constitutional law acknowledged the heterogeneity in matters of "ordinary occurrence" by promulgating religion-based personal codes along with the homogenous all-India civil code. The primary site of difference thus came to be religion and the variability along the axis of locality did not find recognition within constitutional jurisprudence. This not only meant the nonrecognition of colonial customary laws, but also of the north-south divide in Hindu kinship rules (see Uberoi 2002).

The prevailing hope was that over time, familiarity with new legal institutions as well as new legal norms—that is, laws—would result in the closing of the gap and the emergence of a new legal consciousness that was more in consonance with the new ideals. This ostensibly noninterventionist approach was not restricted to the domestic realm, but was part of a more general disposition of optimism surrounding the fate of the postcolonial national community and the advent of modernity. The ten-year time frame for reservations (that is, positive discrimination), the non-enumeration of caste in successive censuses, and the apathy of the political left towards matters of religion are some prominent examples of the hopes vested in the promise of (state-driven) modernity, on the one hand, and, on the other, of the salutary disregard of the culture question in independent India. This nonintervention and non-acknowledgment of the conditions created by the diluted Hindu Code Bill can be seen as the source of the most recent battle between law and culture that *khaps* are currently waging, as the next section outlines.

Towards an Anthropology of Reform

Gender and family relations are regarded both by lawmakers and by scholars as the major axes of reform in the HMA of 1955 and the HSA of 1956 (Kishwar 1994; Majumdar 2009). By outlawing polygamy and introducing the possibility of legal divorce among all Hindus, including upper-caste men and women, the HMA radically altered the legal legibility of the Hindu conjugal unit. But in terms of kinship, the HSA was the more significant of the two. It gave primacy to the conjugal unit as opposed to the joint household composed of male collaterals in succession and, for the first time, bestowed on women the right to inherit property as equal heirs, whether as wives or as daughters. This was a completely new way of imagining not only how property and wealth were to be held, distributed, and devolved in the family but, more significantly, how people were expected to relate to one another within and outside kinship. These laws were formulated to usher in a new society underpinned by a firm belief in equity and equality, where gender and family relations needed to go through radical reform. The sites of reform were not new per se, but what distinguished the Acts from similar efforts undertaken by colonial officials or by anti-colonial nationalists was the scale and scope of the transformations they entailed. These were not examples of piecemeal legislation targeted at isolated social practices such as sati, widow remarriage, age of consent, land alienation, and the like, but were a very conscious and comprehensive rewriting of the grammar of relatedness in north Indian Hindu society.

The starting position for these reforms was the structure of ownership and property rights, even though the HMA was promulgated a year before the HSA. The HSA fundamentally changed principles of relatedness by reimagining the heir and the devolution of property that were to become the primary vehicle through which the constitutional principles of formal equality were to be delivered in the family. The schedule of heirs under the HSA bore little trace of the prevalence of kinship structures, and applied only to (nuclear) family relations. This was not an oversight at all, but a deliberate act aimed at weakening, if not severing, the link between caste and kinship on the one hand, and delivering equal rights to women, on the other. The new schedule of heirs did away with the dominance of male collaterals and instead devolved property along the conjugal household, with the wife and daughter becoming equal heirs to a man's property.

The intent of these two Acts was not misplaced. But the rhetoric on which their promulgation was premised deeply influenced how they unfolded in subsequent years in at least two major ways, neither of which has yet been examined sufficiently in either public debate or in scholarship. First, the Hindu Code Bill and the eventual two Acts conveyed the appearance of giving birth to a new code for arranging matters of daily occurrence. This was not an altogether false appearance, for these were indeed new ways of imagining the workings of the Hindu household. However, these Acts had indirectly drawn on classical texts or, at least, on upper-caste sensibilities (Kapila 2003, 2004; Uberoi 2002). The iteration of newness was understandable because asserting rupture with the past was rhetorically necessary to ensure the success of the reformist agenda. Nevertheless, rupture and its attendant rhetoric made it impossible to explicitly tackle the culture question, in particular its relation to law, even in a germane moment afforded by the debates surrounding the Hindu Code Bill. Furthermore, the state (and, by extension, the law) did not have any discursive or political ground to articulate its disengagement from or disavowal of the culture question. This was because, unlike the colonial state, independent India could hardly claim nonintervention on the grounds of an ostensible sovereignty of the domestic sphere (see Chatterjee 1993). In the all-encompassing self-definition of "Unity in Diversity," there was no such aspect of culture that could be disavowed as not its own by the nation-state. To do so would have implied undermining the sovereignty of the nation-state. Moreover, these new laws were couched less in the spirit of nonintervention and more in the belief in reform. Therefore, aspects of custom (and, by extension, culture) had to be either declared repugnant or outmoded and de-recognized (as in the case of polygamy) or else sidestepped altogether through non-acknowledgment and nonrecognition. The notion of *reform* was key here, for it produced the Acts as the deliverance of the anti-colonial agenda and could thus be deployed to battle the contrarians with unassailable legitimacy. As a result, culture begot a fudging in postcolonial law and neither its content nor its force, particularly in relation to law, were ever explicitly dealt with or, indeed, resolved.

This non-acknowledgment and non-resolution of the gap between cultural and legal norms in domestic matters had a profound, ever more fundamental effect in the following decades, the roots of which lay in the way the new generative grammar of Hindu relatedness was embedded in these two Acts. Although the HMA reduced the conjugal unit to a monogamous one, the HSA reconfigured the principles and patterns of inheritance, as well as reimagined familial relations from the vantage point of the new heirs. The legal categories of kin produced in and through these Acts ("wife," "son," "sister," etc.) bore at best a nominal resemblance to their cultural counterparts, not least because in their transcription of kinship terminology, the prevalent descriptive kinship system was rendered into a classificatory system. The new laws failed to produce the complexity of relationality that is fundamental to kinship. These changes were not merely of academic import, especially when these new forms of sociality and society were combined with prevailing, dominant norms in the new structuration of north Indian society, triggering consequences that were entirely unanticipated and went mostly unacknowledged, as explained below.

The models of the family and household that inhered within the Acts and were borrowed from their Western counterparts bore a deep agnatic bias. In contrast, the motor of Hindu society is primarily driven by alliance rather than descent. Much of the work of culture and society in India revolves around a horizontal axis rather than a vertical one—arranging marriages, keeping and marking ritual distance, and so on. Marriage is not only the central feature of Indian kinship structures, but the very nature of the work it accomplishes is intimately connected to the production of the principles of caste hierarchy. As Dumont writes: "Marriage dominates the Hindu's social life, and plays a large part in his religion . . . It is the most prestigious family ceremony, and at various social levels constitutes the main occasion on which the greatest number of members of the caste and persons gather together . . . By its nature, marriage constitutes to a large measure the link between the domain of caste and that of kinship" (2009: 109–10). Thus, in north India, the production of kinship and hierarchy are intimately linked. Furthermore, as Dumont remarks elsewhere, in north India the twin interdictions against reversing the direction of the exchange of women and against patrilateral cross-cousin marriage are logical elaborations of the wider principles of caste hierarchy: "Caste . . . invades the sphere of kinship in such a way that we cannot speak with any rigour of a 'kinship system' as such. . . . The hypergamous model replaces a kinship element and allows the whole to keep a similar form" (1993:100). For these reasons, it is impossible to disentangle the structures of kinship from those of caste in north India, and any reform aimed at one will have implications for the other. So it was in the case of the Hindu Code Bill and its derivative Acts. Based in the commitment to the wider principle of equality underpinning the constitution, the HSA and the HMA had a deep effect not just on the structure of north Indian kinship but on its very foundation. In making the newly narrowed conjugal unit and its direct descendants primary heirs to property and bestowing on them ownership of hitherto unavailable equal dispositional rights, these Acts altered the bedrock principles of relationality in north India and at once reversed the motor of Indian society. In their unfolding, the two Acts grammatically reconfigured north Indian kinship from descriptive to classificatory and shifted its motor from alliance to descent, the latter now burdened with a hitherto unprecedented weight. The clue to these shifts is to be found in a number of changes that have taken place in north India, which are sometimes all too hastily explained away under bulky rubrics like modernity, globalization, sanskritization (the pursuit of upward mobility by those lower down the caste/tribe hierarchy by emulating upper caste ritual and other social practices), and the like. The effects of such shifts, coupled with the fact that they went largely unacknowledged and unarticulated, are altogether profound, and, in the case of *khaps*, violent, as the next section elaborates.

Khaps and the Clatter of Culture

Let us remind ourselves of what is at issue as far as the *khaps* or caste councils are concerned. In the main, *khaps* have increasingly gained force by issuing retributory diktats against "bad marriages" or "mismarriages" (e.g., intercaste, endogamous, intralocal), none of which is an invalid form of marriage in the eyes of the law. In addition, these councils of patriarchs petitioned the Indian state to amend the HMA to reflect their demands. What poses a special challenge to the state is their growing popular and political influence, and the perpetration of violence at their behest. Let us also recall relevant characteristics of the region where *khap panchayats* are most influential and where the rate of so-called honor killings is on the increase. The region comprises mainly Haryana, western Uttar Pradesh, and Delhi, and it has been marked by at least two distinct waves of affluence in the last fifty years, both of which are tied to the increased value of land.[14] In the first instance, the region was among the

---

14. On the transformation of the region during the colonial period, see Datta (1999). For the effects of these transformation on women in the region, see Chowdhry (1994; 2007).

primary beneficiaries of the Green Revolution in the 1950s and 1960s, which propelled unprecedented growth in the rural economy of the area and made a section of the rural population flush with new wealth. Commentators have elaborated on the relationship between economic growth and new sociological developments, in particular the increasingly unbalanced sex ratio in the region, which currently stands at 850 girls for every 1000 boys (Kaur 2010; Khanna 2010).[15] The rise of *khap* violence is sometimes attributed to the paucity of young women of marriageable age in the region (Kaur 2010). However, neither the adverse sex ratio nor the large proportion of unmarried young men there is an entirely recent development; both these features of north Indian society have long been linked to the rising value of land and the growing political power of landowners (Chowdhry 1994; Chowdhry 2007: 253–54). I want to suggest that although revelatory of the changing social landscape, political economy alone cannot explain the rising influence of *khaps* witnessed today. It is essential that we pay attention to the changes taking place in the structuring of north Indian kinship.

The reversal of the kinship motor of society from alliance to descent has had a profound effect in this area. The work of society has shifted, in that there is a new emphasis placed on vertical as opposed to horizontal relations. This does not imply that the work of alliance has been altogether abandoned, but that social institutions and efforts are now geared more towards achieving the objective of producing descent. Thus, from arranging marriages or circulating women as a motor for moving society forward, increasing its thickness and intensifying the density of relations, the new laws have managed to engender a recalibration of this effort so that the focus is heavily weighted in favor of producing heirs or, in other words, descendants. As a result, social value is no longer being produced simply in and through establishing or reinforcing horizontal networks of alliance, but is now being contested, if not superseded, by an alternative production of social value along the vertical axis of descent. The evidence is most clear from the key shift in this area, where the region's well-established male-child preference has become ever-more prominent in the decades since the Acts were passed (John et al. 2009; John 2011).[16] The need to produce male heirs has now achieved almost

---

15. The sex ratio improved marginally from 801:1000 in 2001 to 850:1000 in 2011, but it was still well below the national average of 933:1000.

16. John (2011) further notes that, although the ratio has marginally improved in the north Indian states, there has been a surprising decline in the same in

an unprecedented level of autonomy such that it has become a goal in itself. Social and reproductive technologies have aided in this objective by freeing it from the conjugal complex. And even though the HSA posits sons and daughters as equal heirs or descendants, these technologies in combination with the policy imperative of the two-children norm have only furthered the dominance of male-child preference (Kaur 2010; Khanna 2010).

But what is curious, and to an extent, remains unaccounted for is that the scarcity of women in the declining sex ratio has not yielded a change in the traffic and direction of marriage payments, as it might have been hoped, if not presumed. Rather, in a bizarre development, two forms of marriage have resurfaced after nearly a century: marriage by capture and child-marriage. The former, also known as marriage by abduction, is now nearly a decade old. Technically, it is not really a marriage, but a contractual "renting" of the womb of women abducted from places as far as Bangladesh for the explicit purpose of producing a male heir. The "wifely" services are usually terminated once her obligation to produce a male heir is completed (Kaur 2004). The abductee has no rights in the household beyond the agreed payment for childbirth. There is no kinship that follows with and for the woman who has borne the child (2004). By contrast, child marriage is touted by *khap* patriarchs and even by some social services agents as a preferred solution for producing the right kind of male heirs, as well as for keeping the circulation of young women under control (Siwach 2010). Unlike womb-renting, child-marriage is very much aimed at sustaining kinship networks, even if it emerges from and consolidates a different principle of kinship (descent vs. alliance). This is not to say that new reproductive technologies, or even contractual arrangements of womb-renting, have arisen as a direct result of these legal reforms. Assisted reproductive technologies are a global phenomenon and their liberatory and exploitative potential is well-recognized in the literature.[17] These technologies have instead become instrumentalized to provide a double-solution to the twin challenges posed by the destabilization of kinship structures instigated by the HSA-HMA. These two acts maintain the prevailing male-preferential ideology that originally

---

central and eastern India, areas which historically have not tended to have a male-child preference.

17. The literature on new or assisted reproductive technologies is too extensive to cite in full. See Strathern (1992) and Franklin (2013). On commercial surrogacy, see Pande (2014).

gave rise to the nihilistic practices of feticide, despite the declining sex-ratio. Further, new reproductive technologies have provided a techno-logical solution to the challenges posed by the fast disappearing women in local populations. Although the paucity of women in the community should have led to an increase in their value (as some may have hoped for), and possibly an eventual reversal in the direction of marriage pay-ments, the likelihood of these changes coming into being is nearly im-possible. Similarly, child-marriages are being seen as the ideal way to return to an age of control of women in this region. This then is the bi-opolitical solution to the challenge of ownership, of fragmentation of es-tates, status, and wealth posed by the law. In the end, gender—that much vaunted axis of reform and the vector of domestic equality enshrined in the original Hindu Code Bill and the pared down marriage and succes-sion Acts—does not and, dare I say, cannot and will not see its imbalance corrected in the long run. The reason for this lies in the way social reform and its axes were envisaged in law, in particular in the Hindu Code Bill, as the next section makes clear.

A Theft of Rights

In discussing the relationship between law and culture thus far, I have ad-dressed some of the strategies and conditions through and under which culture and cultural practices have challenged the legitimacy of Indian state law in recent times. If community patriarchs have found culture to be a conduit for asserting their political and social clout by taking on the law or demonstrating its alien qualities, then in this war of attrition, law has reasserted its position as the a prosthetic extension of the paternal-istic Indian state. In such a self-positioning, law becomes, and presents itself as, not just an arbiter or guarantor, but also as the provider of all things culture could not or did not provide. Chief among these are rights of equity and equality, hitherto unavailable to the citizenry, at least in and through culture. Folded into these rights are notions of liberty and freedom that law deems as its monopoly alone. In doing so, law becomes a critical medium through which the framework of rights becomes the lingua franca for comprehending both political and social life. But as Strathern has cautioned, it is imperative to denaturalize the language of rights, since a "vocabulary that turns on the deprivation of 'rights' must entail premises about a specific form of property. To assert rights against others implies a sense of legal ownership" (1988a: 142). Even though her warning came against certain Marxist-feminist readings of gender relations in Melanesia, specifically regarding the question of owning the product of one's labor, it is nevertheless salutary for understanding the persistent incommensurability between law and culture and why, at this point and in this particular matter, the two end up talking past each other.

Imputed in the way the state frames itself as the provider of everything that is lacking elsewhere is by necessity a restrictive portrayal of all other sources of social and political life. Seen from the eyes of the law, culture, in this all too powerful framework, then becomes a restriction, one that constrains people from realizing the full potential of their rights and liberties conferred in and through citizenship. Speaking within this framework or in its support, sixty years after the constitution first came into force, at such moments of serious challenge from the other side, law and its liberal defendants wittingly or unwittingly position culture as a *thief*, as one that takes away from society all that the law has bestowed. In a neat reversal, law becomes the giver of the gift of rights to its citizens, and culture becomes the thief or the misappropriator. If we locate "theft" in the realm of exchange, then it sits at odds with the "gift"—in fact, almost in opposition to it. Gifts propel exchange, but inasmuch as exchange is written into the gift, so is the grayness of ownership.[18] Theft, on the other hand, disrupts exchange, calls a halt to it, and momentarily disturbs the logic of flow precisely because it disputes and appropriates ownership—not through a process of exchange (whether equal, reciprocal, or asymmetric), but by its disruption, its end. It seeks to end the grayness of ownership, to bring it within the realm of black-and-white clarity. The theft of rights, then, is the greatest crime committed by culture, for it stops certain forms of symbolic exchange—in this case, the rights and obligations between the citizen and the state to continue or even to come into being at all. But what kind of theft, if any, does law commit against culture?

It is here that Strathern's caution comes to bear upon the argument. To talk of rights that law has bestowed and which culture subsequently takes away in the event of efficacious *khap* violence is to assert the existence of those rights in the first place. It also means confirming the location of these rights in the form of legal ownership that people have in themselves and with regard to other people. It is when the edifice of

---

18. The literature on the gift and the *hau* of the gift is too vast to cite. But see, Gregory (2015) and Strathern (1988a). On India, see Parry (1986); Raheja (1988); and Copeman (2011). See also Sanchez et al. (2017).

rights-talk is spliced at this angle that the consequences of the original non-acknowledgment of culture by law become evident. Indian law recognizes culture and cultural difference in very particular forms. The greatest acknowledgment of cultural difference recognized and defended by the Indian Constitution is at the level of religion. The existence of the various personal codes (Hindu, Muslim, Christian) is proclaimed as testimony to the defense of difference by law in India (Bajpai 2011; Bhargava 1998). It is another matter that the impetus to do so is derived not so much from the recognition of difference but from the constitutional guarantee of the right to equality. But what needs to be underscored in the constitutional guarantee of personal codes is the swift and sealed conclusion that the recognition of difference has been completed in this one step. The spirit-level optic that pervades the Indian legal imagination deems that anything that is different can and must be seen as something that needs to be brought up to a level playing field (Chakrabarty 2002: 90). For example, in the landmark 2009 case overturning Article 377 of the Indian Penal Code, which had criminalized homosexuality since colonial times, the judgment was based on the defense of legal minorities—here the rights of sexual minorities rather than on a right to difference per se.[19] This numerical and statistical idiom of equality in Indian law is well noted (Bajpai 2011; Bhargava 1998; Chakrabarty 2002). What remains undertheorized is its monadic calculus of subjectivity as opposed to a relational calculus. As in case of the HSA and the HMA, the law purports to suffuse the citizen with rights (and obligations), but it does so primarily in their status as individuals, in unitary or atomistic fashion. As a result, it is the event or the moment of becoming or unbecoming a certain kind of person (wife, heir, daughter, widower, divorcée) that becomes the focus of juridical attention and elaboration, leeching away the complexity entailed in the relationship per se. The husband-wife relation, for example, is not just a relationship between a man and a woman; it also encompasses and is embedded within an array of relations that go far beyond them. It includes and is constituted by the "obligations entailed in having kinfolk" (Strathern 2004: 208). In other words, composite or dividual personhood cannot be acknowledged or reproduced through the HMA and the HSA, not least because, like Sahlins (2011: 13), law in India categorizes dividual personhood as "premodern." The subjects of the HMA and HSA are monadic individuals

---

19. *Naz Foundation v. Government of Nct of Delhi and Ors* (2009). 160 *Delhi Law Times* 277.

rather than a "composite site of social relations" (Strathern 1988a:13). This discrepancy between legal subjectivity and culturally defined kin categories also explains why individuals opportunistically assume expeditious (or liberal) subject positions as litigants and revert to a cultural type before and after court appearances, or "decision-events," as Humphrey calls them (2008: 368), especially in the case of family disputes (Kapila 2004; Mir-Hosseini 2000).[20] But it also throws light on why, sixty years after these laws were first enacted and equality of status was guaranteed as a fundamental right under the Indian Constitution, sociological axes of difference (e.g., gender) remain mostly undisturbed beyond their formal lives, especially in the domain of kinship. The adverse sex ratio and its expanding territory of influence, as John (2011) pointed out, is only one concrete manifestation of this discrepancy.

Beyond Expediency

In commonplace and some scholarly understandings of the conflict between law and culture, the latter is routinely positioned as a constraining influence, as something taking away from people what law has bestowed on them or inhibiting people's access to these gifts. The public aspirations of law, especially in the case of India, prevent a routine interrogation of its countervailing force because these aspirations are inherently formulated in the future tense. The promise of equality for all in an underdetermined notion of the future therefore presents itself as a powerful and, for most part, incontrovertible proposition that holds an attraction few can deny in a milieu overdetermined by hierarchy.

In fact, it is often the functioning or implementation of law rather than its content and force that usually comes in for criticism. Injustice, too, is not seen to issue forth from the nature of the law itself (Derrida 1990), but from the indolence or sloppiness of its executors. Only in the event of an explicit challenge fielded by representatives of cultural norms, for example, in the famous case of Shah Bano[21] or in the current

---

20. In the literature on socio-legal studies, this is called "forum-shopping". See Merry (1989); and Von Benda-Beckmann (1981).
21. Briefly, Shah Bano, Muslim and immiserated sixty-two-year-old divorcée, was awarded maintenance by the Supreme Court under Section 125 of the Indian Penal Code, which does not allow discrimination on the grounds of caste or religion. The judgment was based on the constitutional principle of

round of *khap*-inspired violence, are public aspirations of law tentatively superseded by the question mark placed on the force of law in Indian society. *Khaps* appear doubly restrictive in this context: they are neither democratic, in that they are not based in equality, nor do they defend it. Moreover, their emancipatory potential and epistemological status are undermined by the fact that cultural norms are not seen to be products of systematic expertise in the way law is, and neither are there recognizable professions attached to them (Galanter 1972: 61).

It is when we turn the argument on its head that the restrictions placed by law on culture reveal themselves in two forms: one is the way in which particular forms of subjectivity find recognition in law, and the other is how its monadic calculus pares down relationality. The narrow field of vision for recognition and the politics it gives birth to is well noted in scholarship on indigenous communities. Elizabeth Povinelli, among others, has discussed at length the "gridlocking" of indigenous bodies and culture by the (Australian) state on two levels: first, by bestowing recognition only on so-called non-repugnant indigenous cultural practices; second, by bestowing legal recognition only on those that can be demonstrated to have an unbroken continuity with the past (Povinelli 2006: 227; see also Clifford 1988). Indigenous communities, for their part, have drawn on culture as an expedient resource for gaining recognition from the state (Yudice 2003: 19). But what we have in the case of the law in India is a very different kind of gridlocking, where culture is rendered anything but expedient. Here, law is premised on a *rupture* with the past; therefore any continuity with the past is precisely what law cannot address or recognize, especially in matters of "ordinary occurrence." In order to redescribe and gain any purchase on the relationship between law and culture, we will therefore need to address both sets of constraints. This means addressing the reasons, not for the conflict between law and culture, but, following Derrida (1990: 951), for their incommensurability that lends the appearance of hostility. And for that, we will need to examine culture seriously, not just expediently—that is, neither as a resource nor as gridlock, which is what the chapters that follow aim to do.

---

equality and was strongly opposed by the Muslim clergy, since it contravened the rights of a divorced woman in the Muslim Personal Code. Ultimately, the government felt forced to rescind the court's order and revert the petitioner to her "cultural category." For discussion on the case and its consequences, see Das (1997); Mullally (2004); Pathak and Sunder Rajan (1989); and Vatuk (2009).

CHAPTER 3

The Truths of Dispossession

> *There is a law of nature that a thing can be retained by the same means by which it has been acquired. A thing acquired by violence can be retained by violence alone, while one acquired by truth can be retained only by truth.*
>
> – M. K. Gandhi, *Satyagraha in South Africa*, 1928

Establishing the fulcrum of liberal law in property and ownership does not exhaust their significance in ordinary life. As the previous chapter made clear, this is especially the case in historically diverse societies such as India, where the law lies amidst a range of competing normative structures which may be either completely at odds with it or even altogether different, even if not expressly or necessarily contradictory. Popularly or locally held ideas of property and ownership, for instance, do not necessarily coincide with legal doctrine for a host of reasons, some of which have to do with the way the doctrine has been codified.[1] Legal doctrine is a late entrant in the normative structures. As the last chapter made clear, India's postcolonial constitutional order was expressly constructed to rewrite the existing grammar of Indian society, especially concerning what colonial officials designated as "matters of

---

1. For a history of the codification of law in colonial India, see in particular Cohn (1996). See also Mukherjee (2010) and Singha (1998).

ordinary occurrence." In this chapter I focus on the distinctiveness of legal concepts of ownership from other ideals. I lean on the notions of property among the Gaddis, a pastoralist community in the western Himalaya, to understand the encompassment of property and ownership in structures of ordinary life, the different scales at which ideas and relations of ownership become manifest, the variety of modes and axes of ownership and accumulation, and why ownership matters. I discuss Gaddi categories and concepts of property to explore not just the relational possibilities made by ownership, but also to understand the obverse: dispossession and its political charge. I examine the different modes and scales under which ownership works and property is accumulated and *disaccumulated* in order to understand the limits of the law and, in turn, the limits of the state. The encompassment of social life in relations of ownership, and the inability of the state (as law) to fold all social life within itself usually form the premise from which to explore ethnographically all that ownership assists and makes possible. While these questions have occupied anthropologists often, I reconsider them here in relation to a less-often investigated corollary: what is dispossession and why is it sovereignty-making?

Anthropology has long attended to questions of ownership, of exchange, and of the relationality born out of transactions.[2] To have property is to be able to have something to give, transact, attract with, hold, and accumulate. As I tried to show through the comparison of two elopements in Chapter 1, to not have any possession, or have very little, is to hold very limited social capacity. Insofar as they are judged by the state to be the embodiment of freedom by the very fact of having a right to hold them, proprietary transactions and accumulation are of central interest to the state. This interest is most visibly routinized in its revenue function. Therefore, holding and transacting are routinely monitored and regulated by the state via its laws and revenue regimes. Though states build an elaborate and ever-growing infrastructure to monitor, record, and regulate these transactions, there remain a number of possessions and transactions that escape the eye and ambit of the

---

2. For relatively recent overviews on the anthropology of property, see Von Benda-Beckmann, et al. (2009) and Hirsch (2010). For a relational anthropology of property, see Strathern (1999). For "real," or landed property, see Verdery (2003). On the anthropology of intellectual property, see Pottage (2001) and Strathern (2005). On the anthropology of cultural property, see Brown (2009).

law. One such holding I explore here to open up a discussion on the limits of the law is women's property. I also discuss intangible property in biogenetic substance that, while being heritable, and capable of being malleable, is completely inalienable. Investigating notions of property and dispossession among the Gaddis outside a purely ethico-legal framework, I discuss ownership of things and relations that are not just "inalienable" (*pace* Weiner 1992), but that can also never be taken away.

As already noted in Chapter 1, the place of ownership and possessions is an ambivalent one in the Indic worldview, where possessions are necessary for both social relations and kinship, yet have the potential to interrupt the ideal progression of a life cycle towards its desired goal of being released from life cycles altogether. Possessions carry the charge of the multiple temporalities and scales in which an individual life is lived: worldly and the cosmic. Possessions and their ownership are important in order to be able to fulfil the obligations of particular stages of a life cycle and, at the same time, may have an effect on the longer temporal cycle of births and rebirths. While not having possessions or abjuring ownership may carry cultural validation for the individual, large-scale, forcible or involuntary dispossessions and voluntary collective dispossession are altogether different, and differently problematic. This contradictory status of possession and dispossession has been efficaciously mobilized by the modern state in India as it attempts to stand in as a proxy for the divine. The insistently egalitarian relationship with the divine makes for a very distinctive relationship with (divine) power and authority. This relation pervades the structuration of several key relationships among the Gaddis, including that of kinship and the relationship with the state.[3] Central to their relationship with the divine are things with which they have a proprietary relationship, which are things they have received in reward from the divine: viz., the landscape, their animals, and their Gaddiness. Possession-dispossession work as a pluripotent dynamic in this relationship, but not in obvious ways. My aim here is to capture ethnographically the everyday multiscalarity at which possessions are held and disposed, and dispossession attempted and thwarted.

---

3. The usage of the collective noun, "Gaddis," is deliberate here and in order to allude to their interlocution with the state *qua* Gaddis, *qua* community, and not in individual or abstract capacities.

Landscapes of Property

The Gaddis are a pastoralist community that live on either side of the Dhauladhar mountains, in present-day Chamba and Kangra districts in the middle-upper western Himalaya. They consider the Bharmaur region of Chamba district in north India as their "home," while from the late eighteenth century an increasing number of Gaddis began to settle on the southern face of the Dhauladhar mountains (see Lyall 1875: 83). Not unlike other communities in India, Gaddis narrate two different types of origin myths: that of the origins of humanity, or the coming into being of the first man and the first woman, and a second myth related to their birth as a distinct community.[4] As is common in India, it is the myth which encodes how Gaddis came to acquire their social and not their human form that is more widely circulated (Banerjee-Dube 2010). It provides a teleology of their current status within the social hierarchy. According to the dominant version of this myth, Gaddis were originally a trading people and inhabitants of the plains, but their ancestors fled to the high ranges of the Himalaya to escape local persecution.[5] Despite

---

4. In the first Gaddi origin myth, many million years ago, there was a very big *jalbimbi* (tsunami) and the earth drowned in the celestial ocean. Only Shiva remained because he is immortal. He created Brahma and Vishnu and told them to populate the world with humans, because without humans there can be no "world." Brahma and Vishnu created an effigy (*putla*) made of silver, and asked Shiva to breathe life (*prana*, vital force) into it. He tried but the effigy remained lifeless. They then created an effigy of solid gold. Again Shiva tried but could not imbue it with *prana*. Human effigies made of iron, brass, bronze and wood similarly failed to gain life. Finally, having come to their wits' end, the three decided to seek out Vidhi Mata (Mother Earth), and asked her how she had created humans. She told them to use ash and use the wood of *tunni* and *dareka* trees to make effigies of a man and a woman. When the two ash and wood effigies were ready, Shiva breathed life into it and the effigies accepted the *prana* and began to breathe.

    In order to walk, these effigies needed bones, which Shiva got for them on a loan from the Ganges (hence one returns one's bones to the Ganges at death). The first seed for agriculture was loaned by a lower caste man and, because that debt is never returned, he periodically holds on to the sun and the moon as ransom, which we experience as eclipses.

5. The motive to flee has been inflected with more recent politics and Gaddis often attribute it to religious persecution at the hands of "Rangjeb," or Aurangzeb.

considerable hardship on their journey north, Gaddi ancestors shared whatever little food they had with each other and with whoever they met on the way, and resisted any temptation for wrongdoing. Finally, they found themselves by the edge of Manimahesh Lake in the Dhauladhar mountains when Lord Shiva assumed his corporeal form and appeared before them. He said he had decided to reward them for their integrity and generosity. Seeing that they were homeless and without a means of livelihood, he flicked off some ash from his body[6] and transformed the specks, which now covered the mountain pastures on either side of the lake, into flocks of sheep and goats. He entrusted the care of the flock to the Gaddi ancestors and promised that as long as they looked after these sheep and goats, they and their descendants would always have prosperity. This is how they say the Gaddis became conjoined with their *khadu-bhedu* (goats and sheep), and became *ghumantu* (pastoralists), moving from pasture to pasture.

In keeping with the usual structure of caste histories, this origin myth at once joins the Gaddis to their present livelihood as an act of divine intervention. However, unlike many other origin myths, Gaddis have been divinely ordained to their livelihood not as an atonement for a misdeed, but rather as reward for ethical conduct and sacrificial disposition. For the community today, looking after flocks of sheep and goats is considered a divine duty, a pledge they undertook simultaneously to propitiate the gods and to secure their own prosperity. To be a Gaddi is to be a pastoralist, looking after sheep and goats, taking the flock from pasture to pasture, all year round. While all Gaddis may not be pastoralists today, and while among those who are pastoralists, plenitude may well be a relative bequest, peripateticism and transhumance nevertheless remains the universally shared starting position of the Gaddi worldview and view of themselves. Any and all difference in status and departure in worldview among the Gaddis comes after this universal starting position.[7]

No matter whether they are currently pastoralists, or indeed prosperous, for the Gaddis, plenitude lies symbolically in two sources: the flock and the landscape. Unsurprisingly therefore, the Gaddi word for the flock is *dhan*, which literally means "wealth." But ownership of animals alone is no guarantee of prosperity, and not all animals constitute

---

6. Shiva is often depicted with an ash-smeared body. On Shiva's place in and beyond the Hindu pantheon, see for example O'Flaherty (1973).
7. Gaddis who follow pastoralism, whether on a modest or a grand scale, are increasingly referred to as "pure" Gaddis.

dhan. A key part of the promissory bond with Shiva is transhumance, their obligation in the mutual pact for prosperity. Transhumance is a way of recognizing and sharing Shiva's domain. Their very name, "Gaddi," is said to be derived from "Gadderan," the name for the mountainous region surrounding Mount Kailash in the high western Himalaya, regarded in mythology as the *gaddi* (literally "seat") of Shiva. The Gaddi transhumant cycle thus echoes the seasonal migration of Shiva from Kailash (Wagner 2013: 41). Landscape therefore is sacred, dotted with material and intangible extensions of divinity. With their flocks, Gaddi herders (men) traverse vast mountainous territory from pasture to pasture all year round, from the cold deserts of the trans-Himalayan Spiti range, when the Himalaya is being lashed with monsoon showers, to the foothills of the Sivalik range in Punjab, when higher pastures are snowbound and the wheat and other *rabi* crops in the plains are in need of manure.[8] Gaddi herders return to their native villages for two short periods in the year (often coinciding with weddings and other ritual occasions), while Shiva's journey takes him further up the mountains to the mythical Meru and then back (Wagner 2013).[9] In my long years of research with the Gaddis, while much has changed, what remains steadfast is the inseparability of herding from transhumance for them. Today, pastoralism may have become waged and thus performed as wage labor even by non-Gaddis, and, over the years, even higher pastures may have become prized with passable roads, nevertheless, for the Gaddis, their ideal of herding remains avowedly pastoralist and transhumant. Journeying across the landscape with the flock is true shepherding: "We are not like the sheep farmers of New Zealand. All they need to do is open the gate of the pen and let their sheep out to graze on the ranch, and in the evening herd them back in the pen. Gaddis walk with our *dhan* to pastures and grasslands up and down the mountains for six months at a time. That is why our wool and the meat is so distinct and valuable."[10]

---

8. There are two categories of crop in India, with distinct cropping cycles: *rabi* (harvested in spring, e.g. wheat) and *kharif* (harvested in fall, e.g. paddy).

9. The echoing of Shiva's life occurs at all key moments in the Gaddi life-cycle, from Shiva's seasonal migration in their own transhumance, to the enactment of Shiva's marriage to Parvati in Gaddi weddings (see also Wagner 2013: 51).

10. Research interview with K. S., male, 60 (2010). The reference to New Zealand, which had taken me by surprise, had to do with the newly inaugurated global trade regime under the World Trade Organization, which had

This long cycle of transhumance is regarded as their fundamental obligation towards the divine and as integral to their pact for prosperity and plenitude. Therefore, transhumant pastoralism is not merely a livelihood strategy for the Gaddis, but is central to their relationship with divine and, as we shall see, also with secular, power. Wealth, well-being, and ownership are folded into their relationship with (divine) power.

Transhumance may join the Gaddis with Gadderan (Shiva's seat), but it separates men's labor from women's labor, men's animals from women's animals, and consequently men's property from women's property. In the late 1990s, Gaddi women in my fieldwork village looked after domestic animals all year round. Domestic animals were often goats, rarely sheep, and sometimes included horses, mules, and cows. Prima facie, looking after domestic animals echoed or mimicked the transhumant cycle in a condensed form. Many Gaddi women preferred to take their domestic animals for grazing in the village commons or *shamlat*, which were usually at the outskirts of the village and at some distance from their homesteads, rather than feeding them at home all the time.[11] Women in the village pooled their animals and took turns to take a small herd of domestic animals to graze, often combining their grazing duty with the collection of firewood. This activity, locally termed as "*bakri* duty" (literally "goat duty") by the women, usually took up the greater part of the day and it was physically demanding. Nevertheless, the labor entailed in the care of domestic animals was never considered by them to be similar to men's transhumant labor, even when it was a Gaddi woman's turn to shepherd the animals. There was little ambiguity about the status of domestic animals in Gaddi women's life. Domestic animals, including their goats, were loved and cared for, and often given names, but these animals were not *dhan*, thereby signaling the inseparability of divinity from pastoral runs, which the village commons hardly matched. Moreover, the village commons were not exclusive either to the Gaddis or to their animals for pasture. Moreover, domestic animals were acquired through

---

resulted in the lifting of protectionist policies towards domestic agricultural products. This had meant that for the first time for domestic wool manufacturers, Gaddi wool had to compete with that imported from New Zealand. When I did this research (2007), Chinese wool had yet to flood the Indian market, and whatever amount there existed, it was considered inferior, if cheaper, than its Kiwi counterpart.

11. See Federici (2004: 72) on the effects of the steady erosion of the commons on the life of women in particular.

the more worldly transactions of kinship exchange (usually as gifts to the bride by her family), or through ordinary commerce (bought), and were considered women's property and wealth. Some domestic animals may have been acquired from the flock itself, but once separated from the main herd, and kept away from the pastures, domestic goats and sheep carried an altogether different valence.

Gaddi women had their own relation to the divine in the landscape but, unlike the men, it was via their substance and not through labor. Kinship-based gods are divided along gender lines. *Kulajs* (sometimes *kul-debi*)), or Gaddi clan goddesses, live in the landscape and are *inherited* along the maternal line. All Gaddi children born of the same mother, regardless of sex, or indeed of father, have the same clan goddess located in or near the original female ancestor's village. Over time, *kulajs* have an echoed presence in the form of smaller shrines dotting the landscape, often along herding or migratory routes. By contrast, clan gods or *kul-debta* are inherited along the paternal line by male children and through marriage by women. These gods are located and worshipped locally, which may even be inside the courtyard of the family house. An unmarried Gaddi girl therefore has no *kul debta* of her own, but shares her husband's on marriage. Thus, while sacredness of the landscape by men is reiterated through their labor and their identification by and with Shiva, it is Gaddi women who transmit this sacred connection to the next generation. No Gaddi, regardless of their sex, is ever without a *kulaj*, even if he or she has not much else by way of possessions. It is in this sense that Gaddiness is inalienable, substantial, and shared.

Though Gaddis beget their livelihood in and through divine benevolence, they understand their commitment to transhumance as a compact, and not as a form of service or worship. Like all compacts, theirs too is rooted in egalitarianism. It is not seen as transactional, but rather regarded as an agreement to uphold a set of mutual obligations in order to create a world in its image. Having gained merit in the eyes of the divine, Gaddis continue to take pride in their generosity. As a local saying goes, "ask a Gaddi for his cap and he will offer you his coat." By entering into a relationship with the divine that is simultaneously based in a recognition of the power of the divine (to bestow) and a response to that gift as not a prompt for servility but of mutuality, Gaddis write the template for their fundamental disposition towards a range of power relations they encounter, including one with sovereignty. Instead of subservience or obedience, the Gaddi relationship with (sovereign) power takes the form of reciprocity, with mutually understood obligations towards each other.

This ideology of mutuality permeates all spheres of exchange among the Gaddis and, therefore, unsurprisingly, the ideal form of Gaddi marriage is *atta-satta*, or isogamy. Even though inegalitarian forms of marriage exchange have begun to take hold of late, the ideology of mutuality persists, at least at the ritual or symbolic level.

Uncommon Property

Clan goddesses, pastures, and flock are thus the first property and the landscape is the first site of accumulation for the Gaddis. But this accumulation is contiguous neither in time nor in space, and therefore takes on specific forms. Clan goddesses and pastures are dispersed in the landscape. Transhumant pastoralism itself sits at odds with, if not counter to, the idea of enclosure of land or landscape. Gaddis do not "own" the Gadderan. Most of them do not even have rights of access to the pastures as much of the landscape today is enclosed, in a manner of speaking, as grazing is now restricted to dedicated seasonal runs known as *jots* (see Saberwal 1999; Axelby 2007). Since the nineteenth century, enclosure of forests by the state has remained the primary technique of governing the so-called wilds and the commons. Over the past two centuries, successive sovereigns have enclosed vast areas of territory and today this quasi-sacred landscape exists as a series of state-regulated "commons" and state-owned "forest land."[12] The colonial process of regulated enclosure was adopted by the contemporary Indian state in toto, which has periodically added new "nature reserves" and protected forests.[13] State

12. Environmental historians of colonial India (e.g. Gadgil and Guha 1992; Sivaramakrishnan 2000) and political ecologists of the region (Saberwal 1999) and beyond (Agrawal 2005; Li 2007; Ostrom 1990; Peluso 1992) have detailed the politics of this process of enclosure of the commons, which under the modern state has resulted in the conversion of this territory into state-owned and regulated "forest land" (Saberwal 1999).

13. On forest enclosure in the western Himalaya, especially as it affects the Gaddis, see Saberwal (1999). Saberwal reveals the alarmist discourse on environmental degradation mobilized by the colonial state to enclose ever greater territories, sometimes for the purpose of converting mixed forests to single-species forests to furnish the needs of the Industrial Revolution. See also Axelby (2007) on the intersection of environmental discourse with the developmental postcolonial state.

enclosure of forests and commons has meant that grazing is highly regulated, and it has had the effect of making pastoralism for the Gaddis not just a divine duty, but also their most readily available form of self articulation with the state.

State ownership of all commons, including forests and pastures, also transformed the Gaddi relationship with the landscape from an identificatory into a proprietary one. Access to enclosed commons and state forests now comes in the form of "permits," which go back to the colonial era, permits which themselves replaced customary and collective grants made by erstwhile princely states in the region. Access to these forests became increasingly curtailed, with greater numbers of forests becoming demarcated and reserved (Saberwal 1999). Today, these are administered by the Forest Department. Permits bestow grazing rights to individual families along earmarked parts of the terrain known as *jots* (runs) and *dhars* (pastures).[14] For the colonial state, to be a pastoralist in the western Himalaya was exclusively associated with being Gaddi and all herders, regardless of their past, were officially classified and returned in the 1881 census as Gaddis. One of the consequences of the official recognition of herding as a "traditional occupation" of the Gaddis was that only those classified as Gaddis were given grazing permits. Although the colonial state's recognition of herding as a "traditional livelihood" was on a collective basis for the Gaddis, permits were bestowed to individual herders at the time of the Forest Settlement of 1881, rather than on the community as such. Only a finite number of herder families "own" grazing rights, which are held along clan lines and are thereby hereditary in status. Since access to pasture comes via only these permits, they are therefore a significant family asset, giving rise to a differentiated proprietary economy in which some families or individual herders not only own flock, but also possess exclusive access to pastures. Those herders who do not own a permit of their own gain access to grazing runs via complex

---

The foundational text for the history of modern forestry and the colonial state in India is Gadgil and Guha (1992). See also Sivaramakrishnan (2000); Prasad (2003). On the successive enclosures of agricultural land, see the two magisterial studies of colonial Punjab by Bhattacharya (2018) and Saumarez-Smith (1996).

14. Following Ostrom (1990), for the erosion of the commons in the western Himalaya, see Saberwal (1999). For Punjab, see Saumarez-Smith (1996); for the transformation of rural northern India under colonialism, see Bhattacharya (2018). I take up the wider material implications in Chapter 4.

local rentier arrangements calculated through long-term kinship and labor-based exchange cycles (see Axelby 2007; Saberwal 1999: 12–43). So, while divine giving in the landscape may have made for symbolically collective prosperity and a collectivizing livelihood, the gifts of the state—such as recognition and permits—have had differentiating and proprietary consequences.

Ordinary Strategies of Accumulation

Despite its symbolic and real connection to prosperity, herding is no longer a popular pursuit for a variety of reasons (Kapila 2008; 2011). From the earliest stages of fieldwork, it was virtually impossible to come across a well-to-do Gaddi household that was not pastoralist. The depth of household accumulation and the scale of pastoralism often went together. Most large flocks (upwards of 1,000 head) were inherited, rather than acquired, or even built up incrementally over a lifetime. In the past, Gaddi men who did not have a herd of their own started their flock from the gift of animals received from the big herder at the end of each grazing cycle in lieu of their apprenticeship or *puhaali*. It was not unusual for *puhaals* to accumulate their own small flock (under 100) in time. Many pooled their herd with other small- to medium-scale herders, while continuing to either do *puhaali* for a big herder, or follow another occupation, such as farming. *Dhan* was and is indeed the source of all value, but this value escalates exponentially with scale and depth of accumulation. Sheep were especially prized because of the prime status of their wool in local markets, while goats were kept for their meat, and both had traditionally brought sizeable cash incomes to Gaddi herders. Today, though, Gaddi wool has lost its once prime position in the local market due to an influx of cheaper wool from Australia, New Zealand, and China. I have discussed elsewhere in some detail the reasons for this devaluation and the effects on Gaddi politics (Kapila 2011). While large-scale flocks remain highly remunerative, it has become more and more difficult to grow from a small-scale herder to a large one.[15] As a result of these and other conditions, though remunerative, pastoralism has slid far down the hierarchy of aspirations for the younger generation.

---

15. This is for several reasons, but significantly because younger Gaddi men do not aspire to become herders anymore. I discuss this in greater detail in Kapila (2008).

Flock and flock size were just one of a myriad forms of accumulation in the village where I have conducted long-term fieldwork. When asked what they had by way of possessions, people invariably listed land, domestic animals, household objects, gold, silver, and sometimes cash savings in terms of money in the bank, or an insurance policy cover. Even those who were precarious always said, "*Matta ha, ghat ha*" or "*Jaraa ki haa*" (literally "I don't have much, I have little" or "I have just a tiny bit"). No one whom I asked about their *jaidaad* ever said they had "no possessions" or had no property, no matter how immiserated they may have been. While people accumulated all manner of things, they enumerated as *jaidaad* only those they considered valuable and heirlooms, rather than simply valuable goods. They also listed "children" as almost a knee-jerk answer to the question from the anthropologist about what they considered was their *jaidaad*. *Mundu* ("son" or "boy," usually used as a generic word for "children"), *bacche* ("children"), they would say, were their most valuable *jaidaad*—"*Satton keemti*" (literally, "most valuable of all"). *Dhan* would follow almost in the same breath as children for those who owned a flock. And yet when asked to generate a more self-conscious list, children featured nowhere. But they were also not the only ones to not make an appearance on these lists. For example, no one listed any so-called white goods, or consumer durables such as televisions and radios, which several families owned at the time, or even refrigerators, which at the time were relatively rare. These somehow were not considered as wealth objects, assets, or property. On the other hand, very specific types of objects counted as wealth objects or prized possessions, usually objects that could be seen to store or hold value, or somehow signal accumulation. Often their value was greater than their material value and ranked quite prominently on *jaidaad* lists I generated with informants. These ranged from ritual objects such as a *daraat* (ritual sickle used in sacrificial slaughter of goat or sheep) and *charotti* (vessel for cooking the sacrificial meat), to objects such as *pedu* (large urns used to store grain), which signify storage or hoarding capacity, as well as size of land holding, and *kapoor mala* (necklaces of yellow jade or amber) that were markers of long-distance trade relations and received from Tibetan traders in the past as ceremonial gifts sealing a trading partnership (Gaddis gifted sheep or goats). Some listed precious metals such as the gold and silver of ornaments, and bronze utensils and pots, usually by weight. Owning *malka ke rupaye* (literally, "empress's money"), or silver coins from the time of British rule, was rare and signaled several things: a longer history of having had very large herds, generational depth of accumulation, and historical exchange relations with the state.[16] *Khaddi*, or loom, used exclusively by women to weave blankets, were the corresponding objects of *pedu*, and signified surplus accumulation not of crop, but of wool from the shearing of sheep and goats, and kept for domestic use. Unsurprisingly, *garam kambal*, sometimes also called *pattu* (handwoven woolen blankets), were a wealth signifier. The only modern consumer durable to enter these lists was motor vehicles (but no other vehicle, such as a motorbike, or scooter, or even a bicycle), primarily because of their use in the pastoralist cycle.[17]

There are possessions that do not turn up on any of these lists but are essentially held in a proprietary relation, even if of a different order. Chief among these invisible or tacit property are herding permits and clan goddesses, the former essentially alienable, the latter inherently inalienable. Children are routinely counted as property when asked about *jaidaad*, but are rarely featured among itemized catalogues of possessions. A reason for this could be that while children start out as one's possessions or "things," they eventually become "persons" and conduits through which possessions flow in time. Matrilineal property in the form of clan goddesses, on the other hand, links all Gaddis to the original Gaddi landscape and provides substantial fluidity between the non-contiguous village and pasture.

Possessions or *jaidaad* for the Gaddis can therefore be seen to be performing two types of work: one, to contain and accumulate (signifiers or *properties* of) Gaddiness, mainly in the form of pastoralist and ritual objects, and, two, to contain and accumulate value that enables exchange or that results from exchange (e.g. grain stores, precious metals, flock). Nevertheless, people were always at first hesitant to talk about property, not in terms of its principles, but in terms of what they owned. Though this reluctance or shyness cut across class and accumulation divides, and was linked to the dangers entailed in the visibility of one's wealth, it stemmed from different types of misgivings. While those at the very bottom of the accumulation hierarchy found it difficult to publicly acknowledge their

---

16. See also Zickgraf (2017) For discussions on "moneyness," and the transformation of value and objects into "money."

17. Owners of very large flock (such as J. and his sons) now drive up from their native village to visit the herd at key points in the transhumant cycle (such as shearing and lambing), rather than accompany the flock on a continual basis. The herd is increasingly looked after by hired wage labor, sometimes from as far as Nepal and Bihar (Kapila 2008).

relatively frugal possessions for the difficulties it may make in terms of social viability, the hesitation of those at the more abundant end of the scale came, not from shyness, but from wanting to actively conceal their wealth so as to not attract extractive interest from others. This hesitation often resulted in what at first appeared as double-speak, where wealthy Gaddis pretended to not have too much, or invoked a subaltern status based not in their immiseration, but in their "tribalness," in a bid to convince one of their modest incomes and assets. The most common extractive fear was that of the evil eye, which could leach your good fortune and prosperity (Da Col 2012; Empson 2012). Others feared the potential diminishing of their assets that may result from being forced into gifting their wares or wealth, usually by less well-to-do kin, either through praise or elicited as acts of forced generosity, akin to what Appadurai (1985) has elaborated for South India.

There was yet another kind of danger which was perhaps represented in the stranger in the midst, in this case, the anthropologist, a danger which lay in making ownership and the value of possessions legible to outsiders. Gaddis would not be able to put a figure on the objective value of ritual objects, but they all know that the value of owning a *charotti* or a *daraat* bore little resemblance to their objective material value. Hence Gaddis never enumerated a *charotti* in terms of its weight (unlike kitchen utensils, for example), but rather in the number of vessels they owned. Similarly, the value of a *daraat* signaled not the ability to afford the metal blade or its wooden handle, but access to an important part of the sacrificial complex (Harrison 1992). At the same time, there were items of wealth that were never on display or in use, for example, *malka ke rupaye*. Similar to the danger of enforced generosity, making the scale of accumulation legible and intelligible in the abstract to outsiders carries the danger of potential future extraction or appropriation. Nowhere was this danger more potent than when it came to the state, which alone carries the ability to extract through taxation, a point made robustly by Maurer in several discussions on offshore finance (Maurer 2004; 2013). Unlike with the super-rich and corporate tax avoiders, whose aim was to conceal their wealth from the state so as to stall its extractive powers over their wealth through taxation, for the Gaddis it was the opposite. The anxiety over revealing their wealth to the state stems not from the threat of the state extracting the wealth from the person, but rather from losing their *own* ability to extract beneficence and welfare from the state.

What has made the continued sequestering of valuable assets away from potentially parasitic or extractive relations possible is the historical mismatch between what people (Gaddis) understand and enlist as *jaid-aad*, and what the state enumerates as property. To meet its governmental aims of regulation and revenue extraction, the state, via the law, makes legible and brings within its field of vision key moments in which property is made or then alienated. As discussed in Chapter 1, the starting unit of modern law is the possessive individual and so no modern legal system—and therefore the state—can exist without the codification of norms surrounding key exchange relations. All modern states have at their core a system that regulates and governs all manner of property relations. While property is crucial for statecraft and the law, as we will see, what the state counts as property and codifies as property relations, captures only partially what people consider as wealth, property, and proprietary transactions. The codification of property and property relations by the state has undoubtedly had a transformative effect on kinship structures and relations but, equally, its aim to be omniscient, omnipresent, and omnipotent with regard to the life of its people remains an aspiration in these "matters of ordinary occurrence," to which I now turn.

The Law Comes Home

The inability of the state to encompass all forms of property within its legal definition and codification originates in the vantage point from which property and ownership is codified within the law more generally, but particularly in the Indian case. Property is conceptualized from the primary vantage point of its separation from the owner, or "dispositional control" (Strathern 1999), and not its ownership. Therefore, it is matters of alienation that find most elaboration in the doctrine for regulation purposes, and this is linked to the law by way of the law's functioning in dispute resolution. Holding and accumulating are monitored by the state in a different register, that of extraction through revenue regimes. Property regimes related to revenue extraction have been foundational to state-making (Chalfin 2010; Scott, et al. 2002) and especially to colonialism (Guha 1996). Regulating the alienation of property became the focal point of colonial attention, whether ownership, whether within kinship (such as through succession), or whether in non-kin-based alienation (such as sale). Title and alienation are common subjects of dispute. To settle them with enduring legitimacy has required the state to formalize social rules with which people alienate their possessions. While the colonial state in India expended considerable effort to codify the existent or shared norms of alienation or introduce new norms to regulate the traffic in and disputes related to land title, the postcolonial state, as the previous chapter shows, set about creating new norms around alienation with specific reparative objectives in mind. Regardless of the intent, codification changed the structure of local society, and yet the state was never able to totally encompass all things over which people asserted personal or collective title.

In my fieldwork village, every single item was inscribed with ownership, even if not always in terms of private property, and possessions were jealously guarded. The village *panchayat* devoted considerable energy to dealing with petty conflicts that fell within its jurisdiction, which largely constituted perceived infringements of these possessions. For instance, every tree in the village had a distinct owner and even its leaves could only be used by the owner as fodder for their domestic animals. A tree may have belonged jointly to a family at a point in time, but once the household has been partitioned between brothers, such partition may limit access to the tree for some. If relations were not the best between the members of the partitioned household, a good use was made of the language of ownership to cement the partition. Sisters-in-law sometimes break into a shouting match in case one of them wrongly takes a few twigs for the hearth or leaves to feed her own goat from the other's tree. On the other hand, despite a partition of property between the brothers upon the death of the ancestor, if the brothers and their respective families were not in conflict, then the language of ownership assumed the idiom of sharing and cooperation.

It was action that makes manifest social relations, as Strathern has pointed out (1999: 16). Women in particular make use of such non-codified actions to make affective relations beyond those prescribed within kinship, such as Buglo at the time of her daughter's wedding (as described in the beginning of this book). Buglo giving away a piece of her jewelry to her brother's wife in some ways is typical of the emotional excess usual at occasions like weddings, but it is also symptomatic of the fact that there are many everyday transactions of things between people which do not fall into either the domain of ritual or that of legal enforcement. While the law is quite clear about certain types of ownership and its rightful devolution, there are categories of proprietors and property that remain at the margins of legal discourse. Women as proprietors and women's property is a good case in point. It is not as if legislation has not touched upon "women's property." In fact, *streedhan* (literally, "women's wealth") has been codified as an important part of many pieces of legislation, from the Hindu Succession Act of 1956 to the Dowry Prohibition Act of 1961. According to these two acts, whatever is gifted to the woman by her natal family at the time of the wedding (and registered officially thus), such gift forms her *streedhan* over which she has absolute ownership and therefore complete and exclusive dispositional control. *Streedhan* was included in the legislation by way of a readjustment of the alienation of natal property from out-marrying female heirs (Uberoi 1996). The empirical reality may tell us quite another story. Despite several decades having passed since the promulgation of the HSA, *streedhan* is rarely registered, and therefore contested claims by a woman can never have legal viability; furthermore, *streedhan* is never really an actual equal share in the natal property (Agarwal 1994).[18]

In legal terms, the property belonging absolutely to a woman devolves differently compared to that of a male proprietor. That is to say, the order of heirs is different in the case of women. While the HSA was created to play an important role in correcting the gender imbalance in property rights, it is by no means a gender-blind law. It conceives men and women as different legal subjects having different legal capacities in terms of how they hold, inherit, and devolve their wealth. This has largely to do with both the descriptive and prescriptive ideals of the Hindu household enshrined in it. The HSA does make a qualification that, while daughters have an equal right in their father's property, they do not have a right to claim a partition to an ancestral dwelling which may be part of their father's property, while the sons do enjoy such a right. In addition, a daughter is also entitled to "a right of residence in that dwelling house only if she is unmarried or has been deserted by or has separated from her husband or is a widow" (HSA 1956). It was not until 2000 that an equal share in ancestral property for women was even considered by the state (Law Commission of India 2000; see also Agnes 2011 and Brulé 2020).

Thus in my fieldwork village, as well as in nearby villages, there were relatively few Gaddi women who were absolute owners of immovable or ancestral property in the form of land or flock. Agricultural land is entered in the records as either property of their husband or of their

---

18. One of the unforeseen consequences of the growth of microfinance in India in recent years is the increased documentation and registration of *streedhan*, especially gold jewelry, largely for its financialization and as collateral. On microfinance in India, see Kar (2018). On the feminization of microfinance in India, see Guerrin (2014).

son(s). The house they live in was also not regarded as female property and always belonged to a male affine or agnate. Unmarried Gaddi women had little by way of possessions. The objects they brought into their affinal homes as dowry (*streedhan*) were seldom seen by them as their exclusive or personal wealth. However, married Gaddi women usually considered jewelry and domestic animals as their property. It was common for Gaddi women to be given animals by their natal family as part of their wedding gift. Depending on the status and wealth of families, these could include horses and donkeys, but goats were by far the most commonly gifted domestic animal. Women owning horses and donkeys earned cash by renting them as pack animals (donkeys and horses), or for transport (horses).

Jewelry is a significant part of a Gaddi woman's property. It passes singularly through the female line: primarily from mother-in-law to daughter-in-law, and in smaller measure from mother to daughter. Women have almost unquestioned power in matters of alienation of these items of wealth. As we saw in the gift-making of Buglo, jewelry is also one of the resources at their disposal for creating links between them and other individuals, and for redefining relationships that are not based solely on normative or prescriptive ties. Unlike laws and rules governing the movement of immovable property, the movement of jewelry remains at the periphery of regulation. Even if the law actually makes the registration of *streedhan* mandatory at the time of marriage, this regulation is hardly ever observed. Jewelry is an important constituent and a marker of wealth for the Gaddis, but it is not an enumerated and registered property in legal documents. Therefore, rancor over its non-egalitarian or objectionable devolution can at best make for bad familial relations, but hardly ever becomes a subject of a legal suit. Since its use is solely by women, women deploy transfers of jewelry to make and mark proximity with their kin. Affective relations are forged, strengthened, or articulated through these transfers women make. Within the conjugal unit too, jewelry plays an important role. A wife may or may not agree to pawn her silver for cash or give it as security to seek a loan, depending on the character of her bond with her husband. On the other hand, it was unquestioningly pawned or offered as collateral to secure money for their children's education, usually at one of the many silversmiths in the village. Ownership of things that women considered absolutely theirs thus played a critical role in the everyday of their affective lives.

Domestic animals too were associated primarily with women. When referring to the pastoral flock, women invariably used the collective possessive pronoun ("our goats," "our sheep"), but always used the singular possessive for the domestic animals ("my goat," "my cow"). Men too used the collective possessive for their flock. The flock animals are seen as a joint resource, similar to land, and therefore are seen to belong jointly to the household because it is not the male members alone who derive benefit or livelihood from them. However, while women may use the singular possessive in relation to domestic animals, most domestic goats and cows technically did not belong to them. For instance, the loan taken to buy their animal may well be in the name of their husband; yet, in day-to-day living, there is little ambiguity about whom that goat belongs to, as it is the women who look after them. Men almost never attended to domestic animals, except for occasionally taking them to the veterinary clinic. While women work the fields as well, especially in households where men still actively herd or are employed outside, a similar sense of entitlement does not necessarily follow. One of the reasons could be that land is seen as a family or household asset which will outlast its current owners and something with clear norms for its alienation. Domestic animals on the other hand are not a perennial resource and rarely survive their owner.

Ownership of flock animals is a wholly male affair and women never own any flock. Though the HSA does not specify the elements of property and a herd is not a fixed asset in any sense, it is devolved along the lines of ancestral property. Flock animals devolve like other ancestral fixed property such as land, and though women are rightful heirs under the law, daughters and wives derive no share of their animals in actual practice. R., now in his late sixties, had served as a *lumbardar* (a hereditary colonial title that combined responsibilities of revenue and rule at the village level) of Meghla village since the age of sixteen. One of the reasons that his family was chosen for the job by the colonial administration would have been their economic status, as there was no indigenous system of local "Big Men" in the region preceding colonial rule (Bhattacharyya 2018). His family owned one of the largest flocks in the village. R. alone owned around 750 head of sheep and goats and, along with the his two surviving brothers, the family flock size was more than 2,000 head. Due to his extensive village-based responsibilities as *lumbardar*, he could not accompany his *dhan* and entrusted his brothers to herd his flock. His brothers' sons were not interested in pursuing herding and wanted to enlist in the army or elsewhere on completion of their education. R.'s own son M., however, has accompanied his father's younger brother, his uncle, on several occasions for stretches of the grazing cycle. He was no enthusiast of herding, but went on the trail as an adolescent to pick up vital skills and herding knowledge, just in case none of his male cousins were willing to become herders in the future.

R.'s brothers had partitioned their agricultural holdings, but continued to herd the flock jointly. In the event that M. became the only one in his family from the next generation to take up herding, his father's brothers would entrust him with their flock. As with land, R.'s brothers told me, it is more profitable to have a larger holding than to fragment it. So, while the brothers kept separate agricultural fields, their flocks were herded jointly. Keeping the arrangement of the previous generations, in return for taking up their herding responsibilities M.'s cousins will work M.'s fields and attend to his other business in his absence. R.'s brother told me that it was possible to herd the flock jointly because herding was more like running a business and it is easier to demarcate the boundaries of interest. Agriculture, he said, had a direct connection with the hearth (*chulla*) and since the brothers ran separate kitchens, it was only wise to partition the land as well. What R. was indicating was the different way men and women deployed ownership in the context of making relations. While men used supra-household strategies of accumulation for maximizing wealth, and used kinship networks to that end, women used possessions such as jewelry to make or strengthen relations that cut across kinship boundaries or other obligations. This is consonant with the supra-household accumulation strategies and the understanding of property ownership and inheritance codified in the HSA, as concepts of joint family property and ancestral property show (See Birla 2009). On the other hand, perceived or real injustices in the division of jewelry from a mother (in-law) to her daughter (in-law) may make for bad family relations, these rarely form the basis of a lawsuit, or even a complaint to the local village council. The state remains marginal in the context of women's property because these transfers must by definition lie outside the area of legal codification of property.

Neither Property, Nor Persons?

As mentioned earlier, in everyday or casual conversations, many Gaddi women and men I spoke to readily and quite early on counted children in their list of possessions, usually calling them "invaluable" (*satton keemti*) or their "largest asset" (*satton vaddi jaidaad*). Such a view that entails ownership rights in another person cannot be accommodated within the law in any formal sense. Advances in new reproductive technologies have facilitated renewed anthropological attention on proprietary notions in law around children, including differential rights of biological fathers, mothers, surrogates, and adoptive parents in a fetus or embryo (Dolgin 1997; Strathern 1992a). The jurisprudence on these matters has emerged from casework related to disputed paternity or abortion rights under newer reproductive technologies. While modern law is clear on the absolute prohibition of ownership rights in other persons due to the legacy of slavery, legal elaboration of reproductive rights and restrictions is always charged because of the potential of personhood inherent in the fetus or the embryo (Strathern 1992a). The landmark case of *Johnson v. Calvert* (1993) brought the fragmented and competing claims of ownership in an embryo and fetus to the fore. The judgement of the US Supreme Court ruled on who had the right to decide whether or not to bring a fetus or embryo through gestation to birth when the disputing parties were respectively the male and female donors of biogenetic substances (sperm and ovum), the gestational surrogate, or the adoptive parents. "Neither person, nor property," ruled the Supreme Court on the status of the disputed fetus itself. While the fascinating details of the case and the judgement are beyond the scope of this discussion, Dolgin (1997) and Strathern (2005), among others, highlight the unstable nature of the relation between a parent and a child, which the law (or other normative orders) help in stabilizing. Not only is the nature of that relation unstable (is it proprietary or not, for example), but its stability can only be achieved in view of its potentiality (potential personhood) or, in other words, a purported future. So when the Gaddis talk of children as *jaidaad*, they seem to use this in the dual sense of the child being an asset, or a valuable possession, but also one that you can invest in for growth in its future value. Like the *pedu*, children are visible repositories of value. But unlike the *pedu*, they are not just receptacles of valued things; they are conduits of flows across temporalities. They are conduits of secular property, of worldly and tangible possessions, and of substance, but they are a prized possession for their parents as they are the conduits of the substance of Gaddiness they beget from their *kulaj* and share with only those who too can be similar conduits.

The Flow of Possessions

Property and ownership work along two rhythms or logics, spatial and temporal, and embodied respectively in and by women and children.

The temporal logic of accumulation (via children) aims at conserving, while the spatial logic of accumulation (via women) is aimed at expansion of one's possessions (whether relations or things), and bringing the outside, or even outsiders, in. The colonial and the postcolonial state both have recognized just one kind of flow, not of the mother's or her *kulaj's*, but agnatic substance in the form of blood. Its recognition of children and heirs therefore codify legitimate heirs based on the government of substantive flow from this point of view. Colonial codification of customary law demonstrated the existence of a more equitable distribution of recognition on both male and female substance in relation to the question of inheritance. The *Manual of customary law of Kangra district* (Middleton 1919) notes the prevalence of two different systems of inheritance in the region and among the Gaddis: the *Chundavand* and the *Pagvand*. The *Pagvand* system recognized all male children as equal heirs of the father's property, regardless of the uterine household. It gave primacy to the male heirs and a de facto exclusion of the wife-mother by omitting her from the legal register of property. In contrast, the *Chundavand* system gave primacy to the uterine household and devolved property not along the agnatic line of descent (number of sons, brothers, etc.) but along the number of uterine households. This agnatic ideology in recognizing children became further entrenched with the HSA, with several unforeseen consequences, as discussed in Chapter 2. But a diminished recognition of uterine households was not the only thing the new agnatic ideology brought about. The new laws also rendered only certain substances recognizable. Older reproductive technologies, such as wills and adoptions, may have allowed transcending blood lines, but these gradually disappeared from ordinary social worlds within communities. Erstwhile categories of heirs among the Gaddis, such as *dahejar* (literally, "one who came in the dowry"—that is, a child from a woman's previous marriage), have disappeared too, socially, as well as in the list of heirs. Their prior recognition, even with circumscribed inheritance rights, at least recognized the importance of the female substance.

For Gaddis, owning particular objects—animals, land, names, gods, goddesses—is crucial to the ability to form and reformulate relations with other Gaddis, non-Gaddis, and also the Indian state. The colonial Land Alienation Act of 1900 was created as a mechanism to address the surge in rural indebtedness at the turn of that century which had led to the traffic in agricultural land in Punjab. However, the effects of this important Act were played out substantially in the domestic domain and the realm of kinship. Agricultural land had come to gain significant commercial value after the introduction of the extensive irrigation network in the province. On the other hand, property rights in agricultural land and tenure had become radically different since the late eighteenth century due to the complete inability or refusal on the part of the colonial state to recognize any other form of ownership other than private and individual (Saumarez-Smith 1996; Bhattacharya 2018). As a result, the increased commercial value in agriculture and agricultural land led to a surge of land disputes and widespread usurpation and sale. Just as the Gaddis were recognized as the only herder community, likewise there emerged a list of "agricultural tribes" who had sole rights to the legitimate ownership of agricultural land. But this maneuver far exceeded the agricultural field: it changed household composition. The Land Alienation Act accorded a clear presumptive force to sons in matters of alienation of agricultural land. While patriliny was a general rule of kinship organization in the region even before the passing of this act, its fuzzy empirical presence gradually gave way to a stricter agnatic *mentalité* over the course of the next fifty years of legal governance. Legal governmentality rendered the making of non-agnates as heirs more difficult. This was amply evident in the procedural stringency with which courts treated matters of adoption and wills, and the systematic marginalization of non-agnatic descendants through family legislation.

Colonial law classified rights according to ancestral and acquired property. Ancestral property was understood as deriving from the patrilineage where any two heirs could be seen to have an ancestor in common, and was to be managed by strict rules of devolution as well as alienation. Rights in ancestral property were very clearly defined and involved intersecting rights for individuals within the various segments of the lineage. The result was that disposal of such property was rare and difficult for any single individual to execute. Property acquired by a person during his lifetime, defined as acquired property, was categorized as non-ancestral and therefore implied a different set of interests and rights. In essence, rights in acquired property were absolute, whereas they were qualified in the case of ancestral property because rights of disposal were circumscribed. Ancestral and acquired property thus defined relationships between members of descent groups and households in different ways, and individuals who had rights in acquired property did not necessarily have the same rights in ancestral property (Asad 1961: 62). A widow, for instance, had no rights in ancestral property, but did enjoy lifelong interest in it. This meant that, while she could derive maintenance from it, she did not have the power to alienate or gift that property away and, after her death, the property was "restored" to the male successors of her late husband. Similarly, daughters too had a legal claim only in their father's acquired property. In consequence, the law codified a singular male descent line in relations to claims to ownership of ancestral family property. These governmental regulations also effected the consolidation of a particular concept of "legitimate children." There were several categories of children who, though not a product of the conjugal unit, were nonetheless an integral part of the conjugal household among the Kangra Gaddis. These were children from previous marriages of a woman (*dahejar* or *pichhlag*), children born to a widow within four years of her husband's death (*chaukandu*), and adopted children (*dharamputar*). All these categories of children in custom enjoyed rights in succession. With the ascent of monogamous conjugality, the rights of these categories of children virtually vanished because the rights of children were increasingly defined by their agnatic proximity.

The Truth of Dispossession

Having things to transact, exchange, and acquire can also be seen as engaging in a non-verbal "dialogue" or "conversation" via these possessions with others who have things to transact or exchange, or engage in what Appadurai has famously called "tournaments of value" (Appadurai 1988). The Kula is one of the most elaborate and spectacular of such conversations. Just as the state views the subject as a possessive citizen, I propose that the Gaddi conversation with the state too is fundamentally embedded in the language of property, that is, the property in their Gaddiness. Similar but different in important ways to the argument made in her classic essay on race as property by Cheryl Harris (1993), Gaddis seek to assert ownership and recognition of their possession of Gaddiness when talking to the state, but that Gaddiness itself is mediated by the specificity of the possession of a flock, or via pastoralism as a livelihood. In the early years of the twenty-first century, the Gaddis of Kangra became successful in gaining this official recognition, thereby suturing what looked to them an increasingly precarious connection between them and pastoralism. Pastoralism itself is now a livelihood under significant threat. With each generation, fewer Gaddis practise this livelihood, and its links with the community look increasingly feeble, if not febrile. As a recognized Scheduled Tribe, Kangra Gaddis now have access to a raft of welfare measures from the state, which are aimed at offsetting the decreasing prices of wool and other historic disadvantages I discuss in the next chapter. Their newly acquired tribal status under the Indian Constitution in 2003 may not have guaranteed a renewed place of pastoralism in the hierarchy of livelihoods and communitarian plenitude, but it certainly guaranteed the beneficence of the sovereign.

> Our relations with the British were fine. But the *angrez* were notorious for their taxation. When we heard that they were coming this way, we had to prepare ourselves. We nominated one person to go and deal with them when they sent for our representatives. Now this Gaddi representative did not respond to their *farmaan* [summons] not once, not twice, not three times. The British general was about to lose his patience. When the Gaddi representative heard about this, he agreed to meet with the British general but turned up for the meeting completely drunk. The general was aghast that someone had dared to come to meet with him in such a state. But the Gaddi told him not to be angry. "I am drunk because I am thrilled our *mai-baap* [literally, "mother-father"] is here. Now who doesn't want to celebrate when they see their parents?! I am simply drunk with happiness." The general was very flattered to hear this. He at once lowered our taxes. You see, this is how we Gaddis deal with situations. We deal with difficult situations through talk ["*gallan te samjhaiyee laiayaan*"].[19]

Most Gaddis I have conversed with over the years were unambiguous about the kind of relationship they have always had with the sovereign. It is not one of war or violence, but one of negotiation, dialogue, or "exchange," they said. The state or the sovereign has to be won over, or then simply transacted with.

> We Gaddis never took up arms against the *angrez sarkar* [British rulers] when they created barriers to our livelihood by enclosing the forest. *Haa hamesha gallan te jitt laayian* ["We always win by conversation, by talking"]. We won over the *badda saab* [colloquial term for colonial officials] and (re)gained access to our pastures by trapping them in our rhetoric ["*gallan te uljhayi laayiaan*"]. We didn't use violence ["*bandookaan naiyyon chakkiaan*"; literally, "We didn't use or lift

---

19. Research conversation, M., 57, Dharamshala, March 2006. "*Angrez*" is the colloquial term for the English/ British.

any guns"], we just kept *saying* we would disband our flock because how else could we feed them. The *badda sahib* had an answer to the guns, but had no answer to talk and eventually gave us permits.[20]

It is true that since archival records exist, every time the colonial or the postcolonial state has threatened to enclose more territory or to impose other restrictions on their livelihoods (such as removal of existing subsidies), Gaddis have always threatened to disband the flock (see Kapila 2008; Saberwal 1999). This threat has thus far been understood—not necessarily erroneously—as an expedient political ploy (Saberwal 1999), or in the pursuit of an identarian politics (Kapila 2008; 2011). Perhaps there is another way to consider the choice of this particular mode of protest, and the effectiveness of this threat, which is to focus on what exactly the Gaddis are saying when they say they would disband their flock. More importantly, why has it always been perceived as a serious enough threat to the state, acceding to their demand as it does every single time? The answer to this may lie outside the calculus of either electoral arithmetic or even political economy.

In threatening to relinquish their flock, what the Gaddis actually threaten is to enter voluntary dispossession. In invoking the threat of such an action, Gaddis seem to reverse the direction of dispossession. Dispossession is usually precipitated by the more powerful, in a bid to become more powerful. Think here of forcible dispossession, in the form of extortion regimes by non-state actors, such as the mafia (Michelutti 2019; Puccio-Den 2019). Depending on the scale, dispossessing someone of what belongs to them is variously called theft, loot, or plunder; it is usually a crime in the eyes of the state and ethically reprehensible in the eyes of fellow men and women. Voluntarily relinquishing one's own possessions, however, summons the ascetic ideal and a theologically ordained renunciatory modality in pursuit of salvation or *moksha*. Such a modality is almost always pursued as an individual as part of the progression of one's lifecycle. But when Gaddis proclaim to the state that they are going to disband their flock if their demands are not met, they are neither threatening to commit a crime, nor indeed professing self-dispossession as renunciatory pursuit of "the good life" (see Laidlaw 2005:

---

20. Research conversation with herder, age 73, Palampur Tehsil, September 22, 2009. On the evolution from the princely *waris* to a grazing permit, see Saberwal (1999: 23–25).

178).[21]. Therefore, their ultimatum is not based in the ethico-moral register of life cycles in which individual lives are based. Instead, by turning the direction of dispossession inwards, they perform self-dispossession as communicative action and not as sacrifice. Just as, following Appadurai (1988), potlatch can be seen as a declamatory speech or a shouting match made with objects, so it is possible to consider the Gaddis' threat of dispossession as a very specific form of interlocution with the state. The threat to disband their flock is tantamount to a negative potlatch. To disband the flock is not to indulge, like the Kwaikutl, in conspicuous wastage in order to gain awe-inspired status from their competitors (or interlocutors); rather, the threat to disband the flock is made precisely to challenge or disrupt the basis of exchange—from the symmetrical reciprocity that underpins compacts to one of asymmetrical exchange aimed at dis-accumulation. Through such a threat, the Gaddis here mobilize dispossession explicitly as a political act, not within a sacrificial economy, nor even as one of competitive consumption, but as a refusal. Such an act on their part is very much in the vein of a proto-Gandhian *satyagraha*, or an act undertaken in the insistence of truth.[22]

Writing after the success of the first civil disobedience he led in Natal, South Africa, Gandhi recapitulates what a member of General Smuts's team had said to him, a sentiment he believed Smuts shared:

> I do not like your people and I do not care to assist them at all. But what can I do? You help us in our day of need. How can we lay hands upon you? I often wish you took to violence like English strikers, then we would know at once how to dispose of you. But you will not injure even your enemy. You desire victory by self-suffering alone and never transgress your self-imposed limits of courtesy and chivalry. And that is what reduces us to sheer helplessness. (Gandhi 1928: 491–492)

Capturing this insistence on truth as a "quiet strength" (1928: 483), Gandhi concluded that those who wield this "priceless and matchless political weapon . . . are strangers to disappointment and defeat" (1928:

---

21. Laidlaw (2005) is talking about the value of fasting and the imbrication of death in notions of "the good life" among the Jains of India.

22. The vibrant scholarship on M. K. Gandhi's political thought is too long to cite in full. For a definitive intellectual biography of Gandhi, see Devji (2012). See also Kapila (2011) and Skaria (2002).

511). This was because this politics was based in active suffering and suffering alone.

The Gaddis' threat of disbanding their flock thus performs two functions: it converts the value of dispossession from a category of exchange (theft) or governance (crime) to a political category (of accumulation of political capital through the insistence of truth), and it invites the state into the competitive frame of this negative potlatch. The idiom of this competitive framing is not to challenge the state monopoly on violence (*contra* Weber). Rather, their threatened dispossession *at scale* makes visible the prerogative the state has held for itself, that of nullification. This is the reason why the state ultimately cannot countenance this threat, for it alone can dispossess people of their *terra*, their *res*, and their *corpus*. It is for a perceived threat to a sovereign monopoly on dispossession that the threat to disband their flock has *always* worked and borne the result the Gaddis have wanted in these negotiations, whether historically to gain or maintain right of pasture or, latterly, to gain greater access to welfare measures from the state. In trying to redirect the Indian state to keep its promises or expand the scope of its provision, the Gaddis are certainly not alone. But what makes them singular is their ability to identify the very nub of sovereignty—that it is not exhausted by the state's monopoly on violence. Their politics works because it remains couched in the truth of how they came to acquire their flock in the first place. In their political locution and illocution with the state, they too are able to move between divine and secular temporalities with a "quiet strength." While the Gaddis are by no means alone in succeeding in countering the state by pursuing its mimesis (Sundar 2014; Taussig 2013), it is what they are able to repeat that is different from others engaged in similar contestations with the state. By understanding that sovereignty exceeds violence, they repeat the state's sovereignty-making relationship with possession, and they do so by animating the structuring potency of *both* ownership and its obverse, dispossession. It is for this reason the threat maintains the relationship of the Gaddis with the sovereign as one of beneficence not as charity, or even as an entitlement, but as compact, in possession and dispossession alike.

CHAPTER 4

Terra Nullius: The Territory of Sovereignty

> *The desire for fusion or the desire for murder constitute the double modality of an essential trouble that agitates us in our finitude. To swallow or to annihilate others—and yet at the same time wanting to maintain them as others, because we also sense the horror of solitude (which is properly the exit from sense, if sense is essentially exchanged or shared).*
>
> – Jean-Luc Nancy, "Church, state, resistance," 2007

The last chapter discussed the potency of dispossession as revealed in and through Gaddi notions of *jaidad* and Gaddi interlocution with the state. In the next three chapters I examine dispossession as a state practice aimed at making, expanding or intensifying its sovereignty. This chapter provides a glimpse into sovereignty-making at the moment of transition from colonial to postcolonial India through two marginal exemplifications.

In September 1948, two British nationals, Charles Holmes and Graham Lockhard, met with Imam ul Majid, the first chief commissioner of Andaman Nicobar Islands of independent India, and asked for a grant of 15,000 acres of forest land in Middle Andamans to be used for a sugarcane plantation.[1] Lockhard was a representative of Gladstone Lyall, a

---

1. *Development of Andaman and Nicobar Islands*. NAI/Home/AN/346/48-AN

Calcutta-based business, while Charles Holmes had recently moved to Port Blair from Calcutta and had already attracted local suspicion.[2] Majid was easily persuaded by their proposal and promptly passed on this request to New Delhi, accompanied with a favorable nod:

> I find certain areas without valuable forest or already worked, which could be made available for sugarcane growing in the middle-Andaman. The forest department will have no objection to us leasing out land for this purpose. In fact, they would, I think, welcome such developments alongside their own activities. From what I gather, sugarcane can be easily grown here and it be [*sic*] very advantageous to the islands if a flourishing sugarcane industry could be established here.[3]

However, this logic seemed to find no favor. Much to the disappointment of all concerned, New Delhi rejected this request, saying:

> [There is already] too much sugarcane . . . being grown in our country at the cost of cereals. It is presumed that as the conditions are suitable for cane growing, they will also be suitable for growing rice, which is at present a badly needed commodity. It would be advisable therefore if this area is used for rice growing and some refugees from East Bengal, etc. may be encouraged to settle in this area.[4]

The use of the Andaman Islands to settle refugees from East Pakistan in the early years after the Partition of India in 1947 has since become common knowledge in India. The interest shown here by the two Britishers and the response of the Indian state both independently capture the imaginary of *terra nullius* that was the prevailing norm in the official, as well as popular, imagination. What is now obscured from popular memory is the extant imaginary of *terra nullius* as a place of fresh starts, shared by the colonial and the postcolonial and also rife among

---

2. From G. K. Handoo, Deputy Director, Intelligence Bureau, to G. V. Bedekar, Deputy Secretary, Ministry of Home Affairs. *Report about the Andamans*. Serial no. 1/ no. SA/ 806

3. I. Majid, Chief Commissioner, Andaman and Nicobar Islands, to Secretary, September 27, 1948, Port Blair. Serial no. 1, 2/1/48. NAI/Home/AN/346/48-AN.

4. December 30, 1948, New Delhi. No. 346/48-AN. Serial no. 2. NAI/Home/AN/346/48-AN.

ordinary people. In the early months after Independence, private individuals regularly wrote to government officials, sometimes even directly
to Prime Minister Nehru, for an opportunity to settle on the islands,
such as done by V. J. Ramdas, who described himself as an "explorer".
Exhorting the prime minister he wrote: "For heavens' sake, take some
interest and give more publicity for the colonisation of the Andaman
and Nicobar Islands. The 200 islands and islets can absorb 2 crores [20
million] of men. It will be a great relief for the already congested cities."[5]
Another letter from one I.C. Verma written to then Home Minister
Sardar Patel, states:

> I decided to approach you with a request that if approved, I am pre-
> pared to proceed to [the Andamans] and start cultivation *as a first
> pioneer*. . . . I suggest that the Government of India should provide
> the following to the *pioneer settlers* to encourage them, either as a free
> gift or otherwise on payment on instalment basis, to each family:
>
> (i) 100 bighas* of land [variable measure of land, equivalent to 32 or
> 64 acres]
> (ii) Two pairs of bullocks
> (iii) One bullock cart
> (iv) Agricultural implements
> (v) Seeds for the first crop only
> The *pioneers* will start growing food crops from the time they [land].
> These crops are badly needed for our millions in India. In addition,
> every one of the migrants should take up social work among the na-
> tives, such as teaching of Hindi, propagating of Hinduism . . . . (em-
> phases added)[6]

How to understand this interest in a part of the world, which until
recently had been a condemned place, and a place for the condemned
(the Islands were a penal colony)? Following Candea and Da Col
(2012), Gamble has argued that migration to new lands was inimi-
cally tied to the deep history of hospitality and its practices of coercive
containment (2014: 158–159). In a later essay, in turn taking Gamble's
insight forward, Da Col conceptualizes visiting as "a social philosophy of access" (2019:15). The anthropology of hospitality is helpful in

---

5. July 22, 1948, Rangoon. Serial no. 9. NAI/Home/AN/1948/25/48-AN.
6. June 7, 1948. Serial no. 7. NAI/Home/AN/1948/25/48-AN.

thinking through and understanding several contemporary conditions, such as the status of the refugee, the rights of asylum seekers, and so on (Derrida 2000). These recent works draw on Julian Pitt-Rivers's hospitality-as-grace model of visitation (2017). Much rests on the ability—or inability—of the host to provide comfort, sustenance, and gracious containment for the stranger and visitor. The anthropology of problematic hospitality has illuminated voracious hosts and parasitic guests (Da Col and Shryock 2017; Candea and Da Col 2012; also Derrida 2000; Serres 2007). But what of murderous and predatory visitation, of gaining access not by invitation but by force? What of those who visit in order not to receive hospitality, but to depose the host? What if visitation is conceptualized not from the point of view of the hospitality offered to the arriving guest, but from the point of view of the hosts of hostile or predatory guests? Following the provocation offered by Candea and Da Col (2012) and Da Col (2019), I ask what the anthropology of hospitality can tell us about settler-colonialism and its attendant doctrine of *terra nullius* by opening up the conceptual terrain of predatory visitation. In the second half of the chapter I explore the corollary concept of indigeneity which arises out of settler-colonialism and read its genesis within this rubric. I take up two familiar instances in which *terra nullius* has been de facto deployed in India and subject them to anthropological redescription. The first is the fate of the Andaman Islands, not in the moment of their British conquest in the eighteenth century, but rather in their incorporation into postcolonial India in the mid-twentieth century. In the second part of the chapter, I take up the related question of indigeneity in postcolonial India and examine its career as a political category for self-identification, as well as excavate the daily life of nullification away from its usually understood eventfulness.

To provide an anthropological account of *terra nullius*, I use Philippe Descola's schema to understand the relational modes at play in dispossessive settler-colonialism, and to map their fundamental reversal under colonial and the postcolonial regimes respectively. According to Descola, "relational schemas can be classified according to whether or not the *alter* is or is not equivalent . . . on an ontological level and the connections . . . with it are or not mutual" (2013: 310; emphasis in original). Though Descola's concern is the sustainability of the nature-culture distinction and the *alter* for him is the Amazonian non-human, these classifications are nonetheless extremely useful to think through the relationality in sovereignty-making.[7] As it will become clear, in the Andamans the relationship between the British state and the Andaman Islanders was based in violence between equivalents. Ironically, the relational mode shifted to non-equivalence under the postcolonial state.

As discussed in Chapter 1, *terra nullius* creates a condition of a permanent present tense, and an "as-if" of timelessness, by erasing any prior social order and settlements. The doctrine of *terra nullius* was foundational to the becoming of settler-colonialism, but until recently it was rarely discussed for other colonial contexts, such as internal and non-settler colonialism. Further, land and territory are often fused, if not used interchangeably, in most discussions of the sovereignty-making technique of *terra nullius*. I provide a distinction between these two—land and territory—as separate domains for sovereignty-making, each with their distinct logic, as revealed in the cusp years of Independence. I begin by examining the extant imaginary of *terra nullius* that accompanied the presumptive incorporation of Andaman Islands into independent India's sovereign territory. This imaginary, I argue, went beyond the state and was widely shared by ordinary citizens, and by business and commercial entities, and at once changed the popular image on the mainland of the Andamans as a condemned place and a place of death to a space of fresh starts. In the second part of the chapter, I examine the denial of claims to indigenous title on the eve of Independence and the permanent consequences of this denial. Reading both these archives in the framework of a "metaphysics of predation" (Vivieros de Castro 2014) and a "metaphysics of attachment" (Descola 2013) allows us to situate sovereignty within a wider anthropology of eliminationist and absorptionist practices. I suggest that far from being "eventful," terra nullification is iterative, routinised, and an ongoing exercise in "disaggregated sovereignty" (Wilder 2015).

A Metaphysics of Attachment

The history of the Andaman Islands is marked by the annihilation, murder, and swallowing that Nancy (2007) speaks of in the epigraph to this

---

7. It is no coincidence that this part of Descola's book begins with the epigraph by René Char: "We need one, we need two, we need . . . nobody is ubiquitous enough to be his contemporary sovereign" (Descola 2013: 307).

chapter. Lying in the Bay of Bengal and just seven degrees north of the equator, the Andaman Islands are at the oceanic crossroads between the African continent, the Indian subcontinent, and the archipelagos of Polynesia, Melanesia, and Austronesia. The British interest in the islands, first recorded in the eighteenth century, inaugurated a relationship of violent incorporation through elimination and destruction.[8] Many original inhabitants and populations of these islands were progressively eliminated. Any rebellion or opposition on the part of the native populations provided a new platform to the colonizer to perpetrate further violence aimed at their so-called "savagery" and based in a civilizational logic (Sen 2009). By the time India became a British colony proper in 1857, the British selected the islands to host the colony's major penal settlement, having successfully created such offshore island fortresses elsewhere in their empire. The most infamous architectural legacy of that history is the Cellular Jail, the panopticon-shaped prison constructed in Port Blair. Built explicitly for the incarceration of Indian subjects from the mainland, a vast majority of whom were charged with sedition and usually serving life-sentences or awaiting death penalties, the islands and the Cellular Jail soon became icons of the punitive colonial regime. A sentence to this offshore prison entered popular vocabulary on the mainland as *kaale paani ki sazaa* ("a sentence to the black waters"), or sometimes simply as the metonymic *Kaala Paani* (literally "Black Waters"). This partly referenced the fact that no one who was sentenced there ever returned. This simultaneously evoked the ritual injunction in Hinduism against sea travel because it begot inauspiciousness (hence *kaala paani*), and its secular confirmation.

The violent colonization of the Andaman Islands by the British in many ways was unsurprising and part of the wider practices of territorial gain though the doctrine of *terra nullius*. To the British, the islands were of interest because of their geo-strategic location, but only after these had been cleansed of their "savagery" (Sen 2009). On the mainland, the Andamans and its Islanders were absorbed into the popular imagination largely in consonance with their colonial purpose. Under colonialism, for most Indians on the mainland, the Andamans were a place of banishment and death, and there was little attachment or identification with the islands or the islanders. A travelogue on the islands by an Indian journalist published in the 1960s noted: "Generally speaking, the average layman

---

8. For a detailed political history of the violence and conquest of the islands by the British, see Sen (2009) and Vaidik (2010).

knows nothing about the Andaman and Nicobar Islands. Barring two hoary volumes useful only to scientists there was no Andaman literature as such, and on the Nicobar, which lie to the south of that archipelago, I had not read even a news item" (Vaidya 1960: 24).[9] In even the decades following Independence, though the islands gradually gained the status of a desirable tourist destination, little about the Andaman Island inhabitants and their ways of life entered popular imagination. This continued until the tsunami of 2004, when images of the Sentinelese people shooting arrows at the circling aircraft of the Indian Air Force went global. A few years later, videos of the islands' Jarawa people made to dance for cigarettes and fruit surfaced in western media to widespread consternation.[10] The latest of these momentary surges of media attention and global interest occurred in 2018 when a young American missionary was found dead on North Sentinel Island, purportedly killed by the Sentinelese people (Bhardwaj 2018). The Sentinelese, along with the Jarawas, are Andamanese people who have lived in voluntary isolation since at least the British discovery of the islands and have consistently rebuffed any attempt at "friendly contact" from all, including efforts made by the colonial and the postcolonial state, as I discuss later.

Suffice it to say that the Andamans were, and remain, at the periphery of the imagined nation as well as the nation-state. Yet, despite such tenuous links, in 1947, the islands were absorbed into the independent state of India with an unquestioned and presumptive force that merits attention. The clues to sources of this presumption lie in the brief window of transition from the colonial state to the postcolonial state in the mid-twentieth century.[11] It is true that under the Government of

---

9.   The writer of the travelogue, Suresh Vaidya, reappears in this book in Chapter 6.

10. "Andaman Islanders 'forced to dance' for tourists," *The Observer*, January 7, 2012. Accessed January 8, 2012. https://www.theguardian.com/world/video/2012/jan/07/andaman-islanders-human-safari-video

11. For non-specialists of the region, independence from colonial rule came with two forms of foundational violence: the partition of India with the formation of Pakistan, on the one hand, and, on the other, the fraught accession of a few princely states into the newly formed Union of India. Before Independence, there were 584 princely states under indirect rule in British India, each of which had to consent formally to accession to the Indian (or Pakistani) Union. With the notable exception of Kashmir, Hyderabad, Junagadh, Bhopal, Benaras, and Travancore, all states within the

India Act of 1935, all territories under British India were to become part of the Union of India at Independence.[12] Yet, smooth accession to the union was neither a given nor universal. British India was a conglomerate of colonies under direct rule (overwhelmingly British, bar a handful under the French and Portuguese) and territories under indirect rule, such as the princely states. In the run-up to Independence, each of the 584 princely states, of varying sizes and hue, had to accede individually to one of the newly independent states of India or Pakistan. While most princely states acceded to either without lingering contest or conflict, the princely states of Hyderabad, Kashmir, Travancore, Bhopal, Benaras, and Junagadh did not join the Union of India on August 15, 1947. The accession of Hyderabad and Kashmir in particular was extremely vexed, and their accession to India came after several months of negotiation with the Indian state.[13] Unlike with these principalities, the incorporation of the Andaman Islands was entirely uncontroversial. There arose no question, let alone dispute, over whether the Andaman Islands territorially belonged to India or to Pakistan after Partition. Along with Lakshadweep—the archipelago on the western coast of India, in the Arabian Sea—the eastward lying Andaman Islands came up for no special mention even in the extensive debates in the Constituent Assembly, the body tasked with drawing up the governmental infrastructure of post-Independence India. This was partly because the Andaman Islands did not have any dedicated representation in the Assembly. The invisibility of the Islands was further compounded by the complete absence of the the Islanders from the minds of the two Constituent Assembly members meant to represent the so-called tribes of India (and whose contribution

newly partitioned territory of India acceded to the union by Independence Day, August 15, 1947. For more on princely states in British India, see Copland (1997) and Ramusack (2003). See also Bhagwan (2009).

12. "Wherein the territories that now comprise British India, the territories that now form the Indian States, and such other parts of India as are outside British India and the States as well as such other territories as are willing to be constituted into the Independent Sovereign India, shall be a Union of them all . . . ," as moved by Jawaharlal Nehru, Objectives Resolution, *Constituent assembly debates*, December 13, 1946. http://164.100.47.194/loksabha/constituent/facts.html.

13. The reasons and conditions were different in each case of negotiated accession. See, for example, Rai (2004) on Kashmir. On Hyderabad, see Purushotham (2021); on Travancore, see Pillai (2016).

I take up in detail in the second part of this chapter). Given the unique conditions of the Islands and the distinctiveness of the Andamanese peoples in relation to even the so-called tribal populations of the mainland, this presumptive force was not only surprising, but also could only be replete with violence.

While historical scholarship on the Islands has discussed in some detail the murder and the annihilation of the Islanders that took place under British colonialism (see for example Andersen et al. 2016; U. Sen 2017; Sen 2009), early ethnographic accounts paid little attention to the wider political conditions or the unique circumstances of the people on the islands (e.g. Radcliffe-Brown 1948 [1922]). Latter-day scholarship has focused on the interrelations between the penal settlement and the Islanders (Anderson et al. 2016), and the ritual and secular change among contemporary Andamanese (Pandya 1993; 2013). While some studies frame the use of the islands to resettle refugees from East Pakistan (present-day Bangladesh) after Partition (Sen 2016) and the effects of wider developmental activities on the islands, such as road building, on the Andamanese people (Pandya 2013) under the arc of *terra nullius*, these do not question the fact of their incorporation into the union itself. To my mind, unpacking the presumptive naturalism inherent in their "accession," rife in that moment of incorporation, and which unwittingly seeps into the scholarship about the islands, is vital to our understanding of the full force of nullification. Here I pay attention to the extant imaginary of *terra nullius* deployed in and through the interventions of the Indian state, business and commercial interests, such as those evinced by Gladstone Lyall, but also, importantly, by private citizens ardent to play the role of "pioneer settlers," even when they knew of the existence of Islander peoples.

Full Attachment

When the British colonizers discovered the Andaman Islands in the eighteenth century and began to assess their viability as British territory, they labelled all aboriginal Islanders as "prowlers" who merely roamed the landscape. In their estimation, the Islanders were not owners of the land in any traditional sense because they did not till the land, but merely roamed it in search of forage and prey (Pandya 2013: 23). "Prowlers" was a familiar denomination within the violent imaginary and eliminationist strategies of settler-colonialism (Birtles 1997). Yet, despite mutual hostility, the British did not aim to eliminate the Islands' aboriginal populations because they were seen to present scientific interest. It was not long before these populations became subjects of curiosity for many a visiting ethnologically-minded explorer or photographer (Pandya 2013; Sen 2009). This framing of the aboriginal Islanders as "mere prowlers" continued to hold true for the postcolonial Indian state, even while the so-called scientific interest in their societies continued to wane (Pandya 2013: 24; U. Sen 2017). While I rely on existing scholarship for the political history of these islands, I part ways with them in their interpretive scaffolding. To my mind, though the colonial officials and the postcolonial state ascribed the same status to the aboriginal Islanders—i.e. "prowlers"—to assist the usurpation of Andamanese territory, there is little carry-over between the two iterations. This is not least because even as they deployed the same doctrine of nullification the aims of colonial and postcolonial sovereignty-making had very different aims. Archival records and historical scholarship are replete with the diminutive status of the Andamanese in the eyes of the British. The "savagery" of the Andamanese served as a benchmark for colonizers' own perceived civilizational superiority (Sen 2009; Pandya 2013). The Indian state worked with the opposite philosophy and on the premise that incorporation within the Indian state lifted the Islanders from the so-called "savage slot" to that of citizenship which automatically inflated their status. In the eyes of the Indian state, citizenship implied enhanced capacities, including rights-bearing personhood and entitlements, something the Islanders had never had access to.

No one of course thought to take any sounding on this matter from the Islanders themselves. In fact, India's first home minister, Sardar Patel, rebuffed the warning of the last British administrator of the islands about the continuation of hostilities after Independence. Responding to the latter's report on the hostility showed by the Jarawa people of the Andamans towards colonial officials, Patel said that Jarawa hostility would cease immediately at Independence, as it was entirely in response to the "colonial attitudes" of the British. He was convinced that the Jarawas would harbor no such hostility towards the incoming Indian officials (Pandya 2013: 20). To assume that even though the Jarawa had chosen to live in voluntary isolation, they somehow had a concept of "India" with which they completely identified and felt a primordial sense of belonging—that the Jarawa were part of India's people, and that their hostility towards the British could only ever have been "anti-colonial", and nascently "nationalist"—was a curious but a powerful assumption to have made, yet not one that was ever put to question. At the same time, there was cognizance that this identification with and attachment to India had to be aggressively cultivated in the early months after Independence. When it was reported that the celebrations for the first anniversary of Independence had been subdued and mellow in Port Blair, officials in the Home Ministry in New Delhi sent detailed directions that the next Independence Day (in 1949) be celebrated with renewed vigor. Eager to show their own enthusiasm for incorporation, local administrators in turn sought permission to make attendance at these celebrations compulsory, which even New Delhi found as "too harsh."[14]

Philippe Descola has argued that, like identification, relational modes too are integrating schemas (2013: 222). He distinguishes between relational modes based on equivalent and non-equivalent terms, where the former include all forms of exchange, gift, and predatory relations, while the latter contain connections forged through and by production, protection, and transmission. Descola's schema helps us distinguish between the relationality of colonial and postcolonial sovereignty-making in crucial ways. Ironically, colonial sovereignty, it turns out, is forged through equivalence, while the latter premises itself in non-equivalence. The non-equivalence of the latter is betrayed in the forcible integration or incorporation aimed at making same (citizen) that which is an *alter* here, the Jarawa and the Sentinelese, who do not recognise the Indian nation-state. The very presumption they do and that they identify with the (Indian) nation-state (such as presumed by Home Minister Patel) is the very technology of achieving forcible integration, assimilation, or incorporation. In thinking thus, the state assumed the hostility of the Andamanese shown towards the colonial forces would end with the end of colonial rule with because that they were automatically aligned with the anti-colonial nationalism of mainland Indians. The aim here was to attribute humanity to the indigenous Islanders such as the Sentinelese and the Jarawa—which had been denied them by the British colonizers—and to establish a relationship based in (forcible) equivalence. The aboriginal Islanders were now not just ordinary citizens, but citizens enumerated among those who were to become the focus of special measures under positive discrimination. This developmentalist logic took on a particularly paternalist face in relation to what became seen as a civilizational deficit in populations identified as tribes, hence speaking

---

14. Report by G. K. Handoo, Deputy Director, Intelligence Bureau. New Delhi, September 29, 1948. NAI/Home/AN/Secret/445/48-AN.

directly to Descola's framework of "protection" and "transmission," as I discuss in the latter half of this chapter. Not only were the Islanders *not* consulted on the territorial incorporation of the Andaman Islands into the Union of India, but that they were instantaneously incorporated within the developmentalist agenda of the state betrayed the forcible, if not false, nature of the equivalence. This is different from the predation mode aimed at incorporation. By transforming the relationship between the Islanders (now called "indigenous"), as a paternalistic and protective relationship, the postcolonial state repositions the status of the Islanders as one of non-equivalence. But what of the Islanders themselves?

Hostility and Friendship in Visiting

The Andaman Islands are exceptional in that they are home to the only two population groups that have held off any contact with other communities since British colonial occupation, the Sentinelese and the Jarawas. The ability of the Sentinelese to remain in voluntary isolation is helped to a certain extent by the fact that they live on a separate, eponymous island in the archipelago. The Jarawa live in the forests of the largest island, South Andaman, which also houses the administrative center, Port Blair, and therefore exist literally on the edge of the nation-state. In light of the disappearance of several aboriginal groups from the Islands, the postcolonial state adopted the policies aimed at their "preservation":

> Whatever remedy modern science can offer to save them from total annihilation must be tried. India with her spiritual background and age-long traditions of humanity has a special responsibility to show before the world by going all out to save the remnants of this very simple and primitive folk, by all means at her disposal. She cannot merely watch them die out in the same ways the Tasmanians, whose total extinction is a lasting shame on civilised man.[15]

These the words of B. S. Guha, the first director of the Anthropological Survey of India, from his brief report on the "near extinct tribes" of the Islands sent to New Delhi in 1948. The report recommended setting up

---

15. Short report on the Anthropological Survey of the Andaman and Nicobar Islands—Welfare of the Aborigines. p.7. July 1948 NAI/Home/ AN/199/48-AN.

a permanent substation at Port Blair to monitor the populations. On a subsequent visit, he wrote: "[O]rdinary methods of amelioration and uplift would be totally useless in the case of the Andaman tribes. We are dealing here with one of the most ancient races of mankind still completely in hunting and fishing state [*sic*] and without any settled habitation. Any attempt to convert [them] to a sedentary mode of living will not lead to anywhere except reducing them to the verge of extinction."[16] The so-called tribes of India were already caught up in a false binary of protectionism versus assimilation, as I discuss later. The aboriginal Islanders too became subject to this policy conflict, but at an altogether different scale and with altogether different consequences. A note by another anthropologist of the Anthropological Survey of India, on the feasibility of a highway in South Andamans, written a few months after Guha's initial report, stated:

[W]e cannot determine whether the Jarawa in this area is really an intruder or whether he is just trying to get back to his home from which he had been deprived by the British, urged on by an increasingly [*sic*] in numbers, or by scarcity of food and water in the western half of the Middle Andamans, concerning both of which we have no knowledge. The fact remains however that so long as our activities in the Middle Andamans are confined to exploration of forest products, the Jarawa can continue to hunt downhill wild pigs or gather as much fruits as he likes and thus eke out an existence as long as he can elude the Forest Guards. This is not likely to be so when the country is opened up by a North South Road running down the middle and the country colonised by agriculturalists from India. The Jarawa is sure to resent this encroachment [via the North South Road] of that what [*sic*] he probably regards as his piggery and the open road will tempt him to raid the settlements to the east and molest travellers, etc on the road. Armed intervention by the government will in consequence be unavoidable and the Jarawa are bound to suffer. . . .

Since the Andamans are no longer a penal colony, there is no requirement for the Jarawa to act as the Jungle Police. Their friendship and their pacification are desirable in themselves. The idea of utilising captured Jarawa for this purpose has proved futile. The principles on which the new government of India are based alone demand this

---

16. B. S. Guha to R. N. Philips, Under-Secretary to the Government of India, Ministry of Home, June 3, 1950. Serial number 31; Demi Official number 1822. NAI/Home/AN/199/48-AN.

pacification and make it indispensable that the Jarawas' right to their food areas and sufficient food is ensured. Once this pacification is effected it would be possible to think of helping this tribe to survive in their struggle for existence.[17]

These passages show the complete reversal of status that the state had effected in relation to the Jarawas, from being hosts that were predated upon by the colonial state, to becoming tolerated guests of the postcolonial state. In variance from the dominant understanding of predation, in the Islands, it was not the host (the aboriginal tribes) that sought to domesticate and convert the visitor in their image (see Costa and Fausto 2019). By incorporating aboriginal Islanders and make them into objects of welfare and development, the state actively converted them unto its image of the ideal citizen, complete with nationalist attachments. Furthermore, the construction of the Andaman Trunk Road in 1978, the voluntary isolation of the Jarawas is increasingly threatened, as they have become ever more vulnerable to exploitation and routinised predation. But what is more salutary is that, regardless of these roads and inroads, both the Jarawa and the Sentinelese have never lost an opportunity to show their steadfast unwillingness to actively join the external world. They have rebuffed each of the numerous and regular attempts of "friendly contact" made by the state and its state anthropologist. But, instead of calling them "hostile," as the colonial state once did, the Indian state chooses to refer to the two as "unfriendly."

"How to analyse this unfriendliness?" asked a senior anthropologist working at the local substation of the Anthropological Survey of India in Port Blair. The substation was set up with the explicit purpose of studying the aboriginal populations on the islands and aiding contact with the Jarawas and the Sentinelese. He continued:

What is the model of friendliness? Strangers smiling at each other? Politicians—who are always smiling at people, are they friendly? We [state anthropologists] are asked to take gifts for them [the Jarawas]. We leave these gifts (usually coconuts and bananas) at the edge of the forest and leave. The Jarawas seldom took these gifts in the past, which we interpreted as "unfriendly." Yet, once when a policeman

---

17. "Report by A. K. Mitra after second visit to Andaman Islands." *Anthropological survey of the Andaman and Nicobar Islands—Welfare of the Aborigines.* p.5. NAI/Home/AN/199/48-AN

insisted on swimming to them, but soon began to drown, they saved him. [And] yet, they would not want to accept any gifts that we had brought. Are they unfriendly?[18]

The anthropologist went on to add: "[W]e ourselves sometimes put [the word] out there that the Jarawa are 'unfriendly,' as a way of protecting them. I know that if they stop being 'unfriendly,' then they will become open to exploitation."[19] A veteran of a number of "contact parties," he said that in his experience "the Jarawa seldom accept food like coconuts and bananas, but will take away any metal objects or scraps they find. Given their preference for wild boar, the Department of Animal Husbandry once left domesticated pigs for them in the forest, but that too came to no avail ... The ATR [Andaman Trunk Road] is a curse as it goes right through their forests, which they do not like at all. They seldom receive us in the forest. The sea-route is the only one which works to some extent."[20]

If contact with the Jarawa has been unforthcoming, then contact with the Sentinelese has always been more fraught. Talking about his experiences, T. N. Pandit, once director of the Anthropological Survey of India substation in Port Blair, said that the Sentinelese were mischaracterized as "hostile" or "unfriendly," but instead always act in in the interests of self-protection. "Since Portman's [the first British colonial official in the Andamans] days, they distrust outsiders. Portman kidnapped two Sentinelese and they did not return alive. So they have reason to be suspicious. . . . When we went in the 1970s, we met them in the water. We took coconuts and bananas for them. I was careful that our party did not make any aggressive moves, and we kept a safe distance. We ensured that we appeared to be offering friendly contact and nothing more."[21] Despite these overtures by the state, such as those made by Pandit's team and others,[22] the Sentinelese remain outside the fold of the nation-state, even

---

18. Research interview with A. (name withheld), Port Blair, November 18, 2006.

19. Ibid.

20. Ibid.

21. Research interview with T. N. Pandit, New Delhi, September 2006. Maurice Portman was a British naval officer who was the superintendent of the penal colony and extensively documented the lives and customs of the different peoples inhabiting the Islands. For more, see Sen (2009).

22. An anthropologist with the Anthropological Survey of India, Madhumala Chattopadhyay, has written about her success in staying with the

as they, their land, and their world are enumerated and folded within the sovereign Indian territory. As with the Jarawa, the Sentinelese too are one among the 400-odd Scheduled Tribes of India. In their refusal to enter the paradigm of either gift exchange or hospitality (as welcoming or reluctant hosts), the Sentinelese have rejected relationality with outsiders. The Indian state, *pace* Descola, continues to make attempts to incorporate them more fully through ostensibly a protectionist framework, and interprets their unwillingness to become incorporated as acts of self-preservation on their part. The state may wish for them to become more than territorially incorporated whilst laboring in the hope of substantialized attachment. But the Jarawas and the Sentinelese have to date taken no cognizance of this recognition, or indeed hope. In doing so they are different from other reluctant citizens who remonstrate against the demand of full attachment to the Indian state, and who protest against their involuntary incorporation through acts of refusal, or insurgent violence against the state. Despite the heterogeneity of political ideologies, these groups of reluctant citizens, in the very minimum, share a recognition of the state as a state, and recognize sovereignty for what it is. In so far as we can tell, the Jarawas and the Sentinelese do not bestow recognition on non-Jarawa and non-Sentinelese worlds. In and through the complete nonrecognition of non-Jarawa and non-Sentinelese worlds, any recognition of their subjectification as colonised, citizens, primitive, tribal, aboriginal, indigenous, hunter-gatherer, and by extension—the categories of state, India, race, empire, sovereignty—are rendered fundamentally meaningless and ineffectual by them. Roy Wagner (1981) argued that tribes living away from contact must definitely entail a "reverse anthropology." Just as we are completely un-interpolated by the reverse anthropology of the Jarawa and the Sentinelese, it is in that very vein that our ways of knowing them and our ways of being in the world are rendered completely meaningless in this resolute self-isolation on the part of the Sentinelese and, to a lesser extent, the Jarawa. Following Wagner (1981), "reverse anthropology" must surely be the most potent form of insurgency against the incorporationist tendencies of the state.

Sentinelese for over a month in 1991, and suggested that it may have to do with her having been the first (and the only) woman to have been part of a "contact party" (Sharma 2018). She later quit her job with the survey and joined the Ministry for Social Welfare (Chattopadhyay 2018). Repeated requests for an interview with her were turned down.

For its part, the state is nothing if not a sovereign. It therefore cannot consign those living within its territory simply as people of scientific interest. Its sovereignty lies in commanding and begetting what Arjun Appadurai (1998) has called "full attachment." Da Col and Shryock point out that the concept of "grace" put forth by Pitt-Rivers crucially moves hospitality into a realm of intentions and not of transactional obligations, thereby inaugurating a powerful theory of affect (2017: xxvii). It is therefore no surprise that the mode of relationality deployed by the state is an affective one, that of attachment, a frame that includes, yet exceeds, sacrifice in Appadurai's sense. The aim of full attachment explains not just the repeated attempts at contact with the Sentinelese and the Jarawa, but also the developmental and discursive apparatus aimed specifically at the so-called "indigenous" or "tribal" people. Most of these measures are aimed at making them in the state's own image, but also at enforcing recognition of its authority and mastery over them. Thus, the purpose of *terra nullius* is the creation of full attachment as a permanent and ongoing condition. By moving the register of encompassment from ownership to attachment, the state may have side-stepped the claims to title, but ironically it gives birth to the political and social category of indigeneity, thereby remaining unable to permanently erase the property question, as the following examination of the question of indigenous title on the mainland reveals.

The Properties of Indigeneity

Indigeneity has had a checkered career in contemporary India, becoming part of the political vocabulary in any recognizable way only in the closing years of the twentieth century (Kapila 2008). The dominant morphological units of Indian society are caste, tribe, and religion. The emergence of indigeneity in recent years has almost exclusively been read in terms of identity politics. This may be true of its latter-day avatar; however, the category of the indigenous emerged not in a cultural politics of identification, but rather in and through a question about property, and that too in that dense moment of transition from the colonial to the postcolonial state. A set of arguments presented in the Constituent Assembly on the eve of Independence explicate the nullification of the property question based in native title, and its rehabilitation through disaggregation.

Dipankar Gupta powerfully shows us the importance of the distinction between *difference* and *hierarchy* for understanding the structures of stratification in any society, and of Indian society in particular. His argument regarding the salience of this distinction is perhaps the most important and productive intervention in understanding the mutability of caste hierarchy in contemporary India, even though it has seldom been taken up beyond the context of caste in politics (Gupta 1991a; 1991b; 2004; 2005). Hierarchy, according to Gupta, is only one principle and not the essence of social stratification, and this is as true for India as it is for other societies. The trouble, he says, is that in our analysis of stratification in Indian society, we have paid too much attention to hierarchy—and as it is represented in the Brahminical worldview, at that—and not enough to difference (1991a: 11). It is when we pay attention to the concept of difference, or the principle of making *qualitative* distinctions (as opposed to *scalar* ones), that we can begin to understand not only non-Brahminical worldviews as competing hierarchies, but, more importantly, how various notions of difference are mobilized to constitute new hierarchies (1991a; 2005).

It is not without reason that hierarchy has remained a dominant trope for understanding the morphology of Indian society. Caste dominates the way we think of Indian society and its basis of differentiation. In scholarship, this owes a great deal to the centrality of Louis Dumont's seminal *Homo hierarchicus* (2009 [1971]). Even though today Dumont's model is no longer dominant in explanations of the caste system, hierarchy remains the dominant trope for thinking and writing about Indian society. The reasoning for this seems to be that caste is, after all, the dominant reality of the vast majority of Indians. Scholarship has rightly highlighted the significance of governmental technologies such as the decennial census and policies of positive discrimination based on these enumerative exercises in bestowing a systemic quality to caste as an interlocutory term with which to address the state (Appadurai 1993; Cohn 1996; Dirks 2001). The intermeshing of scholarship and the political pursuit of caste as the grammar for conducting democratic politics has thus only calcified the dominance of the trope of hierarchy. As a result, other techniques of collective differentiation have remained marginal to commonsensical understandings of Indian society.

Moreover, the marginality rendered to those who have been enumerated as statistically insignificant is replicated in the attention paid to them in scholarship. Until recently, for example, the "tribe question" did not feature in any serious way in any mainstream discussion, scholarly or otherwise, on social stratification or on identity politics. Intellectual agreements and disagreements, social solidarity and unrest, and state making and unmaking had pretty much gone about side-stepping the question of the existence of collectivities in Indian society that cannot be encompassed within either the framework of ritual hierarchy or then under the arc of world religions. This could not simply have come about as a result of salutary neglect in the Burkean sense. Rather, I want to argue, this neglect stemmed largely from the difficulties posed by certain forms of difference. Andre Beteille has argued that in India it is extremely difficult to disaggregate the agenda of government from that of anthropology, so that none of these categories of social distinction are available to study outside of technologies of government (1998). I take Beteille's insight further to suggest that the enumerative technologies of government are just one of the many reasons why until recently the social marginality of tribes was mimicked or repeated in their discursive obscurity.

There has been little systematic and/or extensive discussion of the place of cultural difference (as opposed to the sociological differences of caste, class, and gender, for instance) in relation to either state policy or indeed everyday social life. Moreover, for reasons that have to do with the birth of the postcolonial nation-state, recognition of difference in contemporary India has been underpinned by the discussion on secularism, where religion is seen at once to be the primary and the maximal marker of categorical or heteronymic difference. Beside religion, categorical difference (ontological, cultural) finds no basis for recognition within the constitutional framework because the question of difference has been colonized by sociological modalities such as caste, ethnicity, and gender, not least because they (the latter) form important vectors of equality in postcolonial Indian law. I am not suggesting that there exists in contemporary Indian society a purist separation between cultural and sociological differences. Rather, cultural and sociological differences are distinct assemblages that mobilize specific qualities which are not reducible to each other. For instance, religion as a sociological category encompasses its ability to produce scalar difference in relation to others, whereas the cultural category of religion encompasses its theology, belief structures, ritual practices, etc. The sociological and the cultural overlap and impinge on one another, but are nevertheless involved in distinct forms of production. Discussions of contemporary Indian sociality have been overwhelmed by sociological readings of *difference-as-inequality*, not least because of a nationalist commitment to social reform, including, and especially, that directed at caste. Whilst its reform was unquestionably necessary, its force, combined with its historical preeminence, led to a neglect—in scholarship as well as in public discourse—of forms of difference that were not based in or around a scalar logic. Nevertheless, as the chapter shows, through several processes of translation entailed in creating a coherent agenda of postcolonial social reform, these other forms of difference were incorporated within a scalar logic. Crucially, even though scalarity is not constitutive of the category "tribe," through official processes of social identification and enumeration, it too is now encompassed within a scalar logic of social difference (more developed, less developed, etc.). This has had profound implications for the category "indigenous," especially as it cannot be accommodated within the logic of scalarity. The archive presented here reveals that, ironically, in the attempts to recalibrate difference in postcolonial national society through the pursuit of policies of equity and equality, the logic of hierarchy has become only entrenched further. As a result, it becomes often fused in the capacious category of "tribe," which provides the necessary obscurity to the question of "native title."

In the remainder of this chapter, I focus on the constitutive nature of the category "tribe" in India, especially as a deflection of the question of indigenous title, and discuss the kinds of difficulties posed by what I call the culture question in relation to that of national society. I focus on the discussions on, by, or on behalf of, the tribal people and on their place in the postcolonial nation-state, with a view to excavating the genealogy of their current relationship with the state. I have already discussed the silence on the uncommon conditions of the Jarawa and the Sentinelese, and the Andamans more generally, in the Constituent Assembly Debates. The nature and the language of the claims made by tribal members of the Constituent Assembly bring to light the difficulties in staking a role in the emergent multicultural nation-state from the standpoint of heteronomous (as opposed to scalar) difference, which could not be incorporated within the discussion on secularism either. Examining the discussion on tribes in the Constitutional Assembly Debates from the standpoint of hierarchy and difference enables us to attend to the reasons why the debate on the future of tribes came to be formulated as a potential for modernity and therefore became hostage to the (false) binary between the assimilationists and the isolationists. Within anthropology and beyond, the Ghurye-Elwin debate about whether or not tribes should become incorporated within the national mainstream or in some ways be protected from the advent of modernity is well documented (Guha 1999; Kapila 2008; Skaria 1997; Srivatsan 2005). What has remained obscured from view is *why* the debate on tribes came to be framed in these very terms in the first instance. Contemporaneous discussions on the uplift of dalits, whether in their self-representation or in official and legal discourse, were never posited in terms of their potential for modernity, nor in terms of choice regarding opting in or out of modernity's welfare corollary of "development." The ordinal disadvantage of dalits was framed within an injury discourse and in terms of a historical harm inflicted by ritual hierarchy and its attendant practices that purported to produce species-like distinction between the twice-born and the dalit castes. Positive discrimination was thus cast within a compensatory logic through which this historic injury exacted by ritual discrimination was to be redressed. Whether or not this was adequate measure for dealing with the question of ritual hierarchy is not within the scope of this discussion. What is pertinent here is that in the normative conceptualization of national society that took place in and surrounding the discussions on stratification and modes of redress. Not only were all forms of difference translated into scalar difference, but their redress too was framed within a compensatory logic. If compensatory positive discrimination for Scheduled Castes hinged on the configuration of "bad tradition," state welfare for the tribes was primarily about the understanding of civilizational progress—in other words, modernity of and for the new nation.

In this way, castes were identified by the state with sociality, or the social character of Indian society, the ills within which were to be addressed as a national matter. Tribes, on the other hand, were seen as a matter of "culture," as not integrated within the larger society even discursively, and emerged as a problem arising from modernity, rather than from society itself. In Descola's schema, tribes were non-equivalent and had to be made equivalent, or not. In the case of the tribes, it was assumed that there was no prima facie historical wrong committed by someone in particular that had to be corrected. As a result, the caste question became the object of social reform, whereas that of tribes became that of development. Not all politics of recognition on the eve of Independence, however, was constituted as and through an injury claim. Those who represented either tribal peoples or tribal areas in the Constituent Assembly insisted on a recognition of their contribution to national life, but their claims for recognition were not embedded in, nor emanated from, a cognizance of a historical wrong or a historical injury. And yet, the only way the recognition of their existence was possible was through the encompassment of their claim to difference within the compensatory principle of positive discrimination. The birth of the false debate for tribes has its birth in this encompassment or indeed this misrecognition. This collapsing of difference-as-inequality and difference-as-not-sameness in the policies of redistribution in India as the self-similar subject of justice and welfare in postcolonial India has had profound implications for the status of tribes, their relationship to the state, and their politics. Importantly, it inverted the claim for ownership into a compensatory logic of welfare and upliftment.

Debating Indigeneity in the Constituent Assembly

The Constituent Assembly is aptly described as "an island of calm deliberation amidst the historical currents that swirled through the country" (Khilnani 1997: 33). Its constitution, jurisdiction, and character (i.e., whether public, private, or secret) were themselves matters of much deliberation (Rau 1960: xxxiv), as was its representativeness (Bajpai 2011: 46). Though these debates have been studied to understand the legal framework of the new nation and its democratic and multicultural character (Ambagudia 2011; Bajpai 2011; Khilnani 1997), most discussions have side-stepped an engagement with the question of tribe in relation to group rights and principles of positive discrimination, even when the question of difference has been of central concern (e.g. Bajpai 2010: 126–128; Mukherjee 2010. But see Ambagudia 2011). As a result, the baseline discussions for the category of "tribe" are either the deliberations in and around the classificatory and enumerative exercises such as the census, or then early ethnological accounts. As a result, self and relational understandings of groups classified and identified as "tribes" remain obscured, or, at best, as matters of conjecture in discussions on postcolonial state policies of multiculturalism in India. It is with a view to covering this gap that I focus particularly on the interventions made by the most important representative of tribal India in the Constituent Assembly, Jaipal Singh Munda. In doing so, my aim is to delineate the discrepancy between the self-representation of tribal interests in the Constituent Assembly and the terms of their ultimate translation in the constitution and in public policy, especially in relation to their constitution as a subject of welfare through the Sixth Schedule.[23]

---

23. The Sixth Schedule of the Indian constitution includes a list of all tribes and castes, and areas and constituencies identified for positive discrimination measures.

In the Constituent Assembly, diversity was imagined as the starting point for the formation of national society, thus making the project of Indian multiculturalism already different from other democratic multicultural states, where diversity and difference have tested the robustness of the liberal principles of these polities (Kapila 2008). A complex interlocking of the history of enumeration, the entrenchment of the ethnological imagination, and the contours of the anti-colonial struggle all had paved the way for not only the pursuit of equality as the cornerstone of policy, but also the recognition of only certain forms of difference. For reasons that lay in the very birth of the nation-state, religion came to be the only, and the maximal, categorical difference in Indian society to be recognized by the constitution, which led to the eventual promulgation of its Personal Codes. Simultaneously, the recognition of the violence of historical ritual discrimination led to the strident pursuit of equality and parity of status in law. Whilst religious difference found recognition through the conceptual arc of the minority, legally embedded through Personal Codes, the difference of ritual status was seen to be based in inequality and therefore was sought to be erased from society through legislation (criminalizing untouchability) and active state intervention through policies of positive discrimination. Groups such as tribes, that should have belonged to the realm of categorical difference or even as minorities, since they were statistically marginal, were instead constituted as objects of welfare reform, directed as those who fell under the rubric of difference-as-inequality. The nonrecognition of tribes as categorically different groups had echoes of the historic Poona Pact of 1935, where the demand for separate electorates for tribal members and populations had found no favor with B. R. Ambedkar in Poona in 1935, or indeed with others such as Jawaharlal Nehru and Sardar Patel in the Constituent Assembly (Ambagudia 2011: 35). Instead, the category of tribes in India came to be marked by both categorical difference (*qua* statistical minority) and inequality (through the status of backwardness) at the same time. Hence, it became subject to the twin directives of integration in the national community as minority and development as backward groups. The question of tribes therefore became part of the negotiations between the integrationists and the multinationalists in the debates in the Constituent Assembly, and between the assimilationists and isolationists outside, even though exactly what kind of groups they were remained a subject of contention:

For the first time in the history of India I find the *adibasis* are now "aboriginal" and "hill tribes". I would urge the hon. Minister not to indulge in such disruptive language. Is a man tribal or not? Has he to be up in the hills before he can be a tribal? What is this new language he is trying to introduce in Republican India?[24]

The question of integration of tribes into the national mainstream was of a qualitatively different kind from that of either princely states or indeed religious minorities. Whilst princely states were integral to the discussions on sovereignty and territorial integrity, the same could not be said for tribal kingdoms. Where these may have existed, tribal polities were never recognized as distinct political formations, but were subsumed under the wider territory they were part of. In fact, Alfred Gell has argued that whilst tribal polities such as those in colonial Central India had highly elaborate forms of kingship, they nevertheless eschewed state practices of rent and revenue extraction, prevalent in the surrounding areas under Hindu, Muslim or British rule. It was precisely their inability to develop an elaborate rent and revenue function that distinguished tribal polities from princely India (Gell 1997: 433; see also Grigson 1944: 33). At the time of the framing of the constitution, these factors played a crucial role in the kind of political recognition that was accorded to tribes.

The nonrecognition of tribal polities either by the British or by the national leadership was part of a wider problem. Furthermore, unlike religious minorities whose lifeways and belief systems had gained at least a nominal recognition in law through Personal Codes, tribal religion and lifeways did not find any support or recognition in law. But the tribe question was neither; it was squarely a matter of ownership. The question of minorities thus was neither accurate, nor indeed acceptable to the people themselves concerned:

> I do not consider the Adibasis are a minority. I have always held that a group of people who are the original owners of this country, even if they are only a few, *can never be considered a minority*. They have prescriptive rights. We want to be treated like anybody else. In the past, thanks to the major political parties, thanks to the British Government and thanks to every enlightened Indian citizen, we have been isolated and kept, as it were in a zoo. That has been the attitude of all people in the past. Our point now is that *you have got to mix with us.*

---

24. Jaipal Singh, April 18, 1950. *Parliamentary Debates* 1950, Part 1, Vol. 3, p.1601.

We are willing to mix with you and it is for that reason, because we shall compel you to come near us, because we must get near you, that we have insisted on a reservation of seats as far as the Legislatures are concerned.[25] (emphases added)

The above was the contribution of Jaipal Singh to the *Report on minority rights* tabled by Vallabhai Patel in the Constituent Assembly in August 1947. The Munda leader from Chota Nagpur had been campaigning for the recognition of the rights of the tribal people in the region for some time (Guha 2007: 265–266). Earlier, Jaipal Singh had mobilized the tribal peoples of Chota Nagpur region to form the Adibasi Mahasabha in 1938.[26] Even though tribal interests were picked up and represented by other members such as A. V. Thakkar (Bihar) and J. J. M. Nicholas Roy (Assam), Jaipal Singh was as such the sole tribal member in the Constituent Assembly, and took his representational position both in the Assembly and beyond very seriously.[27] For example, he wrote several missives to Rajendra Prasad, as the senior-most Congress figure from Bihar, reminding him about the inadequacies of the statistical method for understanding the tribal question: "Aboriginal identity must be preserved at any cost. Immediate measures should be adopted to promote aboriginal culture. The statistical confusion that exists in respect of [*sic*] the numerical strength of the aborigines should be removed. An aborigine by embracing Hinduism, Islam or any other religion does not cease to be an Adibasi. Census data are inaccurate."[28] As is evident from the quotation, Singh considered the tribal recognition neither as a matter of statistical minority nor on the basis of scalar inequality. In his

---

25. Jaipal Singh, August 27, 1947. *Constituent Assembly Debates* (hereafter CAD), 5 (8): 226.

26. He later spearheaded the formation of the Jharkhand Party in the early 1950s, the first political association to petition the State Reorganisation Committee in 1955 for a separate state of Jharkhand (Sharma 1976: 38). Singh and his party soon withdrew their petition and movement following a merger with the Congress Party (Sharma 1976: 38).

27. Jaipal Singh was a Munda from present day Jharkhand, and was educated in Oxford. For a brief biographical account of Jaipal Singh in relation to tribal uprisings and movements in Jharkhand, see Sharma (1976). See also Guha (2007). On the history of tribal insurrection in Jharkhand see Guha (1994).

28. From Jaipal Singh to Rajendra Prasad. Dated Ranchi, May 24, 1939. Letter no. 112. In Choudhary 1986: 96. (I thank Rohit De for this reference.)

understanding, the claim was based on a rather different premise—one that was never fully picked up by the political leadership at the time, and pertained to matters of origins, property, and ownership. Consider the very first intervention in the Constituent Assembly made by Jaipal Singh:

> Thank you [Sir], for giving me the opportunity to speak as the representative of the aboriginal tribes of Nagpur. . . . [S]o far as I have been able to count, we are here only five [members representing tribes or tribal areas]. But we are millions and millions and we are the real owners of India. It has recently become fashion to talk of Quit India. I do hope that this is only a stage for the real rehabilitation and resettlement of the original people of India.[29]

The claim to ownership was premised on the originary identification with the territory in question. Singh did not make these claims unaware of the opposition that confronted him, nor the perceived anachronism of these claims:

> [W]herever we have been it has been urged upon us that for several years to come, the aboriginals' land must be inalienable. If I were to fight for that particular, shall we say protection, most members would laugh. A friend of mine, only this morning when I was talking to him, said, "Do you want for eternity that aboriginal land should remain inalienable?" [T]hat is how some of the demands vital to Adibasis are ridiculed. We have been talking about equality. Equality sounds well; but I do demand discrimination when it comes to holdings of aboriginal land.[30]

As is clear from these quotes, there was a lack of fit between the terms in which tribes were being incorporated within the postcolonial state polity and their own self-representation to the Constituent Assembly, thereby revealing the underlying difficulties faced by law and lawmakers on the question of difference. Postcolonial law in India, it seems, was unable or unwilling to recognize difference as discreteness. Even religion—the marker of categorical, heteronomous difference—had to be converted into the statistical model of minorities and majority and could

---

29. Jaipal Singh, December 11, 1946. *CAD* 1 (1): 46.
30. Jaipal Singh, April 30, 1947. *CAD* 3 (3): 449.

thereby guarantee equality finally only through the trope of scalarity. The reasons necessitating the recognition of religion through the trope of majority/minority are beyond the scope of this discussion. My focus here is the discursive moves through which the heteronomous tribe was incorporated within a singular logic of scalarity. I want to suggest that the recognition of the categorical difference that tribes were claiming was transmuted into a scalar one for reasons to do with the *very nature of the claim itself* and made for three distinct but overlapping sets of mis-recognition, as Jaipal Singh's intervention makes manifest:

> We did not go to London for negotiations [*sic*]. We did not go to meet the Cabinet Mission for provisions for our rights. We look only to our countrymen to give us a fair and equitable deal. For the last six thousand years, we have been shabbily treated. . . . Six thousand years . . . that is the time you non-Adibasis have been in this country. . . . Number for number, the Sikhs, the Christians, the Anglo Indians, and the Parsis have been given more than their due, whereas when we come to my own people, the real and most ancient people of this country, the position is different.[31]

Three key elements constitute the core of the claims made here by Jaipal Singh: one, about origins and time; two, ownership claims over territory through primordiality; and, three, the subsequent misappropriation of their property by others. Time and territory as anchors of collective self-identification chimed with prevalent anthropological framings of culture as originary and boundary-making. It was the third element, however, that marked Jaipal Singh's claim on behalf of the tribal populations of India as radical. In these interventions, Singh did not characterize tribes as people who had suffered an injury or harm. Instead, by positioning tribes as the original inhabitants of the land, and by further claiming their inalienable rights of ownership over it, he inherently constituted their demand in terms of *property rights*, and the subsequent claim in terms of *recovery of debt* owed by others and as a problem of hospitality. In other words, this was not a claim of injury that demanded compensation. This was a claim about unpaid debt that demanded recovery and restitution of ownership. A robust corpus of scholarship exists on the usurpation of land and title through the doctrine of *terra nullius* and its effects for settler-colonial contexts (Borrows 2010; Chakravartty and

---

31. Jaipal Singh, January 24, 1947. *CAD* 2 (4): 316.

Ferreira da Silva 2012; Povinelli 2002; Tully 2002). However unlike with aboriginal property claims in settler colonies, Singh had not suggested a comprehensive usurpation or occupation of territory by the non-adibasis, but had gestured more in the direction of bad or problematic hospitality. This allowed for a discursive fragmentation of his claim and a partial recognition of tribal interests.

Distinct from the conceptualization of the claim as an injury or harm whose locus was corporeal (as in the case of caste), the locus of the claim was in the land and the materiality of territory. The state for its part reduced the largest claim of inalienable ownership of territory made by Singh on behalf of the tribal groups to its partial or rather elementary form—by reducing and fragmenting a property claim to one of *resources*, i.e., qualified rights of ownership to elements that may reside in that territory, but not to territory itself. This move disaggregated the main demand for territory into its elemental parts and reduced the temporal claim of origins to merely an affective link to these elemental aspects of territory—forests, produce, etcetera. Francesca Merlan, among others, has argued that "[i]n many instances, including those of the 'classical,' or early-accepted indigenous groups, the introduction in some countries of frameworks that rest on traditionalist assumptions of the centrality of territorial connection have been seen as effectively having a dispossessory effect" (2009: 306). A serious and substantial political claim of the terms through which tribal selfhood was understood shifted registers and came to be recognized through the narrow lens of political economy. Tribes were divested of their claim to ownership of property in the absolute or even substantial sense and placed at a distinct remove from their claim to heterenomous difference. Thus, in these inaugural moments of the new nation-state, tribes became constituted as subjects of welfare and development, profoundly defining not only the politics of development in postcolonial India with respect to tribes, but also their own pursuit for recognition and future claim-making.

New Settlements

The Scheduled Tribe population today is an ever more diverse set with very different social formations and economic realities. Like their nomenclature, the political exigencies faced by *adivasis* ("aboriginal"), *janjatis* ("tribes"), *vanvasis* ("forest dwellers"), *mool bharatiyas* ("original Indians"), to say nothing of the Jarawas or the Sentinelese, are neither the same, nor of the same vintage. Jaipal Singh's query to the Constituent Assembly comes in hand here—is a man tribal or not, does he have to live in the hills for him to be considered as one? Spokespersons of the tribal communities within the Constituent Assembly were categorical about their self-perception as the original inhabitants of India, who as original owners of that land should have inalienable rights in land. Jaipal Singh's disapproval of the descriptor "aboriginal" gestured to the negative anthropological baggage of the appellation. Terminology remains a vexed issue to date, especially because the words "tribal," "aboriginal," "indigenous," and "Scheduled Tribe" do not neatly correspond with each other or, indeed, with their vernacular terms or to the groups thus classified. What we now have by way of redistributive justice for the tribal population in India is an unstable mix of these three positions, i.e. of formal equality, protectionist policies and indigenous politics.

There has been a proliferation of groups demanding a Scheduled Tribe status, especially in the wake of the neo-liberal economic reforms of the last two decades. There is another kind of differentiation that is being given political articulation in recent years. This has to do with the growth in the politics of indigeneity and indigenous status that has given new life to categories such as *adivasi, mool-bharatiya* and *vanvasi*. Every one of these addresses, and is born out of, different political persuasions. But they have also called into being new interlocutors to arbitrate on their state and status that go beyond the Indian state, such as the United Nations International Working Group on Indigenous Affairs. In moving the register of their struggle away from the local and the national to include the global domain, this politics has produced a new axis of inequality that pertains not to ritual rank, nor to civilizational progress—nor indeed to class—but to the question of scale. Within the tribal populations, access to such "global" platforms is not evenly distributed either in the present times or indeed in the potential future. This then is the new creamy layer of the tribal population, which has scaled up its politics beyond the state, but nevertheless remains rooted in the idea of compensatory discrimination for the discursive wrongs committed against its constituents.[32]

---

32. "Creamy layer" is a term coined by the legal scholar Marc Galanter (1984) to describe the narrow reach of positive discrimination measures, whereby just a few families within the scheduled tribes and castes availed themselves of these benefits beyond the one generation.

It is salutary to remind ourselves why this becomes, ironically, a moment of reversal in relationality of the state towards so-called indigenous communities. As Descola puts it: "[P]rotection becomes a dominant schema when a group . . . is perceived both as dependent . . . for its reproduction, nurturing, and survival and also as being so closely linked . . . that it becomes an accepted and authentic component of the collective" (2013: 326). In developmentalist protectionism, the state thus constitutes indigeneity as fundamentally non-equivalent, whereas a prior colonial framing of the indigenous Andaman Islanders, for example, was one based in negative asymmetry of predation, which in fact is rooted in equivalence. Descola writes that "far from being an expression of gratuitous cruelty or a perverse desire to annihilate others, [predation] on the contrary transforms the prey into an object of the greatest importance. . . . Indeed, it is the very condition of that creature's survival" (2013: 318).

In keeping with Descolas's schema, we can say see that at the dawn of Independence, the Indian state found itself "in potentially reversible relations between substitutable terms . . . situated at the same ontological level" (2013: 333) with the indigenous populations—from the Jarawas and the Sentinelese to the Mundas represented by Jaipal Singh, where predation, gift, and exchange could be the veritable modes of relationality. But such modes of relationality ran counter to sovereignty. The early years of Independence were spent in converting these reversible relations into hierarchical and irreversible relations between non-substitutable terms (Descola, ibid.). This meant that instead of being potentially guests and hosts to each other, the relation was converted, first via encompassment and incorporation as a relation of transmission, and then to that of protection via paternalist state welfare measures. Pivotal to this conversion was territory, land, and its control. It was no surprise that the state usurped territory and land as a way of intensifying and expanding the realm of sovereign control.

CHAPTER 5

Res Nullius: The Properties of Culture

Property is theft.

– Pierre-Joseph Proudhon, 1840

How do things acquire properties hitherto not associated with them? This chapter examines the expanding realm of sovereignty from land and territory to that of things. It is based on discussions between private individuals and colonial government officials posted in various locations in India and Whitehall about the disputed status of goods destined for the Indian pavilions at the Great Exhibition of 1851 in the Crystal Palace in London, then referred to as the Exhibition of the Works of Industry and Art of All Nations, as well as the 1862 International Exhibition held in South Kensington, London. In following some of the claims of contested ownership and status, I argue that the differing final destinations (museums, private collections, laboratories, trade catalogues) of these objects not only adjudicated on their value, but also laid the early foundations for the emergence of a more rigid regulation of traffic between the world of commerce and culture. In their reading of these changes, historians of art as well as of empire have tended to explain the shifts in the status of these objects as effects of colonial knowledge and its attendant classificatory regimes (see, for example, Cohn 1996). An anthropological lens, however, allows us to open up this question in an altogether new direction. In following the journeys of these objects, I argue that the change in status was far from a singular reclassification and was instead brought about through a series of exchange transactions through which property in and of these objects was first leeched away and then inscribed anew. Following some of these journeys of acquisition reveals that these objects not only changed hands in terms of ownership, but also acquired new qualities and came to be recognized in new ways that ultimately assisted in stabilizing their sometimes liminal or fragile status. Sovereign power lay in the ability of the state to deliberately misrecognize these objects and the terms of transaction under which they were mobilized. In disaggregating the processes through which new ownership and new qualities were conferred on these objects, the range of exchange and property relations that underpinned colonial state power and sovereignty in British India is revealed.

Property and sovereignty are generally seen to belong to two distinct legal domains: public law and private law (Cohen 1927). But enough instances have occurred in history where sovereignty has been constituted precisely and solely through the ability to (re)define property and property relations. As the previous chapter showed, the doctrine of *terra nullius* in settler colonies or the collectivization of private property under the Soviet and Communist regimes of Eastern Europe in the twentieth century are prime examples of the forcible acquisition of property and dispossession of title as the exercise of sovereignty and state power (see Humphrey 1983; Povinelli 2003; Verdery 2003). For reason of revenue alone, the modern state has had a fundamental interest in all property and property forms. In recent years, advances in information, communication, and biocultural technologies have created new forms of property and new ownership structures in new entities, in turn provoking new challenges for the state. These new forms of ownership structures range from severely restrictive forms of ownership (e.g., non-patentable biogenetic substances) to open-ended ones (e.g., open source software), each posing its own problems in relation to their governance and adjudication by the state, not least because, as property forms, these new entities are inherently translocal.[1] Even as these property forms move from the domain of the real to that of the virtual and intellectual, the difficulties

---

1. Although the list of these works is too long to cite in full, see Hirsch (2010) for an overview of these recent developments. For intellectual property in biogenetic substances, see Pottage (2007) and Strathern (2005: 95–110). For licensing and open source software, see Boyle (2003) and Kelty (2008: 179–209).

in determining or establishing ownership are made more acute (Boyle 2003). But in my engagement with older archives, I find echoes of these current ownership debates in contexts that are not mediated by either the latest advances in technology (as I deal with more fully in the next chapter) or by more enduring questions of land and territory, as discussed in the previous chapter. What the recent contexts of techno-property-making have in common with nineteenth-century objects is the articulation of a more fundamental question—that of property as a power relationship, particularly state power. At the core of this matter, then, is the concern for understanding the state as a proprietor and the place of property in the constitution of its sovereignty—specifically its property in things—through the doctrine of *res nullius*, or the modality of theft. Following the contested journeys from the perspective of the exchange of objects dispatched from colonial India for the exhibitions of 1851 and 1862 allows us to gain insights into the state as a proprietor and its complex modus operandi in acquiring all manner of property. At the same time, it brings a fresh perspective to the anthropology of objects and things on the interplay of the agentive power of objects and the sovereign power of the state.

My interest here is thus not in understanding how "newness" comes into the world and makes it modern, but in deciphering what happens when newness comes to pre-existing objects that make up the world. As an anthropologist, I read this colonial archive to capture the salience of colonial governmentality and its modalities of exchange in and through which new forms of property and property relations emerge. To do so, I engage with the anthropology of things that has come to question hard distinctions between persons and things, subjects and objects, material and symbolic cultures (Henare et al. 2007; Pottage 2001; Strathern 1988a and 1999). Strathern's work on the mutability of persons and things in gift and commodity exchange has been foundational for much of this thinking. In *The gender of the gift*, Strathern alerts us to the indistinct status of persons and things in commodity and gift exchange (Strathern 1988a). Whereas in commodity exchange, both persons and things are rendered as things, in and through gift exchange both persons and things become persons (Strathern 1988a; see also Pottage 2001). Strathern argues for paying attention to the distinction between persons and things as an artifice—an artifice that is revealed or given life-form in our ideology of exchange relations. Henare et al. (2007: 2) have called for an "artefact-oriented anthropology," where "things" are studied ethnographically not as material culture—where culture is read back into them in order to lend meaning to them—but as culture per se, so that they become the very concepts through which we can read social relations. Alain Pottage, following Strathern, dismantles the presuppositions of the separateness of persons and things in the legal imaginary, especially in relation to property and property rights, and the challenge to legal thinking posed by the idea of the potential in configuring biotechnological patents (2001). He is concerned with the legal capacities associated with the notion of "attributes" of a person compared to "properties" of things, particularly in relation to the concept of potential and the limits on their transactability. These distinctions pose great difficulties if they are not torn asunder when the property is composed of a life-form—for example, patents in biogenetic substances. Analogously, Callon et al. (2002) investigate the series of actions that bestow new qualities on goods and transform them into products. This chapter takes up the question of "potentiality" for nonliving things as they become animated through exchange and its significance in the making of new forms of property and property relations. This will enable us to better understand the mutability of objects destined for the 1862 International Exhibition. I enhance the discussions of Pottage, as well as of Callon et al., by bringing to the field the place of power, especially state power, in generating fragility as well as mutability in property forms.

The exhibitions of 1851 and 1862 were pageants of empire (Auerbach and Hoffenberg 2008; Greenhalgh 1988; Harvey 1996; Hoffenberg 2001; Lowe 2015; Nair, 2002) and were at once an archive of the aesthetic, as well as of cultural display (Mathur 2007). Much has been written about their displays of difference (Breckenridge 1989; Hoffenberg 2001; Kriegel 2001), their role in the making of contemporary taste (Lowe 2015; Mathur 2007), and their status as precursors of cultural consumerism (Hetherington 2007; Lowe 2015). The Great Exhibitions articulated the relationship between the metropole and the colony, as well as the significance of the transnational flow of goods that was central to the idea of empire (Breckenridge 1989). Historians of South Asia have attended to these exhibitions as exemplars of the effects of colonial knowledge and its classificatory regimes. Bernard Cohn was among the first to alert us to the deep transformational effects of colonial classificatory strategies, such as the census (Cohn 1996). He brought to light the early colonial conceptualization of India as "a museum of the European past" (1996: 93) and the effects of such a conceptualization on the periodization and classification of Indian art and architecture (1996: 76–105). He explained the transformation of everyday goods into antiquaries in the late eighteenth century as a consequence of the survey and the enumerative modality of colonial governmentality in the late eighteenth and early nineteenth centuries. Following Cohn, scholars have attended specifically to the circulation of colonial scientific knowledge and objects in and through these exhibitions (Nair 2002) and have shown how practices of scientific archaeology, art history, and collecting sensibilities in colonial India made for a very particular imagining of the national pasts (Guha Thakurta 2004; see also Hoffenberg 2001; Kriegel 2001). For historical context, I draw on these accounts, which are valuable interventions in our understanding of the workings of colonial power and the multiple modalities through which imperium was constituted. However, my interest in reading the archives is not so much to reframe the historical argument about empire or to reexamine the role of the Great Exhibitions in the formation of contemporary cultures of consumption. Rather, my concern lies in apprehending what impels the flows through which these objects leave their original location and end up on a different continent. This will entail tracing a phase in their biographies (see Appadurai 1986: 17; Kopytoff 1986) that came to articulate nation and empire as they traveled from one context to another. While scholarly attention has been paid to how these displays came to provide a framework and solidity to empire, I argue that this solidity emerged in and through the malleability, if not fragility, of these objects of display as they moved from one context to another through a series of transactions that rendered these objects into mutable mobiles. Crucial to this stability was the erasure and reinscription of title. As the chapter will show, the stability of status that a reinscription of title achieved was as much for the objects as it was for colonial sovereignty itself. Opening up objects as vectors of sovereignty follows at one level a well-established mode of anthropological inquiry into the "agency" of things (Gell 1998). Scholars have also attended to the political life of circulating objects for their essential or aesthetic qualities per se (see Breckenridge 1989; Lowe 2015; Mathur 2007). However, the objects in circulation discussed in this chapter are unlike the possessions that circulate as political objects acquired through "ritualised friendship" in Kula, as discussed by Annette Weiner (1992: 133–34; also Ssorin-Chaikov 2006). The main difference lies in the very fact of transfer or acquisition being under question. The objects discussed here are to an extent in keeping with Weiner's characterization of items as political objects and trophies, but are acquired through a myriad mechanisms, none of which arise from the frame of friendship. In the recalibration of their status and of their title, these objects assist in expanding the domain of sovereignty from land and territory to include an altogether different domain—of things and objects in and through which empire was made.

From Property to *Res Nullius*

In 1859, W. Grey, Secretary to the Government of India in Whitehall, London, sent a circular to relevant officials in the various provinces of British India, giving them extensive instructions on the process of acquiring articles for the upcoming exhibition in 1862:

> Lists finally prepared . . . should specify against each article in what manner it is intended by the contributor that it should be dealt with. Contributors should be directed to state whether they wish their contributions to be returned to India, or to be sold in England for their benefit. In the latter case the price of the article must be named, and it must be clearly stated whether, in the event of that price not being procurable, it is desired that the article be sold for what it will fetch, or that it be returned to India. In the case of articles being returned to India, every care will be taken to secure them from injury in transit, but it must be understood that the Government cannot guarantee their return undamaged. *When articles are sent without any instructions, it will be assumed that they are intended to be presented to the Exhibition.* These points should be clearly explained to all those who offer to contribute articles to the Exhibition.[2] (emphases added)

The letter set off a chain of transactions and exchange strategies that both articulated and consolidated the colonial state's power over Indians and their possessions. The main emphasis of the letter was to impress upon the officers the need to observe prudence in their expenditures for acquiring objects for the exhibition.[3] (emphases added) Grey underscored to his colleagues that Her Majesty's exchequer would not be able to bear the scale of expenditures that were incurred to purchase articles for the first Great Exhibition of 1851. The total budgetary outlay for 1862 to buy and transport articles from India was set at Rs. 100,000, which

---

2. National Archives of India (hereafter NAI)/Home/Public/A Proceedings/ May 13, 1861/ No. 16.
3. NAI/Home/Public/A Proceedings/ May 13, 1861/ No. 16.

was a significantly lower amount than the previous effort for the 1851 Exhibition.[4] Even though the budget was cut, the number of specimens requisitioned and acquired were far in excess of the previous exhibition: "2699 specimens were sent by sea, exceeding the collection of 1851 by 1237. Valuable textile fabrics, silks and brocades as well as works of art, which remain to be forwarded by the overland route, comprise nearly 2000 articles which will bring up the total number of the collection to nearly 6000 specimens, *double* of what has been sent in 1851."[5]

The cut in the budget also meant that while the volume of articles for display had to increase, the cost of acquisitions for the government had to be brought down. Grey's letter outlined in some detail the kind of measures local officials could adopt to keep these costs low. The circular proposed novel interventions aimed at disturbing and disrupting the usual chain of value accretion in order to achieve this stated goal. Two main forms of disruption to the chain of transactions were suggested: misrecognizing or redefining the mode of exchange, on the one hand, and, on the other, disconnecting owners from their claim to their possessions—or even both. On Grey's suggestion, a new mode of exchange was introduced into the process of acquisitions. He urged his colleagues to encourage so-called private contributions by persuading individuals to send articles for the London exhibition instead of having the state purchase or lawfully acquire these objects, leaving it only the cost of transport:

> But his Excellency in Council would wish that any encouragement and assistance which can be afforded at a moderate cost should be given to private persons who may be desirous to send articles to the Exhibition, and with this object it seems desirable . . . that the Government should signify its readiness to receive contributions for the Exhibition, take charge of them and forward them to England, the cost of conveyance being defrayed by Government.[6]

The expeditiousness of "private contributions" as a mode of acquisition had emerged when government officials settled disputes that arose

---

4. NAI/Home/Public/A Proceedings/ August 2, 1861/ No. 4–15.
5. *Report on the results of the arrangements for the forthcoming exhibition of 1862*, submitted to the Central Committee for Bengal at the meeting held on January 6, 1862. NAI/Home/Public/A Proceedings/ February 1, 1862/ p.1.
6. NAI/Home/Public/A Proceedings/ May 13, 1861/ No. 16.

from handing over articles for previous London and Paris exhibitions. Its expediency lay precisely in the state's capacity to obfuscate the exact terms under which these objects were being sent and received. In one such instance, the family of one Lokenath Sonar of Cuttack wrote a petition in 1858 to the Government of Bengal, stating that, as a family of goldsmiths, they had "contributed" articles of jewelry of considerable value (Rs. 1234) "at the desire of [Mr. Samuels] the then Commissioner of Cuttack for the Paris Exhibition."[7] The petition was written to ascertain from the colonial government what had become of their articles, as these had not been returned to them. The Sonars demanded that in case these articles had indeed been sold, they should be paid their due amount, since they had had to borrow a substantial amount of money to prepare the articles in the first place. The petition thus revealed their perfectly legitimate expectations of the transaction they thought they had entered into with the state. The official investigating this claim confirmed that, although these articles were correctly entered in the original list of freight bound for the Paris Exhibition, the trail ran dry at a crucial point—a fate shared by many such journeys. The existence of the articles belonging to the Sonars could not be traced once they ill-fatedly reached the Queen's Warehouse on New Street in East London, along with the other surplus goods from the Exhibition.

Disappearing from the exchange network or becoming a "lost" article or good was only one way in which title and "owner" became disconnected from each other. In another instance, a private contributor, Baboo Bhyrooprasad of Jaunpur, was convicted of treason and subsequently executed, and his significant contribution to the exhibition of 1851, as listed below, was summarily "confiscated" by the state.[8]

The accounts of Bhyrooprasad and Sonar are hardly startling or unsettling in themselves, as they fall well within the shared, familiar, and in fact ongoing narrative of empire, where theft and expropriation formed routine modalities of exchange. However, what the archive reveals is that this expropriation was achieved in several steps, sometimes propelled by differing logics, rather than in one fell swoop or even by a singular logic.

---

7. No. 510 of March 24, 1858/ pg. 3. NAI/Home/Public/A Proceedings/ April 9, 1858/ No. 84–89.
8. NAI/Home/Public/A Proceedings/ September 3, 1858/ No. 42.

Invoice Number	Article	Price Paid
8540	Piece of Kincob, brown colour	Rs. 295
8544	Red Scarf	Rs. 35
8545	Blue Scarf	Rs. 35
8540	Black Scarf	Rs. 70
8548	Pair of shoes	Rs. 25
8549	Doputta yellow (Silver)	Rs. 575
8550	Doputta yellow (Gold)	Rs. 290
8551	Doputta Blue (Gold)	Rs. 275

List of items contributed by Baboo Bhyrooprasad. Source: Extracted from letter no. 1085, Allahabad, dated May 4, 1858, from J. B. Outram, Secretary, North West Provinces, to Cecil Beadon, Secretary to the Government of India, Home Department, Fort William, NAI/Home/Public/A Proceedings/Consultation of May 7, 1858/ No. 26–27.

Only in a handful of cases was expropriation as neat as in Bhyrooprasad's case, where the original owner had no legal recourse to titular claim. The majority of the cases fell into the blurred zone of appropriation, loss, and disappearance, such as in the experience of the Sonar family. In their case, the proprietary title clearly remained with Sonar, inasmuch as this was his "contribution" to the exhibition. What remained obscured to the Sonars (and others like them) was why the goods from the almirah in the Queen's Warehouse on New Street in East London never made it back to their respective owners. Disappearance from visibility was the first step through which theft proper was put into motion. Obfuscation and loss thus became the grounds on which the Sonar's proprietary title was effaced over time, so the modality of "contribution" became key to bringing about an osmotic transfer of ownership. Contribution as a mode was imbued with voluntarism, and therefore it made any claim of reciprocity—whether of symbolic or material equivalence—redundant.

Contributions were not the only mode through which such redundancy of reciprocity claims was sought to be achieved. The other ambiguous transaction of "presentation" too raised all sorts of problems. As put by one official: "In 1851 and 1855, large contributions were obtained from private individuals, the greater portion of which was returned in the lists as 'presented' to the Exhibition, yet none of the articles were made over to the Commissioners for the Exhibition; they were considered the bona fide property of the late East India Company and disposed of accordingly."[9]

It was clear that the modality of presentation did not clinch the proprietary status unambiguously in favor of the recipient, which was further complicated by the fact that the recipient was deemed to be the exhibition itself. What was the exhibition? A legal person vested with the capacity to "receive" presentations and participate in the cycle of exchange? Or was it an event merely marked by exchange relations occurring during its limited duration rather than having the capacity to participate itself? It was not exactly clear who "owned" the exhibition or whose exhibition it was—the Crown's or the East India Company's?[10] In any case, those making the presentations were in fact quite clear to whom they were making those presentations and under what conditions: "I deemed it right to ascertain the sentiments of the several gentlemen at the Presidency who have presented a variety of articles to the 'Exhibition', and each and all state that their contributions are presented to Her Majesty's Indian Government, and *not* to the 'Exhibition.'"[11]

It was important for the government to assert its status as the one to whom these contributions were made. As Dowleans wrote to Grey, cautioning against the misuse of ambiguity over the exact recipient, and citing examples from the 1851 collection drives:

> A variety of specimens of local manufactures and natural products, which in the lists of the several local Committees are returned as *"presented* to the Exhibition." The aggregate value of these contributions is but small, still the majority of the specimens is such as will form a valuable addition to the India Museum in London; but if forwarded as *"presentations"* to the Exhibition it might happen that they may be claimed by Her Majesty's Commissioners for the Exhibition as their property.

---

9. A. M. Dowleans, Secretary to the Central Committee for the Collection of Works of Arts and Industry, Government of Bengal, to William Grey, Secretary to the Government of India, Whitehall, No. 178, dated November 4, 1861; NAI/Home/Public/A Proceedings/ November 15, 1861/ No. 18–19.

10. India was under the East India Company's rule until the revolt of 1857, after which paramountcy passed on to the Crown. The 1851 exhibition therefore was organized by the Company and not the Crown, thus leading to the ambiguity of post-hoc responsibility.

11. Dowleans to Grey, November 4, 1861.

In 1851 and 1855, large contributions were obtained from private individuals the greater portion of which was returned in the lists as "presented" to the Exhibition, yet none of the articles were made over to the Commissioners for the Exhibition but were considered the bona fide property of the late East India Company and disposed of accordingly.[12]

While the East India Company had deemed itself, and not the Crown, to be the recipient, the presenters were in fact making a prestation to the Crown in order to initiate a different kind of cycle of exchange and reciprocity. To seal off such competing claims for these prestations and the status accruing from them, Grey suggested that the category of "contribution" be given primacy: "I think that to prevent any misunderstanding as to the real meaning of the term 'presented' it would be better to substitute the word 'contributed,' leaving it to Her Majesty's Secretary of State for India to decide that question, should His Excellency the Governor General in Council not feel disposed to pass any definite orders on the subject."[13]

Hence, senior colonial officials in Whitehall and in India repeatedly instructed their district commissioners to enlist private contributions. These contributions towards the Exhibition took the form of a variety of goods, including raw materials, textiles, manufactured and industrial goods, as well as "philosophical instruments," such as survey tools. In doing so, they were asked to enlist them as a "contribution to Her Majesty's Indian Government," not as a "contribution to the Exhibition." They reasoned that since "the whole of the expense of the transmission of such contributions is defrayed out of the public revenue, the articles themselves must fairly be considered as the property of the government."[14]

This was the first maneuver to secure state ownership of these goods in transit. The second was the emphasis on "private contribution," which ensured that, although the budget outlay was half of what is had been for 1851, the "contributions" collected were nearly three times the amount of goods collected for the previous exhibition.

Thus, in two swift moves, ownership shifted from the original, rightful owner to the imperial state. In bearing the cost of the freight, the British government inserted itself in the value chain and thereby, in its

---

12. Ibid.
13. Dowleans to Grey, November 4, 1861.
14. Ibid.

own reasoning, acquired a claim to the good itself. Converting the nature of transaction to the more ambiguous category of contribution imbued the presentation with volition rather than forcible acquisition and thereby divested it of any claim to reciprocity, propitiation, compensation, or return—whether for a gift, sale, or loan. Thus, by the time these goods reached the almirah of surplus goods in the warehouse in New Street, there remained no other rightful owner on the horizon other than the Crown itself. This then was *res nullius*, the "thing" version of *terra nullius*: both classes of objects were treated as if there were no prior relations of title that needed to be attended to or, indeed, to be recognized and respected. It was in these moves of misrecognition and nonrecognition that sovereignty was exercised and produced, where the real terms of exchange were never revealed to the presenter, contributor, or trader. The senders of these presentations, prestations, gifts, and trade samples were repeatedly frustrated by the recipient (the colonial state) failing to meet its obligation to return, protect, reciprocate, or pay back these items. Nowhere in this extensive correspondence—replete with instructions— were these obligations of the recipient ever clarified, while, all along, the emphasis remained singularly on acquisition.

The Properties of Things

While the Great Exhibition of 1851 showcased objects from different parts of the world that had been selected for display due to their aesthetic difference (Mathur 2007), objects for the 1862 exhibition were chosen not for their aesthetic qualities alone, but also for their industrial potential. As many as 7,358 specimens of indigenous manufacture were dispatched from India, as can be seen in the Borgesian catalogue below:

No. of specimens	Specimens Type
345	Ores and non-metallic substances
42	Mineral products
46	Alkalies, earths and their compounds
68	Oilseeds
70	Oils
19	Essential oils
25	Starches

No. of specimens	Specimens Type
35	Resins and gum resins
29	Gums
21	Intoxicating drugs
549	Medicinal substances
297	Cereals
84	Pulses
8	Dried fruits and seeds
71	Spices and condiments
30	Sugars
18	Distilled spirits
146	Substances used in preparation of drinks
25	Substances used in the preparation of food
36	Raw wool
48	Raw silk
23	Downs and Feathers
4	Furs, skins and hides
18	Ivory, horns and shells
85	Pigments and dyes
13	Tanning substances
220	Fibrous substances
657	Tines, reeds and grasses
67	Cordage materials
5	Railway plant
25	Manufacturing machines and tools (models)
67	Armour and accoutrements
1	Philosophical instruments
11	Photography
1	Horological instruments
251	Manufactures in cotton
22	Manufactures in flax and hemp
193	Manufactures in silk
29	Manufactures in Woollen and Worsted

No. of specimens	Specimens Type
35	Carpets
1062	Tapestry, Lace and Embroideries
37	Skins, furs, feathers and hair
10	Leather, including saddlery and harness

Specimens dispatched from India. Source: Extracted from the Final Report of the Central Committee for the Collection of Arts and Industry on the results of the arrangements made in furtherance of the objects of the Exhibition of 1862, A. M. Dowleans, Calcutta, March 15, 1862; NAI/Home/Public/A Proceedings/ April 2, 1862/No. 1–3.

The collected goods and articles were classified into raw materials, machinery, manufactures, and works of art. Protocols of description were standardized, culminating in the production of an exhaustive catalogue of the displays from India (Dowleans 1862). One of the enduring legacies of these descriptions and catalogues is the standard format we associate with museum displays today—composed of place names, craft type, and material used. Despite extensive work going into the catalogue format and protocols, many of the collected objects were neither easily works of manufacture nor works of art in the prevailing sense, thus posing a significant challenge of how to account for assessing their value, as well as their rightful place in the display.

It was decided that the classification of objects and the assessment of their value were both to be derived from the production process, which also did not get rid of the problem. For example, classifying stoles, shawls, and *doputtahs* proved to be difficult. As unstitched items, they were originally classified as "textile," but as they were handwoven products, the task of assessing their so-called "intrinsic value" was even trickier. Some stoles were displayed by their descriptive name, such as the *kinkob* (or *khimkhab*). This brocade from Benaras (Varanasi) was classified simply as a textile manufacture, even though it had been woven and embellished with "pure thread" (thread made of real silver or gold). For most other stoles and *doputtahs*, classification was decided after much debate. They were eventually entered as "items of clothing" as opposed to "textiles," emphasizing their original and intended usage. As handwoven items, most of these articles were pegged low on the scale of industrial manufacturing and, as such, were considered to be low in value. But it was argued that much of the value of these stoles and shawls lay not in the process of manufacturing of the fabric but, rather, in the secondary work done on them. Embroidery, which involved manual labor and hence was considered even more primitive than their process of manufacturing itself, led to a very low assessment of these shawls and stoles:

> Most valuable fabrics of India are of a description which would render it somewhat difficult to assign to them the proper class in which they ought to be exhibited. Thus, for instance, Class 27, "Articles of Clothing" would comprise an immense variety of fabrics, which constitute "clothing" in *India* [emphasis in original], but which in Europe come within the meaning of manufactures in "cotton," "in silk," "embroideries," etc. To overcome the difficulty, I have adopted the plan of classifying all such manufactures according to the peculiar workmanship for which they are valued. Thus, for instance, though Cashmere shawls most undoubtedly would come within Class 21, "Manufactures in Wool," their great merit consists in their embroidery and thence they have been classed among embroideries. The splendid *doputtahs* or shawls from Benaras are articles of clothing worn by wealthy natives, but their beauty consists in the fineness of the texture of the silks and the interweaving of the gold and silver threads and I have accordingly classified them among manufactures of silk.[15]

Since the exhibition of 1862 was explicitly concerned with the manufacturing potential of the colonies and with the place of Britain in the industrial world, the specimens from colonies such as India had to be adjudicated not only in terms of their intrinsic value or aesthetic qualities, but now also from the viewpoint of their industrial potential. Historians have alerted us to the self-identification of metropolitan superiority that was relied on as well as produced in the transformation of these goods into inferior products (Breckenridge 1989; Hoffenberg 2001). Specimens were noted to have had no special quality unless there was an explicit British intervention that had been inserted into the production process. Judging the collection sent to England, one official remarked: "Passing to the collection sent, I would first observe that in making it the Committee was forced to set aside the rule that 'all works of industry

---

15. Report on the Results of the Arrangements for the Forthcoming Exhibition of 1862, submitted to the Central Committee for Bengal at the meeting held on January 6, 1862. NAI/Home/Public/A Proceedings/ February 1, 1862/ No. 1–2.

intended for the Exhibition should have been produced since 1850.' Had the Committee bound themselves by this rule they would have had little to send to the Exhibition beyond raw produce."[16]

This revealed a further difficulty—that of innovation in relation to culture. According to the committee overseeing the collection of goods for shipment, there had been hardly any "improvement" in the manufacturing process or, indeed, in the quality of the manual work. They thus considered it difficult to meet the demand for an emphasis on goods with industrial potential and manufacture for display in the exhibition. The committee thought that one of the ways this difficulty could be overcome was if these goods were accompanied with illustrations of their manufacturing process. The illustrations could highlight the *potential* not in the good itself, but in the production process of so-called primitive goods, one that could yield an increase in value through European intervention, for they believed that only under European superintendence could the potential of native skill and art be fully realized: "Apart from being interesting and instructive, it would be the means of showing the crudeness and almost primitiveness of the implements and machinery by which some of the most valuable fabrics and staple articles of this country are produced and it may thus lead to considerable improvement."[17]

Moreover, India had well been established in the colonial imaginary as a place of timeless traditions; not only were these production processes "primitive" when compared to industrial mechanization, but they had also been insulated from any discernible technological improvement for centuries. Because innovation was conceptualized purely in incremental and industrial terms—that is, as an *improvement* in the production or manufacturing process—none of the articles were considered to be particularly innovative. The odd philosophical instrument (used for the trigonometric survey of India) and an assortment of medicines from the Bombay Bazaar thus comprised the handful of "scientific objects." Their potential lay in what Callon et al. call "the possibilities of qualification and requalification" of their status (2002: 200). They describe the series of transformations of things as they change their status from goods to

---

16. From *Publication of the Catalogue of Exhibits Collected for the London Exhibition of 1862: Report of the Central Committee Bengal.* NAI/Home/Public/A Proceedings/ February 1, 1862/No. 1–2.

17. From A. M. Dowleans to E. H. Lushington, Secretary to the Government of Bengal, No 44, dated July 20, 1861; NAI/ Home/A Proceedings/ August 15, 1861/ No. 73–75.

products (ibid.). This process of singularization is achieved through a sequence of negotiations in which the qualities and their intrinsic value or status becomes temporarily stabilized until the next moment of transformation (Callon 2002: 199). While this insight finds resonance with the material on the exhibitions, the domain of these negotiations, as well as action, are radically different in the two contexts. Callon et al. are interested in the production of consumer goods or products, and how qualities and characteristics become attached to them as they are presented in the market. In the context of the exhibitions, objects underwent qualification and requalification not in the process of production, but in and through exchange and adjudication involving a colonial state. Here, the critical actant that defined the career of these objects was sovereign power and not market forces. The adjudication of their qualities and characteristics was nevertheless intended to ascertain their potential in the world of market goods and trade. The colonial conceptualization of potential was as a form of incremental improvements aimed at ultimately achieving an industrial status. Whatever these Indian goods appeared to lack in intrinsic value they more than made up for in their *potential for intervention*, their capacity for improvement as raw materials that could be transformed and service the processes of industrial innovation afoot in Europe.

The potential lay in not just the improvement that processes of manufacture could be subject to, but also in the kind of exchange relations these objects could precipitate and participate in. Their capacity for participation and precipitation of exchange in part depended on the status of their owners and their potential for participating or precipitating certain kinds of exchange relations. Utilitarian objects, such as wooden chests and caskets— sometimes inlaid with expensive ivory and therefore arguably of a level of fine craftsmanship comparable to a *kinkob* or Benaras brocade—were considered of too little value to justify the cost of their freight. The procurement committee asked the manufacturers of such caskets and chests to supply these in greater numbers than the one-off piece, so that the volume of sales could generate adequate surplus value. Such assessments of qualities and characteristics produced an enduring legacy, since it was in these differentially attributed values that early distinctions between tradeable (artisanal or handicraft) and collectible objects emerged, each governed by a different mode of exchange and circulation. Artisanal goods or "handicrafts" such as caskets and similar goods were supplied directly by the manufacturers themselves, with the explicit aim of generating interest from potential buyers in the future. At the time, they were summarily decried for their low value, and manufacturers were asked to send these in bulk in order to recover costs:

> The blackwood furniture and inlaid work of Bombay and the agate of Cambay however leave nothing to be desired. The quantity of inlaid work would indeed be excessive were it intended for Exhibition simply. But the Committee has had another object in view in purchasing articles that were likely to sell well at the close of the Exhibition, viz. to reimburse Government so far as possible the expenses incurred by them on the Indian contributions and as the expenditure on the bulk of these would be a dead loss, it was considered desirable to multiply so far as was not inconvenient such as were likely to realise a profit.[18]

In due course, these handicrafts were "requalified," in the sense used by Callon et al. (2002), and became desirable consumption articles in their own right, available to be bought in departmental stores such as Liberty in London (Mathur 2007: 27–42), or viewed on display as a stable category at future industrial and art fairs (Mathur 2007: 52–79; Stuart 1911).

The contributors of the so-called collectibles tended to be members of the landed aristocracy and wealthy Indian merchants, some of whom may well have pawned these articles in lieu of patronage in the wake of the Mutiny of 1857:

> Among the collection of works in silver, I would draw attention to a fountain of solid silver, presented by Rajah Deonarain Sing [sic] of Benaras. Though the workmanship is extremely rough, and indeed much below the average of what native silversmiths produce, it is distinguished by novelty of design, which is entirely oriental. The same Rajah has contributed to the Exhibition, a splendid silver vase, manufactured by native artisans under the superintendence of Messrs Allan and Hayes, the Government Jewellers of Calcutta, and presented to him by His Excellency the Governor General and Viceroy

---

18. From George Birdwood, Secretary to the Bombay Central Committee, to the Secretary to the Government, General Department, Bombay Town Hall, No. 26 of 1862, Dated April 11, 1862. NAI/Home/Public/B Proceedings/ May 9, 1862/ No. 55–56. George Birdwood went on to become a renowned authority on Indian crafts and the author of *The Industrial Arts of India* (1880). On his career and contribution to this landscape, see Mathur (2007: 30–33).

of India in acknowledgement of his faithful attachment to the British Government during the rebellion of 1857.[19]

As the date for the 1862 exhibition drew closer, more and more private individuals refused to make contributions, insisting that their goods be purchased. The subsequent usurpation of many of these articles—whether tradable or collectible—was contested, even if for differing reasons. But only in a handful of cases was the usurpation as easy as that of Bhyrooprasad of Calcutta, who was charged with treason in January 1861. His *kinkob* and Benaras brocade *doshalas* were declared to be confiscated for the exhibition by the state. Many petitions and letters asked the government to send back these unsold goods or to have the sale money reimbursed to the original owners. That, of course, never happened. In the almirah of surplus goods—now deemed to be gifts to the Crown or simply its property—they came to form, among other things, the resources from which the India collection of the Victoria and Albert Museum was built.

Sovereignty in the Almirah of Surplus Goods

The ability to annex, capture, or deny property to another has been one of the common and most legible marks of sovereignty (Benton and Straumann 2010). At the same time, the ability to possess private property was held to be a basic individual right and a building block of legal personhood under liberal law. For India, the centrality of property in configurations of sovereignty or its lack was most famously elaborated by Ranajit Guha in *A rule of property for Bengal* (1996). Guha argues that colonial rule was inaugurated in the reconfiguration of property relations with a view toward introducing a new revenue regime, but one that had deep social and political effects well beyond the agricultural and land-owning classes. Guha's work brings to center stage the foundational work of the land, ownership, and revenue regimes, and its restructuring in providing solidity to colonial sovereignty. Scholarship on property and property relations in India has since been dominated by the centrality of land and land reform, and the role of the state in influencing patterns of private property holding (see, for example, Agarwal 1994; Wahi 2014). Recent

---

19. A. M. Dowleans, Calcutta, March 15, 1862. NAI/Home/Public/B Proceedings/ May 9, 1862/ No. 55–56.

work on intellectual property, especially on the politics of pharmaceutical patents (Chandra 2010), shareware and copy-left activism (Liang 2005; Sundaram 2011), and geographical indicators (Rangnekar 2010) has undoubtedly begun to broach those property forms that are assisted by technological advances, where state sovereignty itself may be undermined. In this chapter, it has become clear that the property question needs to be addressed afresh for colonial and postcolonial India, and, also, that there is a need to examine a diversity of property relations in landed, as well as non-landed, forms of property, in and through which sovereignty came to be constituted.

As the previous chapter showed, the imaginary of *terra nullius* that pervaded the settlement of titular claims of indigenous communities and the underdevelopment of the question of indigenous title in the Constituent Assembly Debates at the cusp of Independence was crucial to the configuration of postcolonial sovereignty. Although in non-settler colonies like India, a fundamental reconfiguration of property relations may not have come about explicitly through the doctrine of *terra nullius*, reconfiguration wrought by *res nullius* was a much more pervasive experience (Benton and Straumann, 2010). Nevertheless, the state as a proprietor or an omnipresent potential proprietor was a key constituent of its sovereign power. Unlike *terra nullius*, where the lack of recognition of any prior title was achieved in one swift movement through the promulgation of the doctrine, *res nullius* was achieved through a progressive leeching away of proprietary title. Moreover, in contrast to the commonly held view in legal scholarship that *res nullius* was mostly invoked positively to defend native ownership in things and resources (Fitzmaurice 2007: 8–9), I show that for objects that were acquired, contributed, or presented for the exhibitions, this was simply not true. These objects were detached from their original owners and locations as they moved from households to museum display cabinets, acquiring along the way qualities of collectability, heritage, craft, and artistic or industrial potential while simultaneously becoming stripped of other prior qualities. Their requalification was not achieved in one single move of forcible possession or straightforward theft; instead, it required a series of acts of misrecognition—of title, or the terms of exchange itself, which endowed these objects with new qualities. It was in this capacity to misrecognize or deem that an article was actually sent as a trade sample or loaned for limited period of time—that is, as an intentional or voluntary "contribution"—that the violence of the (colonial) state in the making of public and cultural property was located.

These disputed journeys also provide a window into the emergence of cultural property and its distinctiveness from other property forms prevalent in India at the time. It was precisely in the disputed claims to ownership that things came to be recognized as cultural property, differentiated from other objects of similar age, function, or source (Flessas 2003: 1094) in terms of ownership and circulatory regimes. Scholarship has tended to focus on the reverse journey of many such objects from appropriation, museumization, and cultural commodification (Brown 2003; Flessas 2003; Mathur 2007; Mezey 2007). In attending to their onward journeys instead, this chapter has shown that some of the journeys were more legible and stable than others (for example, those that ended in the Victoria and Albert Museum). Even though the journeys of a vast number of objects remain opaque, what is clear is their connection with the birth of heritage as the prime property of Indian culture, and the importance of this notion to the ideals and ideas of national and cultural history, and, not least of all, to sovereignty itself.

CHAPTER 6

Corpus Nullius: The Labor of Sovereignty

The Indian citizen does not have absolute rights in his body.

– Mukul Rohatgi, Attorney General of India, July 2015

The veiled slavery of waged labour . . . needed for its pedestal, slavery pure and simple in the new world.

– Karl Marx, *Capital*

In 1944, Suresh Vaidya, an Indian journalist working in London, was sentenced to prison for refusing compulsory military service in the British forces fighting in the Second World War. At the time, Vaidya was on the staff of *Time* magazine and also part of the editorial team of *Indian Writing*, a periodical brought out by the Indian Progressive Writers Association based in the UK.[1] Vaidya was not the first to refuse conscription

---

1. The Indian Progressive Writers Association was formed in London in 1935 by Indian students studying at Oxford, Cambridge, and London universities. *Indian Writing* gave way to *Marg* when the association moved its base to India after Independence, with Mulk Raj Anand as editor. On the progressive writers' literary movement, see Ranasinha (2020). See also Open University's research project "Making Britain: How South Asia

or be arrested for it. But unlike a number of those who had been similarly sentenced, he had not refused military service on anti-war or pacifist grounds. Rather, Vaidya declared that he did not wish to fight a war that was not his, and nor did he want to fight on behalf of the colonial state. These contrarian views and his subsequent arrest generated a fair deal of interest at the time, prompting support from many quarters, including from George Orwell. Warning that the colonial power had more to lose than to gain from commandeering Indians to die on the battlefields, Orwell wrote: "No Indian, whatever his views, admits that Britain had the right to declare war on India's behalf or has the right to impose compulsory services on Indians" (1944). Vaidya contested his arrest in court, and won his case after a closely watched and much talked about trial. The case went on to became legal precedent and helped secure the release of scores of colonized subjects similarly imprisoned in British jails for having refused to fight a war that was not theirs.[2]

Vaidya's refusal was grounded in the relationship between a colonial state and its subjects, and the place of labor within that relationship. At the heart of Vaidya's arrest and trial was the question of the capacity of the state to command the labor of its people against their will. Colonial sovereignty is premised on exaction. Commandeered labor brings into view underlying assumptions of freedom and liberty, and when this labor is commandeered by the state, it gains a particular force, one that was foundational to colonial sovereignty. But as others have pointed out, the nexus between unfreedom, labor, and sovereignty has continued to persist (Brace and Davidson 2018; Federici 2004), and the plantation imaginary continues to find new economic forms (Besky and Blanchette 2019). In the final part of the triptych, I explore how the relationship between the laboring body and the state is being reconfigured under the sign of erasure in contemporary India. Having examined sovereignty through dispossession of land and things, I turn to the dispossession of personhood as sovereignty-making. In this chapter, I explore the making of *corpus nullius*, as constituted in the breach of the final frontier of

---

Shaped the Nation 1870–1950," http://www.open.ac.uk/researchprojects/makingbritain/.

2. Vaidya's case was fought by two leading members of the Independent Labour Party of the UK, Fenner Brockway and Reginald Sorenson. The trial took place in Kent County Court and formed the subject matter for Vaidya's novel, *An English Prison* (1953). Sorenson subsequently became a champion of prison reform in post-war Britain.

appropriation, the human body. Appropriation of the body or any of its aspects renders persons into things. This category switch, despite prevailing legal, political, and moral injunctions, has taken place time and again in history and in various contexts. However, since Abolition, any attempt at collective or categorical enslavement has had to be made either surreptitiously, or in a disguised form and analogically, such as in trafficking or sweat-shop work.[3] The abolition of slavery was underpinned by the universalization of the liberal legal universal of the free, rights-bearing, possessive individual as the subject of natural justice. In this universal, the principle of self-ownership has included all aspects of the self, including labor. Under this ideal of the free (wo)man, human labor therefore can only be offered voluntarily, and its appropriation must be duly compensated on mutually agreed terms. This condition of voluntarism extends to the state. However, in some contexts other intervening or qualifying arrangements or social contracts may precede or supersede many freedoms, for example conscription, or other forms of compulsory service for the state. Given that the state is itself the guarantor of those freedoms, such relationships of enforced labor are limited and often part of the repertoire of techniques aimed at fostering "full attachment" (Appadurai 1998).

Enforced or involuntary misappropriation of labor continues and has thrived in leading many into modern-day slavery and precarity (Calvao 2016: 452; Precarity Lab 2020), as these relations are integral to contemporary capitalism and its entailed value-chains. Most of the recent literature on newer forms of misappropriated or uncompensated labor, therefore, tends to focus on capital-labor relations, whereas scholarship on the enforced labor of citizens by the state has mostly dwelled on the extraction of forced labor under confinement, for example in prisons or detention centers. I stay with the question of the rights of the state over a citizen's labor, and I discuss it in the relation to the emergence of a new property form: data. I argue that in the new and fast-growing data economy, not only are Indian citizens being conscripted into a regime of uncompensated labor, but, more specifically, the laboring body of the citizen is being constituted as the newest realm of appropriation as a sovereignty-making practice of the Indian state. Ironically, the making of data into property is itself predicated on the erasure of title in one's body and its labor, where labor is not just misappropriated by private

---

3. Human trafficking and individual cases of enslavement fall beyond the scope of this discussion.

capital, but such misappropriation is fundamentally enabled by the state. In its becoming, data-as-property reveals in fullness the hollow center at the heart of the possessive, rights-bearing citizen in India.

The rise of data as a major source of economic and political value in India was significantly boosted by the adoption of an ambitious biometric identification infrastructure, Aadhaar. It was first launched in 2007 and has increasingly become mandatory and the sole mode of verification in a range of state and non-state transactions. Elsewhere in the world, the challenge of data ownership involves a contest between the state and private capital or giant tech corporations, such as Google and Facebook, that have acquired monopolistic status in this new economy (Fourcade and Kluttz 2020). In India, however, the most data-fecund technology platform, Aadhaar, is owned by the state. This makes propriety and regulatory questions for this emergent zone of economic activity radically different than in other jurisdictions. How does the sovereign rein itself in?

Aadhaar has rightly attracted a fair amount of scholarly attention to date. But academic and popular discussions of Aadhaar, especially on the relationship between the state and data, have been captivated by privacy and surveillance concerns (See Cohen 2019; Khera 2019; Nair 2018; Rao and Nair 2019; R. Singh 2020). While privacy and surveillance concerns are obviously major fall-outs of digital identification, these are ultimately instrumentarian questions that concern the *uses* of data, which as such can provide only a utilitarian explanation for the state-data relationship. I diverge from this approach in order to deepen its critique by opening up a new aspect for inquiry, and consider the role of Aadhaar as a technology not in what it enables (surveillance), but how it enables this. I place the citizen's body right in the middle of the technological apparatus of Ranjit Singh's (2020) ground-breaking study and argue that the citizen's body is a critical part of Aadhaar's infrastructure, and not just its object of control. Such an approach allows us to approach data not simply as something "always-already formed." Rather, in the specific context of Aadhaar, I investigate here what data is, how it is created and how it is subsequently transformed into a thing, a property form. It further allows us to investigate what kind of value is contained in this emergent property form and how, or rather *where*, that value is produced. Strathern (1988a; 1992b) argues that the value of something lies not only in ratios and equivalences but, crucially, also in its *origins*. Value cannot be understood apart from the web of relations within which it is embedded and its simultaneous ability to be detached from those relations (Strathern 1988a; also Graeber 2001: 42). I take this insight as my starting point to attend equally to the origins of value production in data and the process of detachment or alienation of that value, for it is in the latter that we can find clues for the transformation of data into a property form. In doing so, we discover that at the heart of data-*making* lies the question of labor. Given that in India Aadhaar underpins the emerging state-data relationship, to understand the state-data relationship, we therefore cannot ignore the state-labor question. It is the mode of detachment or alienation of one's labor by the state in and as biometrics that throws light on this newest sovereignty-making technique. As the rest of the chapter describes, the working of Aadhaar and its architecture of ownership rely on citizens to perform a particular type of labor for the state, a type for which they cannot be compensated. But *contra* Fourcade and Kluttz (2020), this is not "gifted" labor, or even tributary labor, such as the voluntary contributions of wealth objects to the sovereign as discussed in the previous chapter. The labor of Aadhaar is a labor embedded in a particular form of servitude that has echoes in prior forms of labor relations. Drawing on Gaddi understandings of the transformative potential of the different forms of servitude, I show that the questions posed by Aadhaar exceed its surveillance capacities and I examine it here as a fundamental question of labor and in its becoming a property form. Although a relatively new property form, and even a novel "thing" in the world, in its relationship to the state in India, data summons echoes of, if not continuities with, the older relationship of the sovereign with labor.

The Biometric Citizen

In 2012, a retired High Court judge, Justice K. S. Puttuswamy, filed a public interest litigation (PIL) in the Supreme Court of India challenging the mandatory status of Aadhaar.[4] As a biometric identification

---

4. A Public Interest Litigation is the provision in the Indian constitution for any citizen to file a writ in either a High Court or the Supreme Court on matters of public interest, where a simple letter, if it meets the criteria of justiciability, can be considered as a legal petition by the court. This provision has been considered essential in the making of judicial activism in India. On the history of the provision and its recent uses as an audit tool in local governance, see Bhuwania (2017).

program of the Indian government, Aadhaar allocates a unique, randomly generated twelve-digit number based on demographics (name, age, gender, address, etc.) and biometric data points (ten fingerprints, two iris scans, and one facial photograph). This program was first mooted in 2007 as a voluntary form of digital identification available to all Indian citizens and residents, which emerged from the particular brand of technoscientific economic thinking of the late 1980s. In his PIL of 2012, Puttuswamy questioned the constitutionality of the rapid adoption of Aadhaar as mandatory for identification in order to access key state services and subsidies, a requirement that he asserted had no backing in legislation. In the long-running case that followed, the main argument of the government in its defense was that Aadhaar is aimed primarily to gain administrative efficiencies and improve the governance of state-run welfare programs, chiefly through its capacity for de-duplication. It stressed that Aadhaar enabled the state to efficiently prevent the duplication of recipient lists for various centralized and state programs, and thus prevent leakages of welfare funds and target delivery of welfare benefits to deserving recipients more accurately. Making biometric identification mandatory for citizens to access such services could therefore not be interpreted as any breach of the constitution.[5]

As the case progressed through various levels of judicature, the right to privacy came to be its linchpin. The petition claimed that the enhanced surveillance capacities of the state enabled by making Aadhaar mandatory fundamentally compromised the right to privacy of India's citizenry. The government argued that the petitioners had misunderstood the constitution: privacy was not an absolute or even a fundamental right under the Indian constitution and therefore was not justiciable.[6] Privacy is not a separate or a discrete right under the constitution; instead, it is derived from the encompassing fundamental right to freedom (Articles 18–21), especially the right to life (Article 19). It was in the hearing on whether or not there existed a fundamental right to privacy in the "spirit" of the constitution that the Attorney General, acting as government's counsel, declared that a fundamental right to privacy entailing a freedom from surveillance would rest on having absolute rights in oneself. This, he said, was not a sustainable claim because, under the constitution, "Indian citizens do not have absolute ownership of their body."

---

5. *Indian Express*, July 23, 2015.
6. For an excellent analysis of the case, see Gautam Bhatia (2018).

Janet Dolgin (2020) has recently pointed out the slippage between status and contract in litigation. Discussing this in the case of reproductive technologies, she says that these technologies have dismantled the presumed difference between home and work (metonymically rendered through the difference between love and money) and forced the erstwhile separate domains of family and marketplace to inform each other (2020: 140). In litigation, this domain-crossing finds a parallel proliferation in a number of cases making demands of status from a domain of contract, and vice versa, for example, as in "libel" and "privacy" related litigation. Dolgin maps this shift on to the separation of tort law from contract law that predates these new technologies. In jurisdictions where it is already a well-established and well-developed branch of the law, such as the US, tort becomes the natural home for such cross-domain lawsuits (Dolgin 2020: 140). Drawing on Henry Maine's *Ancient Law*, by contract, Dolgin means "negotiated relationships that endure only as long as those involved choose for them to endure" (ibid.: 139–140). Status-based relationships, on the other hand, "[support] fixed roles and [hierarchies] that once formed are expected to endure" (140). This slippage between status and contract, or between fixed and negotiated relationships and hierarchies, has had a particular bearing on the debate surrounding the very nature of the state-citizen relationship as reconfigured by Aadhaar.

Aadhaar is seen by many as only the latest example of the ever-expanding security state in India and its ever-enhancing capacities to track the life of its citizens (Ramanathan 2010; Ramanathan, personal communication).[7] Some have wondered whether there exist "Indic" notions of privacy that exist outside the realm of law, which could potentially become aligned with or mobilized for understanding biometric identification under Aadhaar (e.g., Manzar 2017. Also Bhatia 2014). For the most part, arguments made by both sides in the Puttuswamy case, and the judgment itself centered on the constitutional basis of privacy and its relationship to sovereignty and liberty. Critics claimed that even though the amassing of identificatory information by the state may have originally been intended to gain administrative efficiencies, Aadhaar had given the state access into citizens' lives at an unprecedented scale and scope, with not enough regulatory checks in place. As a member of Puttuswamy's wider legal team remarked to me, "How else to read this other than as an assault on privacy?! . . . The government's argument of lack

---

7. Research conversation (via Zoom) with Ramanathan, April 2020.

of any constitutional basis for privacy is legal sophistry."[8] Underlying these critiques of biometrics is an assumption—not unlike the argument made for the anti-colonial struggle—that certain aspects of people's lives are "sovereign" and must remain out of bounds for the state (Chatterjee 1994). Whereas anticolonial nationalists were clear that the state had no right to interfere in the interior worlds of religion and family, the contours of the sovereign realm of privacy which must remain beyond the purview of the "biometric state," *pace* Breckenridge (2014), are nebulous in these arguments.

The question of consent—or rather the lack of it—by which biometrics are collected emerges as one clear watermark for privacy violation. The Attorney General spoke directly to this concern in his arguments. A right also paid significantly high attention to the question of consent—or rather the lack of it—by which the biometric data was taken from the people.

The Attorney General spoke directly to an assumption of sovereignty of the citizen's body in the claims of the petitioners. A right to privacy, he said, could not be derived from the existing right to life under Article 19, since Indian citizens did not have absolute rights in their body. Refuting the argument of any a priori notion of liberty, he claimed that there have always existed constitutional limits on the extent to which a citizen's body could be deemed sovereign. The Attorney General stated that accessing the citizen's body by the state was not in and of itself a breach of the constitution, since citizens did not have absolute ownership of their bodies, and that the state always retained rights of access to the citizens' body, with or without consent (Livelaw Research Team 2017). Giving examples of the regulation of organ donation and the legal restrictions on abortion after twenty weeks, he argued that there was also no presumed entitlement to bodily integrity under the constitution. In his opinion, Aadhaar was analogical to the elicitory technology of fingerprinting. Consent may sometimes be required in blood-based identification techniques because they require the extraction of bodily substance, but no consent was needed to take anyone's fingerprints because of the non-invasive nature of that technology. According to him, Aadhaar too elicited information by taking impressions or images rather than extracting substance from the body. Therefore, the question of consent did not arise for taking biometrics. Even in the case of technologies of identification that were invasive, such as those based in

---

8. Research interview with Apar Gupta, New Delhi, October 2017.

blood, an absolute right to bodily integrity on the part of the citizen could not be assumed. The right analogy to understand the limitations on liberty, he argued, was to think of the revocation of the right to freedom and other constitutional protections of those serving sentences for committing crime. In concluding this set of arguments, he made the infamous submission that Indian citizens do not have absolute ownership of their body.[9]

This was the first time such an argument had been proffered in the highest court of the land, and that too by the state's counsel in defence. Yet, even though Aadhaar's footprint has become larger in the everyday life of Indian citizens, and though the strengths of biometrics-based identification become more widely debated, the Attorney General's statement on bodily ownership has remained a minor controversy. It has drawn little to no commentary, whether now, or at the time. The outrage that followed was relatively short-lived, and certainly no one followed up on the legal underpinnings of the Attorney General's position on bodily ownership. Secondly, insofar as one can tell, no objections were made to the Attorney General's distinction between impressionistic and invasive technologies to determine consent.[10] In my reading, both points made by the Attorney General—of the limited or qualified ownership of one's body and the linked characterization of the nature of the technology for recording biometrics as impressionistic—have been missed opportunities, in court and in scholarship. Paying attention to them, and not dismissing them in outrage has allowed me to move the discussion on Aadhaar in new directions. Discussions and debates around biometrics are dominated by the attention to the "metrics" in biometrics—of data and the datafication of persons. What has received relatively less attention is the "bio" in biometrics, the corporeal, and the vital. What indeed is the relationship between the body and its digital or informational impression, such as the fingerprint, the image of the iris, and the facial scan? To what extent are one's iris, fingerprint, and facial scan merely indexical of the body? Taking seriously the Attorney General's provocation, I attend to Aadhaar as a corporeal technology—a technology that is fundamentally based in or emanating from the body. Seizing the opening provided

---

9. The preceding discussion of the Attorney General's views relies on Livelaw Research Team (2017).

10. Supreme Court proceedings are not recorded or, at least, available for public access. The only publicly available documentation from the Supreme Court cases are judgments and depositions.

by the Attorney General's reading of corporeal ownership in Indian law allows us to refute his claim that biometrics is not *extractive* and therefore does not require consent. The questions before us are thus: What is the relationship between the corporeal and the digital? If the citizen does not indeed own her own body, who does? What are the ownership regimes that underpin the relationship between the corporeal and the digital in Aadhaar, and what relationalities do they engender? Parsing the elision between the informational and the corporeal is not only vital for understanding how and why the elision is made in the first place, but it also helps us to situate Aadhaar in new and necessary terms that surpass issues of surveillance and its corollary, consent.

An Anthropology of Biometrics

Like most states, the Indian state too considers enumerating and collecting statistical information about its citizens and their activities as integral to government, and indispensable for achieving its developmental mission (Ghosh 2016). The original purpose behind setting up the Unique Identification technology platform was both enumerative and auditory, and partly aimed at the rationalization of the developmental state. Aadhaar was primarily proposed as a solution for a de-duplicated and leakage-free distribution of welfare claims (Cohen 2019; Ramnath and Assisi 2018; R. Singh 2020). As such, Aadhaar is neither unique as a technocratic solution to the problem of systemic leakages nor for its enumerative logic. Aadhaar is in fact a summation of several existing initiatives, and yet a radical shift in gear. Its aggregative form was integral to its design and purpose, but what its design architects had not been fully understood or even anticipated when it was first mooted was the platform's potential for a 360-degree encompassment.[11] This lapse in foresight was perhaps a logical outcome of the times. In the mid-1980s, when the Indian state, in collaboration with national and multinational

---

11. Research interview with Sam Pitroda, May 2020. Pitroda was the prime architect of India's IT revolution. He was Chief Technology Advisor to the the Government of India, which gave the green light to Aadhaar in 2007. Pitroda was also the architect of the Indian government's Telecom Mission from 1984–1990, the flagship programme that is indirectly responsible for India's technology boom in the decades that followed. For more on Pitroda, see his autobiography, *Dreaming big: My journey to connect India* (2015).

corporations, took its first steps towards the IT revolution that later enabled Aadhaar, the world was still analog and state enumerative efforts
were directed at gathering statistics rather than collating "big data."

A biometrics-based identification system, however, is not simply the
metrics it collects and the indices it collates. Although states have been
collecting information about their subjects and citizens in some form
or the other for centuries, a quasi-mandatory, universal coverage-based
biometrics identification system is a radical departure from any prior
or similar enumerative exercise. The most easily comparable of these
is the decennial census on the one hand, and more descriptive forms
such as gazetteers and colonial ethnologies, on the other (Appadurai
1993; Cohn 1987; Dirks 2001). An exercise like the decennial census
is primarily summative and its operative unit is a population. In contrast, a biometrics-based identification system is simultaneously aggre-
gating, but necessarily individuating. A census enumerates and sum-
mates, thereby producing a population within a given territory, while a
biometrics system creates a permanently identifiable individual, and a
precisely retrievable link between an individual body and its indexical
records, such as facial scans or fingerprints (Cole 2001: 4). Even though
population-level indexical records have sometimes been collated for the
explicit purpose of identification of suspected individuals (for example,
fingerprint registries), these records are usually mono-indexical (nasal,
cephalic, fingerprint) and seldom collected for entire populations. A
rare hybrid, particularly salient for India, is the decennial anthropometric survey, first introduced in India the late nineteenth century by the
colonial state (Bates 1995; Nair 2018) and conducted almost uninter-
rupted to date (Kapila n.d.). Though based in multiple bodily indices,
an anthropometric survey is only and precisely just that—a *survey* of
characteristics (albeit physiological) that are statistically correlated with
each other or compiled for deriving generalizations about the particular
population under consideration, rather than a searchable database that
may be used for identification of individuals.

Aadhaar at once combines the enumerative logic of the census and
the identificatory rationale of the fingerprint. While its enumerative logic is based in its population-wide remit, its identificatory brief is enabled
by a unique and altogether new composite metric that combines the
biological and the sociological. It includes three corporeal indices and
attributes, such as age, sex, address, etc. This composite data set, or "digital dossier" as Orlove (2004) calls it, that is collected at the level of the
individual is designed to ensure a greater precision and faster retrieval

(Sengoopta 2003:18). The ability to infinitely add new indices is a critical part of its architecture, and the nub of its value. The immutability or fixity of biological indices ensures accuracy of retrieval, while the more dynamic attributes make the dossier infinitely capacious as well as malleable. Changes to any given dossier may occur circumstantially through movement (e.g., change of address, or travel), accretion (such as acquiring a new mobile telephone or bank account), or individual actions—understood in the data universe as "micro-behavior" (e.g., individual financial transactions, telephone usage, etc.). Each of these variations can be tracked and logged, changing the individual dossier, as well as the composite data set. This infinitely recombinant and generative potential is the linchpin of its value and that which fundamentally separates biometric identification systems from other types of informational repositories and statistical data sets.

As an identification infrastructure that has recombinance built into its architecture, individual attributes may be combined to understand not only their interrelations (such as to compute a statistical correlation), but potentially also to predict future attributes of the digital dossier. Take the repercussions of the now-mandatory linking of one's Aadhaar with one's bank account. A log of an Aadhaar number with a store of financial information (e.g., a bank card) can both *individuate* data (e.g., summate all financial transactions of an individual related to a particular good or service in a given period of time, which can potentially be used algorithmically to predict their future financial transactions) and *aggregate* data (e.g., all transactions from one locality, or by one gender, or caste, etc.). Moreover, multiple operations of data individuation and aggregation can be carried out in real time, thereby making live and growing (big) data sets. The ability to link up Aadhaar as a universal verification device has been called its "hourglass design," where other technologies can be funneled through the Aadhaar platform, creating a generative and proliferating infrastructure based in biometrics (R. Singh 2020). One of the members of the original team that designed the architecture of Aadhaar, clarified that in any such instance of combining, the data is anonymized because, in and of itself, Aadhaar does not store any information other than the collected biometrics. Even the record of where this data was collected, with which machine, by whom, is automatically destroyed after a period of time.[12] Aadhaar-based verification is today mandatory not just for accessing state services, such as welfare programs and subsidies,

---

12. Sanjay Jain, research interview, September 2019; Bangalore.

but also to conduct commercial transactions, such as buying a mobile phone or opening a bank account, which in turn can and are aggregated and recombined for information and insights. Thus, Aadhaar may have provided the state the ability to track its citizens *qua* citizens, but its real and potential value today lies in its malleability to recombine transactions across realms into an infinite value chain. The infinitude of this value chain lies not in a sui generis capacity of the "thing" (data) itself. Rather, Aadhaar's value goes well beyond the creation of an individual profile or identity number or card for every single resident and citizen of India. Its size and the universality of its database is not the only reason why Aadhaar is a uniquely valuable asset.

Aadhaar's value is neither intrinsic nor stable, but rather, something that is achieved anew and increased through routine human action. Restacked individual dossiers and reaggregated data sets are now the new site of value production and the latest commodity to animate capital and make it "lively" (Sunder Rajan 2012). Commercial firms in India and elsewhere have been sloughing off data generated from digital interactions for some time now (Sundaram 2017; Orlove 2004), thus contributing to the proliferation of "surveillance capitalism" (Zuboff 2019) or "platform capitalism" (Srnicek 2016).[13] In securing the mandatory linkage to Aadhaar, commercial firms have the unprecedented ability to gain access to the universal database comprising of the entire population of India and, as a result, to an astonishingly high volume of transactions. While one can see the obvious benefits and attraction of the mandatory status of Aadhaar in private transactions to data-based enterprises and entrepreneurs, less clear are the motives of the Indian state in allowing Aadhaar to be linked for non-state services. The interests of private capital and enterprise are not my concern here; instead, I want to explore what value exists for the sovereign or the state in making mandatory the linking of Aadhaar to access to non-state services (such as mobile telephony). It is here that Strathern's (1987) discussion of Melanesian value is illuminating.

As said earlier, data sets are "live" in that they are hermetically open and can be disaggregated and reaggregated in any number of ways, potentially endlessly. Aadhaar is a composite data set, made up of different data points or data dividuals of each enumerated person (their biological,

---

13. These are not necessarily the same but can overlap. "Platform capitalism" is conceptualized by Srnicek (2016) to be based in the ownership of information.

geographical, and sociological metrics). At the same time, as a single twelve-digit number, it is also itself one such data dividual that can become an autonomous actant. Every time an Aadhaar profile is used as proof of identity, it adds to a different data set, which is simultaneously profiled at the level of the individual holder of Aadhaar, as well as added to the second data set that comprises the entity or transaction ("exchange") for which that proof is required. For example, in making Aadhaar mandatory for buying a new telephone SIM card, a change is made in at least two types of data sets. The first is the individual's digital dossier that can be potentially collated around their Aadhaar number; the second is the data set collated by the SIM card vendor, the SIM card provider, or indeed the bank or other digital mechanisms (such as e-wallets) that may service that exchange. Thus, Aadhaar cardholders, by virtue of their participation in discrete exchange through their actions or "behaviors" are inserted in a potentially endless sequence of transformations in innumerable data sets. The Aadhaar-bearing citizen is doubly implicated in this recombining: once as a dividual composite in the form of their unique biometrics, then as an actor/actant in the process that propels the first change in the data sets to occur (Deleuze 1992: 5). These *actions* of the bank cardholder (or "owner") thus change the nature of the existing databases by mutating them or incrementally multiplying them. This connection of data to bodies, refracted in the stored biometrics and in the physical actions underpinning the transaction, is what keeps data forever in a raw state and therefore forever live. Value is therefore produced precisely at these points of attachment, refraction, fission, and fusion. Databases such as Aadhaar are therefore made and proliferated by a series of actions, big and small, and the value of Aadhaar is therefore crucially dependent on this labor. The value is created by not just the intellectual labor of the analyst, but by the citizen in performing the labor of small and big transactions. In Aadhaar, the citizen's body is thus doubly imbricated: in and through the bodily impressions, in the corporeal indices, and as the laboring body that performs these transactions. For this reason it is crucial to pay attention to the "bio" in biometrics in order to understand the relationship between a body and its impression (fingerprints, iris scans, facial photos), as well as its transformation into information as "data points."

The value of Aadhaar infrastructure lies as much in the capture of biological attributes as indexical of the individual body, as it is in the mandatorily tethered laboring body whose labor acts further on the value of these aggregated indices. These dividuals become the laboring dividuals as indices of the laboring body in the digital sphere (Deleuze 1992: 5). It is therefore no surprise that the micro actions that precipitate change in the data set are called "data-work." It is data-work that produces the prime commodity in this sphere—the algorithm, which in turn is deployed to create new and directed data-work. Indeed, data-work is the subject of considerable debate globally, coalescing at the interrelation between privacy and ownership (Gray and Suri 2019). But it is precisely the point at which data sets become (more) valuable that those transacting in these sets as already formed commodities are reckoned, as generative of nothing more than "[behavioural] surplus," of junk, or "[data] exhaust" (Bouk 2017: 104). Ethnographically attending to the point at which something new is put into circulation allows us to reveal the work that has gone into making new things appear, including the relationships that inhere in the new thing (Strathern 1992b: 249). If the point of addition of value is characterized as "worthless" by the entrepreneur, then one can see the profit-making motive of private capital all too clearly. The state is at least one of the parties involved in any transaction that involves Aadhaar-based verification. The very moment in which value is made in data-work is the moment that the data entrepreneur conceals by deeming it as the point of digital exhaust. They do so to conceal the extraction of surplus. But what of the state? In recent years, regulators have struggled globally to determine an adequate way of compensating people for the use of personal data infringements from technology and data companies that have predated on people's online lives without consent, what Zuboff has called "dispossession by surveillance" (2019: 98). I contend that in the Indian context, though dispossessing, data-work under the sign of Aadhaar takes on a distinctly different relationality.

Investigating the emergence of data as the newest property form in India, not as an already formed thing, but, crucially, in corporeal actions and transactions helps reveal the moments of transformation as well as the locus of value-generation. The entailed modes of its appropriation provide us with an insight into how value is generated in this process of transformation, which renders data into a property form (i.e., as something that can be owned, or possessed and disposed of), but also with insight into the critical entanglement of the state as an appropriator of data. In compiling the biometrics of all its citizens into individual identificatory numbers, and then creating a database of all citizens, it may appear to be no different than the average tech entrepreneur discussed by, among others, Zuboff (2019). Reading these transactions and their entailed asymmetries through the relationality engendered in their appropriation necessitates understanding the original relationship in which this new economy intervenes. At the heart of this lies the question of ownership and the related question of its erasure in data-work. Akin to the mode of erasure of title in land and territory, integral to the the creation of digital political geography as *vacuum domicilium* is key for the expansion of state sovereignty. Sovereignty-making practices in the erasure of title in land differ from those in data in one important way however: the latter (data) is not an inert or finite physical resource, but potentially infinite and immortal primarily as a consequence of human activity. Further, as the rest of the chapter shows, Aadhaar is the latest manifestation, if not the culmination, of the central contradiction between accumulation and anti-accumulation as simultaneous pursuits of proprietorial logic in contemporary India. In this respect, data bears only a slight resemblance to other jurisdictions, crucially because of the deep and extensive involvement of the state, which cannot be understood simply as "surveillance capitalism." In light of the missing or incomplete right to property in Indian law, mandatory data-work invokes older histories of servitude and an older settlement on the question of labor and its ownership. To explain this, I take a detour and explore Gaddi distinctions among different types of servitudes that helps us isolate the erasure at play in the labor of Aadhaar.

The Bonds of Labor

It was not until a few years into my research among the Gaddis that I first heard the word *baziya,* or perhaps first made any note of it. It was 2005 when I first met D., who happened to drop by at someone's house I was visiting. Not put off at all by the anthropologist in attendance, but instead rather enthusiastically joined in to say, "I am a Gaddi too, Madam," he said, choosing to use the English form of address rather than an appropriate and more usual kin term, perhaps to signal his professional or salaried status and the resulting upward mobility. "I am a Gaddi too, Madam, but my origins are very different from most in the village. I may be working today as a government employee in Shimla [the provincial capital], but you see, my mother and father worked for a *baziya* in this village." He quickly gathered that I did not quite follow, and said: "You know Madam, *baziye* [pl for *baziya*] … they were a little bit like *bandhua,* but not quite." In common parlance in north India, *bandhua* was shorthand for bonded labor and, thanks to some vivid depictions in popular

144

cinema, just using the word provoked all manner of ill ease. Bonded labor in commonsensical understandings was hereditary servitude that came from unpaid debt. This inhumane practice was a hallmark of feudal agrarian relations in large parts of the country, at least until 1976, when it was finally outlawed and several families *finally* liberated from the shackles of eternal servitude. And what would be the difference, I asked. He replied:

> Madam, workers with the *baziya* lived like family, but their children did not necessarily enter servitude. So, my mother educated me and I was able to escape the fate. But she lived in the *baziya's* house 'til the day she died. I remember my time in the village as a child very well. And I remember my mother working the fields and doing the household work in their house. While my father was alive, he did manual work for the family. They had not entered the *baziya's* house out of indebtedness but to perform servitude. Some people would leave their sons behind with a *baziya* while they went on the trail as minor shepherds or as *puhaals* because the school cycle did not work well with the herding cycle. I was left behind to be given a school education who would give them *taleem* [education] but not for free, in lieu of labor.

Why was it not the same as *bandhua*? I asked him. It was simple, he said. Working for a *baziya* was not a debt relation, nor indeed kinship or potential kinship. The former, he said was *pahchari*. Sometimes, in this (male) labor-short Gaddi community, *pahchari* would end up as *mundai*, or bride-service labor,[14] though Gaddis who migrated from Chamba to the southern slopes of the Dhauladhars by *pahchari* could rarely hope to end up as sons-in-law of their paymasters. The lingering existence of *pahchari* was always spoken of in hushed tones, its disappearance as a common practice taken to be a sign of how far they had come from their past.

Gaddi pastoralism contained within it myriad forms of labor and methods of recompense. The most straightforward of these was performed by herd-owning families, where the men accompanied the herds on their annual cycle of transhumance, keeping away from their villages for long stretches of time for most part of the year. Occasionally, women

---

14. "*Mundai*" was the labor that young men performed for older men as bride-service, and it can involve herding or farming, depending on the requirement.

accompanied the men or reached them on the trail at certain parts of the cycle. More often than not, Gaddi women stayed in the village where they worked the land and looked after their domestic animals, as discussed in Chapter 3. Prior to the reorganization of the Gaddi household in the mid-late twentieth century, which I have discussed in some detail elsewhere (Kapila 2003; 2004), the practice of bride-service was not uncommon.[15] Even though bride-service was not the only way by which men could acquire wives, labor was certainly one of the ways by which a man who was too poor to pay bride-price and who did not have a sister to offer in the preferred form of isogamous exchange (*batta-satta*, or *atta-satta*, marriage), could acquire a wife. A number of elderly men in my fieldwork village had first arrived from the other side of the Dhauladhars in *mundai*. Through labor, younger men with no flock of their own transformed this relationship of servitude into a kinship relation and not only gained ownership of their own labor, but were also set to inherit the flock and land that once belonged to the wife's father.

But not all forms of servitude entailed the same transformatory potential. *Puhaals* were hired as shepherding help on the trail, and looked after the flock and at times also performed odd jobs on the trail, such as cooking and washing for the herd owner. A herder with a large flock (upwards of a 1000 head of sheep and goats) could have more than one *puhaal* in his retinue on the trail. In the past, *puhaals* were Gaddi men who did not own any flock and were usually from a lower ranked *al* (or clan) than the herder. To a *puhaal*, servitude to the herder meant being an apprentice, having food for the entire year, and receiving two or three kid goats and lambs at the end of the herding cycle as compensation. Many Gaddi men start off as *puhaals* and later become owners of moderate herds themselves (Kapila 2003; Saberwal 1999). For the *puhaals*, servitude transformed their status from servant-laborer to herder, but not kin. In more recent years, when young Gaddi men, especially those who do not come from large herd-owning households, have been less keen to enter herding as livelihood, *puhaals* have been recruited from the wider pool of migrant wage labor, sometimes coming from as far as Nepal (Kapila 2008). Waged *puhaals* however, remain just that—*puhaals*, irrespective of the years of servitude, not least because they rarely receive animals at the end of the cycle, partly because of their status as migrant labor, but also because they are not part of any ritual or extended Gaddi

---

15. To date, though, the institution of *mundai* has all but disappeared, and marriage prestations move in the direction of the wife-giver, not the wife-taker.

exchange networks. Unsurprisingly, wage labor carries none of the established transformatory potential in any recognized sense other than catapulting personhood into the framework of a modern market economy, or "veiled slavery," as Marx called wage labor (Johnson 2004: 302).

"To labor mean[s] to be enslaved by necessity," says Hannah Arendt (1998: 83). Neither *mundai* nor being a *puhaal* entailed any negative status connotations. *Pahchari* and servitude to a *baziya*, on the other hand, were and continue to be stigmatized because they signaled a debt relation that was singularly defining of the person (or household), robbing them of their liberty, as well as their children's. These forms of servitude were neither in the realm of kinship nor entailed any potential to enter that domain, such as *mundai*. The difference between *pahchari* and servitude to the *baziya* was the heritability of servitude, or the temporal cycle of debt. It was the *puhaal's* ability to maintain a household separate from the herder that marked debt-derived servitude away from that of *pahchari*. Labor when performed to service a debt relation was seen as "unfree," and the practice was considered unsavory both by people themselves and by the authorities.

Ironically, unfree labor was a source of much anxiety for the colonial state. Colonial records are replete with anxious references to the existence of forms of labor that hinted at uncompensated labor, or unwaged servitude, referred to as *begaar*. Most of these records reflect state efforts to investigate, curtail, or then arrest the guilty party for practicing this (outlawed) form of servitude. But often what looked like the sale of persons in fact revealed the complexity within which labor was mobilized and deployed in society. On July 11, 1879, the Government of Punjab alerted one of its secretaries to the "existence of slave trade" in Kangra: "A vernacular newspaper *Koh-i-Noor* . . . complained that slave trade prevailed in Kulu, that women were publicly sold and bought and that there was an office for the registry for the deeds of sale."[16] This newspaper report had caught the attention of the Secretary of State, who had asked for further investigation on the matter. The Lieutenant-General had gone on to inform the Secretary of State that the alleged slave trade was "clearly a rude and inexpensive method of divorce."[17] This was not the first time officials in the colonial state had either misrecognized a practice as slavery, had expressed anxiety over it (Eaton and Chatterjee 2006; Pinch 2013; Prakash 1990), or had not recognized its existence

---

16. Letter from the Government of Punjab, No. 427 of July 11, 1879. NAI/ Home/Public/A Proceedings/ September 1879/No. 150–152.

17. Ibid.

altogether, especially when it lay within the domestic sphere (see Chatterjee 1999; Pinch 2013). The misrecognition was often prompted in instances where an exchange involving persons (for example, women, as in the case above) accompanied a monetary exchange, especially one for which accounts were kept. Slavery had only recently been abolished in the metropole and so any actual or presumed exchange that had a whiff of it, especially in the colonies, was a source of anxiety, as it was seen to undermine the legitimacy of the colonial presence (Major 2012).[18] But, as historians of the period have argued, the supposed state of "unfreedom" of any section of the population was a curious concern for a colonizing power to hold about the colonized (Major 2012; Prakash 1990).

In his influential work on servitude and labor in colonial India, Gyan Prakash queries the usefulness of the freedom-unfreedom paradigm to all too readily understand non-waged labor as slavery by the (colonial) state (1990: 6–7). He points out that *bhatta*, the Hindi term for "wage," is derived from the word for rice, *bhaat*, and therefore contains in it traces of wage relations that preceded the time of capital (1990: 7). Such traces can also be found in certain types of labor relations among the Gaddis (e.g., *puhaali*), as discussed above, where workers were paid in heads of animal rather than cash. Prakash argues that the singularity of liberty and the emergence of man in post-Enlightenment discourse as "essentially free" coincided with the rise of capitalism, and though forms of servitude may have existed in registers other than that of free and unfree labor, today it is difficult to speak of it in any other framework, given the universalized reign of capital. In the multiplexity of servitude, it is a relation of permanent and heritable debt that carries with it the potential for non-personhood. What distinguished other forms of servitude from bonded labor, or *pahchari* in the case of the Gaddis, was the debt-relation that results in unfreedom for generations to come.

Primordial Debt and the Economy of Vitality

Today, the discourse of freedom is enmeshed not just with that of capital, but also with modern law as its enabler and guarantor (Pistor 2019).[19]

---

18. Major (2010) contends that this repugnancy towards slavery was maintained with an even greater zeal in the colonies than in the metropole.
19. On the relationship between law and capital in India, see Birla (2010). Birla discusses the creation of a new legal infrastructure under colonialism

The bulwark of freedom in modern law is articulated through rights, which have their basis in the idea of the possessive individual. This is especially pertinent in understanding how or why the relationship to labor, ownership, and self-ownership, or what Quigley calls a "coherent property approach" (2018: 19), has been particularly difficult to establish even in independent India. This is because central to the framework of rights is the ownership rights in one's own person, recalling the shadow of slavery and its abolition that modern law is built on. If slavery renders persons into things, the body into a commodity, and its labour of no exchange value, then in the Aadhaar ownership architecture lies the eradication of ownership in one's person. The ownership of one's body was already qualified due to all types of constraints placed on it, which the state abrogated to itself, as reminded by the Attorney General. The Aadhaar cardholder's body is permanently integrated into the network of the state with enhanced visibility and traceability, but also in permanent performance of ostensibly "value-less" labor from which there is no escape. Like the slave, this networked and laboring body of the "cybernetic citizen" (Liu 2019) through its ostensibly value-less labor produces the valuable good (data, plantation commodity), extracted or appropriated by the state with no recognition of their person or humanity in that value-chain. The state offers no compensation to the citizen enslaved under Aadhaar other than a generalized sense of belonging (through citizenship with the nation-state), and territorial encompassment, which here, instead of the plantation, is the network. It is in the context of the ensnared and enslaved body of the cybernetic citizen that the full import of the missing fundamental right to property is made visible, and final and absolute owner revealed.

What makes data-servitude possible? If the Gaddi material tells us anything, it is that servitude that comes with no transformative potential is only possible in conditions of indebtedness, where infinite labor is promised and performed in lieu of the burden of debt. Gaddis in servitude to a *baziya* seldom passed on their servitude to the next generation. Kamias on the other hand, as Prakash tells us, became tied in debt-serfdom during the colonial period, partly because of the misrecognition of the relation between labor and debt by the colonial state. In both cases, the relation between servitude and slavery is premised in debt. Having

---

that underpinned the government of indigenous capital through commercial legislation and other legal instruments aimed at reshaping kinship and market practices of local mercantile communities.

forfeited absolute ownership of her body to the state, the Indian citizen is now forever indebted for the very essence of humanity the state has bestowed on her—i.e. freedom, as permanent debt. In the absence of the fundamental right to property, this debt can always be recalled by the state and the citizen made to pledge her laboring body without any expectation of recompense.

In India, data as a property form has emerged simultaneously with the denial of ownership and erasure of title, and as an exemplary form of sovereignty-making practices of the state. Attending to this simultaneity allows us to ask new questions of the becoming, or the emergence, of data both as a property form and of its amenability for appropriation. Attending to the processes of becoming helps us liberate the state-data relationship from the straitjacket of consent and surveillance concerns. An anthropology of data, rather than its political economy or sociology, allows us to approach this new property form not from the point of view of the state, or of private capital, which forms the focus of most work in this field (notably Zuboff 2019), but from a different starting position, that of relationality. In order for us to understand the relationality generated under Aadhaar, it becomes necessary to describe the nature and conditions of the (asymmetric) exchange that characterizes data-work, which has all too readily been read under the sign of the gift. Marion Fourcade and David Kluttz (2020) have called the accumulation by dispossession perpetrated by data companies where customers are lured into parting with their data under the lure of a "free" service a "Maussian bargain." A similar argument is made by Joanna Radin (2017) in her influential paper on how indigenous communities come to be configured as "donors" of data harvested for medical studies, later repurposed for use in machine learning. It is tempting to see the sloughing of biometrics as the citizen's gift to the state, but this may not be wholly accurate, or then even the full picture. For what we have under Aadhaar—and any biometrics based identification system—is not asymmetric exchange, or "gift," but instead, a negative reciprocity, a "not-gift," which seizes and wrests but offers nothing in return (Descola 2013: 318). Under Aadhaar, biometrics are extracted mandatorily—there is neither escape, nor is there compensation. I instead propose a different reading of the relationality in which Aadhaar is based and the biometric person it engenders out of the citizen.

The Aadhaar complex is akin to what Fernando Santos-Granero characterised in Amerindian societies as the "native regimes of capture and servitude" (2009: 5).[20] In a highly sophisticated account of six indigenous systems of enslavement predating colonial conquest, Santos-Granero argues that in these societies servitude worked within a political economy of life, where vitality, being a scarce resource, is accumulated through the servility and enslavement of others (2009: 14, 209). The "other," or the enemy, is enslaved in order to be made into an affine, or kin. In these societies, there exist a range of servile relations, which are not restricted to the economic relationship: from property-form slaves (rare) through to pets and servants (2009: 177). It is the master's productive agency which includes but also exceeds the act of capture itself, that produces the servile relation (2009: 168). Therefore, in these communities, children are said to be "owned" by their parents because they are fed and clothed by them, and the parents are responsible for causing them into existence (2009: 170). To me this dynamic of capture echoes the mode of relationality underpinning Aadhaar. I would like to argue that India's mandatory biometric identification too is an economy based in the capture of life. However, in contrast to the regimes and ethos of capture in Amerindian societies that Santos-Granero and others have described,[21] the capture of vitality under Aadhaar is not driven by scarcity. Instead, the political economy of life in Aadhaar is is based in its excess and never-ending potential. The same excess which is deemed "waste" or "worthless" by the entrepreneur, is sovereignty-making in and through its appropriation.

The Indian state is able to spawn this new political economy of capture through the vitality of impressions, of the bio in biometrics. As an economy of vitality, Aadhaar allows the Indian state to join a longer, if spatially and temporally dispersed tradition of thinking on the vitality of impressions. Anthropologists since Frazer tried to understand why people associated the magical qualities people associated with impression-based technologies of capture such as photography. This was because, magic is based in either of two principles: contagious and homeopathic. Contagious magic, Frazer argued, required contact with the person on whom the magic was being enacted, whereas "homeopathic" magic was enacted on the image of the person, such as voodoo dolls, which he thought was the principle on which photography was seen to work (Pinney 2011: 65). Lévy-Bruhl extended this insight to understand the resistance of indigenous communities when they first encountered

---

20. I thank Luiz Costa for this reference.
21. Notably Costa (2017); Costa and Fausto (2019); Taylor (2001); and Vivieros de Castro (2009).

photography, who thought it to be a theft of their soul, their vitality. According to Lévy-Bruhl, this was because in their cosmology there was no conceptual distinction between a person and their shadow. They saw the relation between the person and their photograph not as one of resemblance, but of identity. The photograph *is* the person (Pinney 2011: 77). In biometrics similarly, the corporeal is kept permanently alive through its appropriation. Hence what is captured here is vitality of the citizen itself. Keeping the citizen permanently unrecompensed for their labor and their vitality is the making of *corpus nullius*, or *persona nullius*. Unrecompensed labor is enslavement, and permanent enslavement is premised in a debt relation. Biometrics as a technology of capture transforms the state-citizen settlement from one of mutual obligations through rights and responsibilities to that of primordial debt. Any release from a primordial debt is temporary and takes the form of sacrifice as a deferment, or as "interest payment," since the original debt can never be repaid (Graeber 2011: 56–57; Malamoud 1983). As the state calls on them to repay their primordial debt, Indian citizens perform the permanent and ongoing sacrifice of their freedom by and forfeiting their labor in this final frontier of erasure.

Conclusion

The entanglement of servitude, biometrics, and excess has a surprising genealogy. In 1907, Gandhi was practicing as a barrister in Transvaal (South Africa) when the intolerable conditions of servitude of Indian indentured laborers caught his attention (Gandhi 2018). His encounter with Balasundaram had a profound bearing on Gandhi's career in South Africa. An indentured laborer, Balasundaram in particular had approached Gandhi the barrister after he was beaten up violently by his owner. Indentured laborers were not at liberty to wander beyond a set distance from their master's estate. Balasundaram's owner had severely beaten him for "straying" beyond the permitted distance. Gandhi was able to secure Balasundaram's release from his particular owner. The release did not mean liberty from indenture itself, but simply a transfer to a more benign employer, which too Gandhi was able to secure (Gandhi 2018: 266). This victory led to a stream of Indian laborers indentured in South Africa seeking Gandhi's help for release or transfer to new employers. But at the time, Gandhi considered himself more as a technocratic ally of the South African state rather than its political opponent (Breckenridge 2011; Nandy 1981). In this techno-utopic phase, Gandhi had championed the setting up of the Asiatic Finger-print Registry in South Africa and at the time believed in the scientific basis of identity (Breckenridge 2014: 92). Indentured laborers from India in South Africa were required to register with the local police. To enforce the strictures related to "straying" and deal with the large-scale flux of laborers following Balasundaram's victory, the government decided that every laborer was to henceforth carry a photo identity. For the purposes of monitoring laborers fleeing their owners, the govern-ments of Alfred Milner and later J. C. Smuts suggested maintaining a registry of photographic identity of all Indian laborers. To Gandhi and many of his clients, photo identification imputed criminality to the individual and, moreover, it went against their religious sensibility (Breckenridge 2011: 337). With an aim to circumvent the problem of photo identity while ensuring the dignity of the laborers, Gandhi proposed and helped set up the National Registry of Fingerprints in South Africa. It was when he realized that not just the excess (all ten fingerprints when one thumbprint could do), but that the permanence of biometrics was itself an instrument of repression by the state that he pivoted away from managerial progressivism to develop his unique antimodern, anti-technological politics.[22] The immediate product of this turn is his de facto political manifesto, *Hind Swaraj* (Breckenridge 2014: 90–131).

As Deleuze argues: "Types of machines are easily matched with each type of society—not that machines are determining, but because they express those social forms capable of generating them and using them" (1992: 6). It is not impossible to relate data-work as *animal labo-rens* (Arendt 1998), that is, labor that leaches human interiority away from the person performing the labor, leaving behind a mechanical life. Aadhaar is not simply a technological enhancement tacked on to an older state apparatus, or a further proliferation of the documentary

22. Keith Breckenridge (2014) writes about this little-known episode in Gan-dhi's life as an important milestone in the history of the surveillance state in South Africa. *Hind Swaraj* is often thought of by scholars as having emerged from Gandhi's encounter with Tolstoy and Ruskin, and their in-fluence on his anti-modern politics. Breckenridge argues that this has re-sulted in the neglect of Gandhi's prior enchantment with techno-utopia and managerial progressivism and reason behind his shift in his relation-ship with the South African state from 1904–1909.

state with added technology.[23] It is based in the political economy of vitality.

In making Aadhaar mandatory, the sovereign has opened a new register in its relationship with the people, a more familiar one that is based in the language of debt and the labor of indebtedness. The techno-utopia imagined by the advocates of Aadhaar, of de-duplication and transparency, is little more than latter-day managerial progressivism, for which Gandhi saw no other solution other than a political one. This chapter began with a little-known incident that showed the consequences of refusing to perform commandeered labor. It may be worthwhile to note that it was the recognition of the rapaciousness of the arrangement of laboring bodies, technology, and sovereign power that gave us one of the most famous political baptisms of the twentieth century.

---

23. On the documentary state, see Torpey's magisterial study of the history of the passport (2000). See also Caplan and Torpey (2001). For South Asia, see Hull (2012); Mathur (2016).

CHAPTER 7

Coda: The Illusion of Property

How one can propose an anthropology of sovereignty in its own (anthropological) terms, while keeping alive the engagement with the legal canon, political paradigms, as well as historical context? In this book I have tried to provide some potential ways in which the anthropology of the state can be revisited away from liberal political categories and understood within the disciplinary canon. This is not by way of making a parochial point, but to highlight the new perspectives and terrains such a move affords. In the specific context of this book, by relying on structural anthropological frameworks to understand the workings of sovereignty across temporal and spatial scales, I try to extricate some of the debates (such as the relationship between law and culture) from analytical dead-ends. Similarly, recasting the anthropology of sovereign power away from the Schmittian-Agambenian-Foucauldian frames, shows that the anthropology of the state is exhausted neither in and by biopolitics nor necropolitics (see Mbembe 2003).

To reprise the questions I put forth in the introduction: What is left when something is taken away? Is the obverse of *hau* sovereignty? These questions manifest in their fullness when one is confronted with the hollow center at the heart of India's modern legal framework—the absent right to property. Sovereignty lies in the power to take, but also in the ability to create illusions. The ability to dupe, transform, and self-transform is a singularly divine potency, which cannot be acquired through knowledge, penance (or labor), or merit (or conduct). To create an illusion is to dispossess the other of their discrimination between the real and the unreal.

The *Garuda Purana*, the scripture that focuses on, among other things, ancestral rites, describes the fate of the soul (*atma*) of a person whose dead body has not yet been consigned properly to the next world, usually as a result of improper or incomplete mortuary rites (*Pretakhanda, Garuda Purana*). This is because, just as life is staged, so is the journey from death to the next world. The aim of a mortuary ritual is to rehome the *atma*, or soul of the deceased. Once the outer shell (or the physical body) of the person has been consigned to the funeral pyre, and before its soul or *atma* has been sent properly home or converted fully into an ancestor through the ritual of *pind-daan*, the not-as-yet ancestor is represented by a drawing of its twin—a ghost (*pret)* which is fed and sated, accompanied by recitation of specific chants (Parry 1994: 192–93). Sometimes, depending on the type of error or deficit that may occur in the mortuary ritual, the soul or *atma* may roam restlessly, looking for an abode or a resting place until such time it can be calmed. But of course, nowhere other than a new body can be a rightful abode, which the ritual error or deficit has permanently deprived the *atma* of, and thereby from becoming an ancestor. Folk-tales and mythology are replete with tales of restless spectral beings, from friendly ghosts to vampiric *pishaches* through to story-telling *baitaals*. What is common to all these beings is their uncanny ability to keep returning not just because of an improper consignment, but also as a sign of unfinished business.

Proprietary ownership is akin to an illusion in the absence of Article 19 (Fundamental Right to Property) of the constitution of India—an illusion at best, and a ghostly revenant at worst. A *pishach*, because it has not been properly put to rest and is not a full ancestor, and therefore keeps returning, and not always in a benign form.[1] Despite being underpinned by the modern legal framework and its attendant universalist language of rights, it is not just ordinary people (as the literature on legal pluralism and forum shopping tells us), but the state too, mobilizes pre-constitutional relational modalities between the sovereign and the subject. Mimicking the divine, the state deploys the illusion of

---

1.　The latest return of this spectre was witnessed in the abrogation of Article 370, which had provided for a special status to Jammu and Kashmir. One of the primary planks of its legitimation was the scrapping of Article 35A, a constitutional protection that prevented non-Kashmiris to buy land and hold title in the territory of Kashmir.

ownership in three different realms—land, persons, and things—while hoarding ever greater sovereignty for itself. Ownership therefore lurches between the steadfast fixity of rights and the illusory danger posed by accumulation. Like the improperly consigned ancestor, the property question returns time and again, as a *pishach*, a revenant throwing light at the hollow center of the work of law in India.

References

Abrams, Philip. 1988. "Notes on the difficulty of studying the state." *Journal of Historical Sociology* 1 (1): 58–89.

Abu-Lughod, Lila. 1991. "Writing against culture." In *Recapturing anthropology: Working in the present*, edited by Richard G. Fox, 137–154. Santa Fe: School of American Research.

Agamben, Giorgio. 2005. *State of exception.* Chicago: Chicago University Press.

Agarwal, Bina. 1994. *A field of her own: Gender and land rights in India.* Cambridge: Cambridge University Press.

Agnes, Flavia. 2011. *Family law, Volume 1: Family law and constitutional claims.* Delhi: Oxford University Press.

Agrawal, Arun. 2005. *Environmentality: Technologies of government and the making of subjects.* Durham: Duke University Press.

Ambagudia, Jagannath. 2011. "Scheduled tribes and the politics of inclusion in India." *Asian Social Work and Policy Review* 5 (1): 33–43.

Ambedkar, Bhim Rao. 1935. *The annihilation of caste.* Speech prepared for the Jat Pat Todak Mandal, Lahore. 3rd ed. Accessed September 14, 2012. www.ambedkar.org/amcd/02.Annihilation%20%of20%Caste.htm

Anand, Utkarsh. 2015. "Where's right to privacy? You decide, Govt tells Supreme Court." *Indian Express.* July 23, 2015.

Anderson, Clare, Madhumita Mazumdar, and Vishwajit Pandya. 2016. *New histories of the Andaman Islands: Landscape, place and identity in the Bay of Bengal, 1790–2012.* Cambridge: Cambridge University Press.

Appadurai, Arjun. 1985. "Gratitude as a social mode in South India." *Ethos* 13 (3): 236–245.

———. 1986. "Theory in anthropology: Centre and periphery." *Comparative Studies in Society and History* 28: 356–361.

———. 1993. "Number in the colonial imagination." In *Orientalism and the postcolonial predicament: Perspectives on South Asia*, edited by Carol A. Breckenridge and Peter van der Veer, 314–340. Philadelphia: University of Pennsylvania Press.

———. 1998. "Full attachment." *Public Culture* 10 (2): 443–449.

———, ed. 1988. *The social life of things: Commodities in cultural practice.* Cambridge: Cambridge University Press.

Arendt, Hannah. 1998 [1958]. *The human condition.* Chicago: Chicago University Press.

Asad, Talal. 1961. *Some aspects of change in the structure of the Muslim family in the Punjab under the British rule.* Unpublished B. Phil Thesis. University of Oxford.

———, ed. 1993. "Multiculturalism and British identity in the wake of the Salman Rushdie affair." In *Genealogies of religion: Discipline and reasons of power in Christianity and Islam*, 239–268. Baltimore: Johns Hopkins University Press.

Auerbach, Jeffrey A., and Peter H. Hoffenberg, eds. 2008. *Britain, the empire, and the world at the Great Exhibition of 1851.* Aldershot: Ashgate.

Austin, Granville. 1999 [1966]. *The Indian constitution: Cornerstone of a nation.* Delhi: Oxford University Press.

Axelby, Richard. 2007. "'It takes two to clap': How gaddi shepherds in the Indian Himalayas negotiate access to grazing." *Journal of Agrarian Change* 7 (1): 35–75.

Bajpai, Rochana. 2011. *Debating difference: Group rights and liberal democracy in India.* Delhi: Oxford University Press.

Banerjee-Dube, Ishita. 2010. *Caste in history.* Delhi: Oxford University Press.

Banner, Stuart. 2005. "Why *terra nullius?*: Anthropology and property law in early Australia." *Law and History Review* 23 (1): 95–132.

Bataille, Georges. 1991. *The accursed share: An essay on general economy.* Vols. 2 and 3. Translated by Robert Hurley. New York: Zone Books.

Bates, Crispin. 1995. "Race, caste and tribe in central India: The early origins of Indian anthropometry." In *The Concept of Race in South Asia*, edited by Peter Robb, 219–259. Delhi: Oxford University Press.

Baviskar, Amita. 2007. "Indian indigeneities: Adivasi engagements with Hindu Nationalism in India." In *Indigenous Experience Today*, edited by Marisol de la Cadena and Orin Starn, 275–304. Oxford: Berg.

Baxi, Pratiksha, Shirin M. Rai, and Shaheen Sardar Ali. 2006. "Legacies of common law: 'Crimes of honour' in India and Pakistan." *Third World Quarterly* 27 (7): 1239–1253.

Bayly, Christopher A. 2012. "Recovering liberties: Indian thought in the age of liberalism and empire." *Britain and the World* 5 (2): 294–295.

———. 2011. *Recovering liberties: Indian thought in the age of liberalism and empire.* Cambridge: Cambridge University Press.

Benhabib, Seyhla. 2004. *The rights of others: Aliens, residents, and citizens.* Cambridge: Cambridge University Press.

Benton, Lauren, and Benjamin Straumann. 2010. "Acquiring empire by law: From Roman doctrine to early modern European practice." *Law and History Review* 28 (1): 1–38.

Besky, Sarah and Alex Blanchette, eds. 2019. *How nature works: Rethinking labour on a troubled planet.* Santa Fe: School of Advanced Research.

Beteille, A. 1998. "The idea of indigenous people." *Current Anthropology* 39 (2):187–192

Bhagwan, Manu. 2009. "Princely states and the making of modern India: Internationalism, constitutionalism and the postcolonial moment." *Indian Economic and Social History Review* 26: 427–56.

Bhardwaj, Deeksha. 2018. "Sentinelese are peace-loving, leave them alone, says anthropologist who has met them." *The Print*, 18 November 2018. Accessed April 3, 2019. https://theprint.in/features/sentinelese-are-peace-loving-leave-them-alone-says-anthropologist-who-has-met-them/154548/.

Bhargava, Rajeev, ed. 1998. *Secularism and its critics.* Delhi: Oxford University Press.

Bhatia, Gautam. 2014. "State surveillance and the right to privacy: A constitutional biography." *National Law School of India Review* 26 (2): 127–158.

———. 2019. *The transformative constitution: A radical biography in nine acts.* Delhi: Harper Collins India.

———, ed. 2018. "The Aadhaar judgement: A roundup." *Indian Constitutional Law and Philosophy*, October 5, 2018. Accessed October 6, 2018.

https://indconlawphil.wordpress.com/2018/10/05/the-aadhaar-judgment-a-round-up/.

Bhatia, Udit, ed. 2017. *The Constituent Assembly: Deliberations on democracy.* London: Routledge.

Bhattacharya, Niladri. 1985. "Lendors and debtors: Punjab countryside 1880–1940." *Studies in History* 1 (2): 305–342.

———. 1996. "Remaking custom: The discourse and practice of colonial codification." In *Tradition, Dissent, and Ideology,* edited by R. Champakalakshmi and S. Gopal, 20–51. Delhi: Oxford University Press.

———. 2018. *The great agrarian conquest: The colonial reshaping of a rural world.* New Delhi: Permanent Black.

Bhattacharyya, Debjani. 2018. *Empire and ecology in the Bengal delta: The making of Calcutta.* Cambridge: Cambridge University Press.

Bhuwania, Anuj. 2017. *Courting the people: Public interest litigation in post-emergency India.* Cambridge: Cambridge University Press.

Birla, Ritu. 2009. *Stages of capital: Law, culture, and market governance in late colonial India.* Durham: Duke University Press.

Birtles, Terry G. 1997. "First contact: Colonial European preconceptions of tropical Queensland rainforests and its people." *Historical Geography* 23 (4): 393–417.

Bonilla, Yarimar. 2015. *Non-sovereign futures: French Caribbean politics in the wake of disenchantment.* Chicago: Chicago University Press.

———. 2017. "Unsettling sovereignty." *Cultural Anthropology* 32 (3): 330–339.

Borrows, John. 2010. *Canada's indigenous constitution.* Toronto: University of Toronto Press.

Bouk, Dan. 2017. "The history and political economy of personal data over the last two centuries in three acts." *Osiris* 32 (1): 85–106.

Boyle, James. 2003. "The opposite of property?" *Law and Contemporary Problems* 66 (1–2): 1–32.

Brace, Laura, and Julia O'Connell Davidson, eds. 2018. *Rethinking slavery and anti-slavery.* New York: Routledge.

Breckenridge, Carol A. 1989. "The aesthetics and politics of colonial collecting: India at world fairs." *Comparative Studies of Society and History* 31 (2): 195–216.

Breckenridge, Keith. 2011. "Gandhi's progressive disillusionment: Thumbs, fingers, and the rejection of scientific modernism in *Hind Swaraj*." *Public Culture* 23 (2): 331–338.

———. 2014. *Biometric state: The global politics of identification and surveillance in South Africa, 1850 to the present*. Cambridge: Cambridge University Press.

Brown, Michael F. 2003. *Who owns native culture?* Cambridge, MA: Harvard University Press.

Brulé, Rachel. 2020. *Women, power, and property: The paradox of gender equality laws in India*. Cambridge: Cambridge University Press.

Callon, Michel, Cécile Méadel, and Vololona Rabeharisoa. 2002. "The economy of qualities." *Economy and Society* 31 (2): 194–217.

Calvao, Felipe. 2016. Unfree labour. *Annual Review of Anthropology*, 45: 451–467.

Candea, Matei. 2019. *Comparison in anthropology: The impossible method*. Cambridge: Cambridge University Press.

Candea, Matei, J. Cook, C. Trundle, and T. Yarrow, eds. 2015. *Detachment: Essays on the limits of relational thinking*. Manchester: Manchester University Press.

Candea, Matei, and Giovanni da Col, eds. 2012. "The return to hospitality." *Journal of the Royal Anthropological Institute* 18: S1–S19.

Caplan, Jane, and John Torpey, eds. 2001. *Documenting individual: The development of state practices in the modern world*. Princeton, NJ: Princeton University Press.

Carrithers, Michael, Matei Candea, Karen Sykes, Michael Holbraad and Souhmya Venkatesan. 2010. "Ontology is just another word for culture." Motion tabled at the 2008 meeting of the Group for Debates in Anthropology, University of Manchester. *Critique of Anthropology* 30 (2): 152–200.

Chakrabarty, Dipesh, ed. 2002. "Governmental roots of modern ethnicity." In *Habitations of modernity: Essays in the wake of subaltern studies*, 80–99. Chicago: Chicago University Press.

Chakravartty, Paula and D. Ferreira da Silva. 2012. "Accumulation, dispossession, and debt: The racial logic of global capitalism." *American Quarterly* 64 (3): 361–385.

Chalfin, Brenda. 2010. *Neoliberal frontiers: An ethnography of sovereignty in West Africa*. Chicago: Chicago University Press.

Chandra, Rajshree. 2010. "The role of national laws in reconciling constitutional right to health with TRIPS obligations: An examination of the Glivec patent case in India." In *Incentives to global public health: Patent law and access to essential medicines*, edited by Thomas Pogge, Matthew Rimmer, and Kim Rubenstein, 381–405. Cambridge: Cambridge University Press.

Chatterjee, Indrani. 1999. *Gender, slavery, and law in Colonial India*. Delhi: Oxford University Press.

Chatterjee, Nirmal Chandra. 1954. *Hindu sanskriti par aaghat: Hindu code ka vishleshan*. Delhi: Hindu Mahasabha.

Chatterjee, Partha. 1994. *The nation and its fragments: Colonial and postcolonial histories*. New Jersey: Princeton University Press.

Chattopadhyay, Madhumala. 2018. "What is Christianity to those who pray to sky and sea, says first woman to contact the Sentinelese". *The Print*. Accessed February 2020. https://theprint.in/opinion/whats-christianity-to-those-who-pray-to-sky-sea-says-first-woman-to-contact-sentinelese/156801.

Choudhary, Valmiki, ed. 1986. *Dr Rajendra Prasad: Correspondence and select documents*. Vol. 3. New Delhi: Allied Publishers.

Chowdhry, Prem. 1994. *The veiled women: Shifting gender equations in rural Haryana 1880–1990*. Delhi: Oxford University Press.

———. 2007. *Contentious marriages, eloping couples: Gender, caste, and patriarchy in northern India*. Delhi: Oxford University Press.

Clifford, James, ed. 1988. "Identity in Mashpee." In *The predicament of culture: Twentieth century ethnography, literature, and art*, 277–346. Cambridge, MA: Harvard University Press.

Cohen, Lawrence. 2019. "The 'social' de-duplicated: The Aadhaar platform and the engineering of services." *South Asia: Journal of South Asian Studies* 42 (3): 482–500.

Cohen, Morris R. 1927. "Property and sovereignty." *Cornell Law Review* 13 (1): 8–30.

Cohn, Bernard S. 1987. "The census, social structure, and objectification in South Asia." In *An anthropologist among the historians and other essays*, 224–254. Delhi: Oxford University Press.

———. 1996. *Colonialism and its forms of knowledge: The British in India*. Princeton, NJ: Princeton University Press.

Cole, Simon A. 2001. *Suspect identities: A history of fingerprinting and criminal identification*. Cambridge, MA: Harvard University Press.

Copeman, Jacob. 2011. "The gift and its contemporary forms in contemporary India." *Modern Asian Studies* 45 (5): 1051–1094.

Copland, Ian. 1997. *The princes of India and the endgame of Empire 1917–1947.* Cambridge: Cambridge University Press.

Costa, Luiz. 2017. *Owners of kinship: Asymmetrical relations in indigenous Amazonia.* Chicago: HAU Books.

Costa, Luiz and C. Fausto. 2019. "The enemy, the unwilling guest, and the jaguar host: An Amazonian story." *L'Homme* 231/232: 195–226.

Da Col, Giovanni. 2012. "The poisoner and the parasite: Cosmoeconomics, fear, and hospitality among Dechan Tibetans." *Journal of the Royal Anthropological Institute* 18 (1): 175–195.

———. 2019. "The H-factor of anthropology: Hoarding, hosting, and hospitality." *L'Homme* 231/232: 13–40.

Da Col, Giovanni and A. Shryock, eds. 2017. *From hospitality to grace: A Julian Pitt-Rivers Omnibus.* Chicago: HAU Books.

Das, Veena. 1997. *Critical events: An anthropological perspective on contemporary India.* Delhi: Oxford University Press.

———. 2006. *Life and words: Violence and the descent into the ordinary.* Berkeley: University of California Press.

———. 2014. "Ethics, the householder's dilemma, and the difficulty of reality." *HAU: Journal of Ethnographic Theory* 4 (1): 487–495.

Das, Veena and Deborah Poole, eds. 2004. *Anthropology at the margins of the state.* Santa Fe: School of American Research Press.

Datta, Nonika. 1999. *Forming an identity: A social history of the Jats.* Delhi: Oxford University Press.

De, Rohit. 2018. *A people's constitution: The everyday life of law in the Indian republic.* Princeton, NJ: Princeton University Press.

Deleuze, Giles. 1992. "Postscript on the societies of control." *October* 59 (Winter): 3–7.

Derrida, Jacques. 1990. "Force of law: The mystical foundation of authority." *Cardozo Law Review* 11 (5–6): 920–1045.

———. 1994. *Specters of Marx: The state of the debt, the work of mourning, and the new international.* London: Routledge.

———. 2000. *Of hospitality.* Translated by Rachel Bowlby. Stanford: Stanford University Press.

Descola, Philippe. 2012. "Beyond nature and culture: Forms of attachment." *HAU: Journal of Ethnographic Theory* 2 (1): 447–471.

———. 2013. *Beyond nature and culture*. Chicago: Chicago University Press.

Devji, Faisal. 2008. *The terrorist in search of humanity: Militant Islam and global politics*. London: Hurst.

———. 2012. *The impossible Indian: Gandhi and the temptations of violence*. London: Hurst.

Diamond, Cora. 2003. "The difficulty of reality and the difficulty of philosophy." *Partial Answers: Journal of Literature and the History of Ideas* 1 (2): 1–26.

Dirks, Nicholas B. 2001. *Castes of mind: Colonialism and the making of India*. Princeton, NJ: Princeton University Press.

Dogra, Chander Suta, Neha Bhatt, and Arpita Basu. 2010. "Justice by death." *Outlook*, July 12, 2010. Accessed August 24, 2010. http://www.outlookindia.com/article.aspx?266074.

Dolgin, Janet. 1997. *Defining the family: Law, reproduction, and technology in an uneasy age*. New York: New York University Press.

———. 2020. "Response to *Birth Rights and Wrongs*." *Boston University Law Review Online* 100: 139–142.

Donner, Henrike. 2005. "'Children are capital, grandchildren are interest': Changing educational strategies and parenting in Calcutta's middle-class families." In *Globalizing India: Perspectives from below*, edited by Jackie Assayag and Chris Fuller, 119–140. London: Anthem Press.

Dowleans, A.M. 1862. *Official classified and descriptive catalogue of the contributions from India to the London exhibition of 1862: Prepared through the central committee of Bengal, Government of India*. Calcutta: Bengal Printing Company Ltd.

Dumont, Louis. 1993. "North India in relation to south India." In *Family, Kinship, and Marriage in India*, edited by Patricia Uberoi, 91–111. Delhi: Oxford University Press.

———. 2009 [1970]. *Homo hierarchicus: The caste system and its implications*. Delhi: Oxford University Press.

Eaton, Richard M., and Indrani Chatterjee, eds. 2006. *Slavery and South Asian history*. Bloomington: Indiana University Press.

Ellis, Thomas P. 1917. *Notes on Punjab custom*. Lahore: Civil and Military Gazette Press.

Empson, Rebecca. 2012. "The dangers of excess: Accumulating and dispersing fortune in Mongolia." *Social Analysis* 56 (1): 117–132.

Ewick, Patricia, and Susan Silbey. 1998. *The common place of law: Stories from everyday life*. Chicago: Chicago University Press.

Fabian, Johannes. 1983. *Time and the other: How anthropology makes its object*. New York: Columbia University Press.

Fazal, Tanweer. 2019. "The mosque as a juristic person: Law, public order, and inter-religious disputes in India." *South Asian History and Culture* 10 (2): 199–211.

Federici, Silvia. 2004. *Caliban and the witch: Women, the body, and primitive accumulation*. New York: Autonomedia.

Fitzmaurice, Andrew. 2007. "The genealogy of *terra nullius*." *Australian Historical Studies* 28 (129): 1–15.

Flessas, Tatiana. 2003. "Cultural property defined, and redefined as Nietzchean aphorism." *Cardozo Law Review* 24 (2): 1067–1097.

Fourcade, Marion and Daniel Kluttz. 2020. "A Maussian bargain: Accumulation by gifts in the digital economy." *Big Data and Society*, January–June 2020: 1–16.

Franklin, Sarah. 2013. *Biological relatives: IVF, stem-cells, and the future of kinship*. Durham: Duke University Press.

Gadgil, Madhav, and Ramachandra Guha. 1992. *This fissured land: An environmental history of India*. Delhi: Oxford University Press.

Galanter, Marc. 1972. "The aborted restoration of 'indigenous' law in India." *Comparative Studies in Society and History* 14 (1): 53–70.

———. 1984. *Competing equalities: Law and the backward classes in India*. Delhi: Oxford University Press.

Gamble, Clive. 2014. "The anthropology of deep history." *Journal of the Royal Anthropological Institute* 21 (1): 147–164.

Gandhi, Mohandas K. 1928. *Satyagraha in South Africa*. Translated by V. G. Desai. Madras: S. Ganesan.

———. 2018. *An autobiography, or, my experiments with truth—A critical edition*. Translated by Mahadev Desai. Annotated and introduced by Tridip Suhrud. New Haven: Yale University Press.

Gell, Alfred. 1997. "Exalting the king and obstructing the state: A political interpretation of royal ritual in Bastar district, central India." *Journal of the Royal Anthropological Society* 3 (3): 433–450.

———. 1998. *Art and agency: An anthropological theory*. Oxford: Oxford University Press.

Ghosh, Arunabh. 2016. "Accepting difference, seeking common ground: Sino-Indian statistical exchanges 1951–1959." *BJHS Themes* 1: 61–82.

Goodale, Mark. 2017. *Anthropology and law: A critical introduction.* New York: New York University Press.

Graeber, David. 2001. *Toward An anthropological theory of value: The false coin of our own dreams.* New York: Palgrave.

———. 2011. *Debt: The first 5000 years.* New York: Melville Publishing House.

Graeber, David and Marshall Sahlins. 2017. *On kings.* Chicago: Hau Books.

Gray, Mary L. and Siddharth Suri. 2019. *Ghost work: How to stop Silicon Valley from developing a new global underclass.* Boston: Houghton Mifflin Harcourt.

Greenhalgh, Paul. 1988. *Ephemeral vistas: The Expositions Universelles, Great Exhibitions, and World Fairs 1851–1939.* Manchester: Manchester University Press

Gregory, Chris. 2015. *Gifts and commodities.* Chicago: Hau Books.

Grigson, W. V. 1944. "The aboriginal in the future India." *Journal of the Royal Anthropological Institute of Great Britain and Ireland* 74 (1–2): 33–41.

Guerrin, Isabelle. 2014. "Juggling with debt, social ties, and values: The everyday uses of microfinance in rural South India." *Current Anthropology* 55 (S9): S40–S50.

Guha, Ramachandra. 1999. *Savaging the civilised: Verrier Elwin, his tribals, and India.* Delhi: Oxford University Press.

———. 2007. *India after Gandhi: The history of the world's largest democracy.* New Delhi: Macmillan.

Guha, Ranajit. 1994. "The prose of counter-insurgency." In *Culture/power/history: A reader in contemporary social theory*, edited by Nicholas Dirks, George Eley, and Sherry Ortner, 336–371. New Jersey: Princeton University Press.

———. 1996 [1963]. *A rule of property for Bengal: An essay on the idea of permanent settlement.* Durham: Duke University Press.

Guha Thakurta, Tapati. 2004. *Monuments, objects, histories: Institutions of art in colonial and post-colonial India.* New Delhi: Permanent Black.

Gupta, Akhil. 1995. "Blurred boundaries: the discourse of corruption, the culture of politics, and the imagined state." *American Ethnologist* 22 (2): 375–402.

Gupta, Akhil, and James Ferguson. 1992. "Beyond 'culture': Space, identity, and the politics of difference." *Cultural Anthropology* 7 (1): 6–23.

Gupta, Dipankar. 2005. "Caste and politics: Identity over system." *Annual Review of Anthropology*, 21: 409–427.

———, ed. 1991a. "Hierarchy and difference: An introduction." In *Social Stratification*, 1–21. Delhi: Oxford University Press.

———, ed. 1991b. "Continuous hierarchies and discrete castes." In *Social Stratification*, 110–141. Delhi: Oxford University Press.

———, ed. 2004 *Caste in question: Identity or hierarchy?* New Delhi: Sage.

Gygi, Fabio. 2018. "The metamorphosis of excess: 'Rubbish Houses' and the imagined trajectory of things in post-bubble Japan." In *Consuming life in post-bubble Japan: A transdisciplinary perspective*, edited by K. Cwiertka and E. Machotka, 129–151. Amsterdam: University of Amsterdam Press.

Hansen, Thomas Blom, and Finn Stepputat. 2006. "Sovereignty revisited." *Annual Review of Anthropology* 35: 295–315.

———, eds. 2005. *Sovereign bodies: Citizens, migrants, and states in the postcolonial world*. Princeton, NJ: Princeton University Press.

Harris, Cheryl I. 1993. "Whiteness as property." *Harvard Law Review* 106 (8): 1709–1791.

Harrison, Simon. 1992. "Ritual as intellectual property." *Man* 27 (2): 225–244.

———. 1993. *The mask of war: Violence, ritual, and the self in Melanesia*. Manchester: Manchester University Press.

Harvey, Penelope. 1996. *Hybrids of modernity: Anthropology, the nation state and the universal exhibition*. London: Routledge.

Hegel, G. W. F. 1967 [1952]. *The philosophy of right*. Translated by T. M. Knox. Oxford: Oxford University Press.

Henare, Amiria, Martin Holbraad, and Sari Wastell, eds. 2007. *Thinking through things: Theorising artefacts ethnographically*. London: Routledge.

Hetherington, Kevin. 2007. *Capitalism's eye: Cultural spaces of the commodity*. London: Routledge

Heywood, Paolo. 2015. "Freedom in the code: The anthropology of (double) morality." *Anthropological Theory* 15 (2): 200–217.

Hirsch, Eric. 2010. "Property and persons: New forms and contests in the era of neoliberalism." *Annual Review of Anthropology* 39: 347–360.

Hoffenberg, Peter H. 2001. *An empire on display: English, Indian, and Australian exhibitions from Crystal Palace to the Great War*. Berkeley: University of California Press.

Holbraad, Martin and Morten Pedersen. 2017. *The ontological turn: An anthropological exposition*. Cambridge: Cambridge University Press.

Holbraad, Martin, Morten Axel Pedersen, and Eduardo Viveiros de Castro. 2014. "The Politics of Ontology: Anthropological Positions." Theorizing the Contemporary, *Fieldsights*, January 13. https://culanth.org/fieldsights/the-politics-of-ontology-anthropological-positions

Hull, Matthew. 2012. *Government of paper: The materiality of bureaucracy in urban Pakistan*. Berkeley: University of California Press.

Humphrey, Caroline. 1983. *Karl Marx collective: Economy, society, and religion in a Siberian collective farm*. Cambridge: Cambridge University Press.

———. 2008. "Reassembling individual subjects: Events and decisions in troubled times." *Anthropological Theory* 8 (4): 357–380.

Islam, M. Mufakhural. 1995. "The Punjab Land Alienation Act and the professional moneylenders." *Modern Asian Studies* 29 (2): 271–291.

Jaffrelot, Christophe and Pratinav Anil. 2020. *India's first dictatorship: The Emergency 1975–77*. London: Hurst.

John, Mary E. 2011. "Census 2011: Governing populations and the girl-child." *Economic and Political Weekly* 46 (16): 10–12.

John, Mary E., Ravinder Kaur, Rajni Palriwala, and Saraswati Raju. 2009. "Dispensing with daughters: Technology, society, and economy in north India." *Economic and Political Weekly* 44 (15): 16–19.

Johnson, Walter. 2004. "The pedestal and the veil: Rethinking the capitalism/slavery question." *Journal of the Early Republic* 24 (2): 299–308.

Kapila, Kriti. 2003. *Governing morals: State, marriage, and household amongst the Gaddis of north India*. Unpublished PhD dissertation. London School of Economics and Political Science.

———. 2004. "Conjugating marriage: State legislation and Gaddi kinship." *Contributions to Indian Sociology* 38 (3): 379–409.

———. 2008. "The measure of a tribe: The cultural politics of constitutional reclassification in north India." *Journal of the Royal Anthropological Institute* 14 (1): 117–134.

———. 2011. "The terms of trade: Competition and cooperation in the western Himalaya." In *The Indian state after liberalisation*, edited by Akhil Gupta and K. Sivaramakrishnan, 197–212. New York: Routledge.

———. 2014. "Old differences and new hierarchies: The trouble with tribes today." In *Interrogating modernity: Essays in honour of Dipankar Gupta*, edited by Surinder Jodhka, 99–116.Delhi: Oxford University Press.

———. nd. "The location of culture in Indian anthropology." Paper presented at online workshop, "The Other Within." Universities of Leeds/Manchester. October 2020.

Kapila, Shruti. 2011. "Gandhi before Mahatma: The foundations of political truths." *Public Culture* 23 (2): 431–448.

Kar, Sohini. 2018. *The financialisation of poverty: Labour and risk in Indian microfinance*. Stanford: Stanford University Press.

Karlsson, Bengt G. 2003. "Anthropology and the 'indigenous slot': Claims to and debates about indigenous peoples' status in India." *Critique of Anthropology* 23 (4): 403–423.

Kasturi, Malavika. 2009. "Asceticising monastic families: Ascetic genealogies, property feuds, and Anglo-Hindu law in late colonial India." *Modern Asian Studies* 43 (5): 1039–1083.

Kaur, Ravinder. 2004. "Across-region marriages: Poverty, female migration and the sex ratio." *Economic and Political Weekly* 39 (25): 2595–2603.

———. 2010. "Khap panchayats, sex ratio and female agency." *Economic and Political Weekly* 45 (23): 14–16.

Kelty, Christopher M. 2008. *Two bits: The cultural significance of free software*. Durham: Duke University Press.

Khaitan, Tarunabh. 2018. "Directive principles and the expressive accommodation of ideological dissenters." *International Journal of Constitutional Law* 16 (2): 389–420.

Khanna, Sunil. 2010. *Fatal/fetal knowledge: New reproductive technologies and family-building strategies in India*. Belmont: Cengage Learning.

Khera, Reetika, ed. 2019. *Dissent on Aadhar: Big Data meets Big Brother*. Hyderabad: Orient BlackSwan.

Khilnani, Sunil. 1997. *The idea of India*. London: Hamish Hamilton

———. 2002. "The Indian constitution and democracy." In *India's living constitution: Ideas, practices, controversies*, edited by Zoya Hasan, E. Sridharan, and R. Sudarshan, 64–82. London: Anthem Press.

Khosla, Madhav. 2020. *India's founding moment: The constitution of a most surprising democracy*. Cambridge, MA: Harvard University Press.

Kishwar, Madhu. 1994. "Codified Hindu law: Myth and reality." *Economic and Political Weekly* 29 (33): 2145–2161.

Kopytoff, Igor. 1982. "Slavery." *Annual Review of Anthropology* 11: 207–230.

———. 1986. "The cultural biography of things: commoditization as process." In *The social life of things: Commodities in cultural practice,* edited by Arjun Appadurai, 64–92. Cambridge: Cambridge University Press.

Kriegel, Lara. 2001. "Narrating the subcontinent in 1851: India at the Crystal Palace." In *The great exhibition of 1851: New interdisciplinary essays,* edited by Louise Purbrick, 146–179. Manchester: Manchester University Press.

Krishnaswamy, Sudhir. 2010. *Democracy and constitutionalism in India: A study of the basic structure doctrine.* Delhi: Oxford University Press.

Kumar, Aishwary. 2015. *Radical equality: Ambedkar, Gandhi, and the risk of democracy.* Stanford: Stanford University Press.

Kuper, Adam 2003. "The return of the native." *Current Anthropology* 44 (3): 389–402.

Laidlaw, James. 1995. *Riches and renunciation.* Oxford: Clarendon Press.

———. 2002. "For an anthropology of ethics and freedom." *Journal of the Royal Anthropological Institute* 8 (2): 311–332.

———. 2005. "A life worth leaving: Fasting to death as telos of a Jain religious life." *Economy & Society* 34 (2): 178–199.

———. 2013. *The subject of virtue: An anthropology of ethics and freedom.* Cambridge: Cambridge University Press.

Landecker, Hannah. 2007. *Culturing life: How cells became technologies.* Cambridge, MA: Harvard University Press.

Lau, George. 2013. *Ancient alterity in the Andes: A recognition of others.* New York: Routledge.

Law Commission of India. 2000. "Property rights of women: proposed reforms under the Hindu Law." *Report of the 174th Law Commission.* Government of India.

Li, Tania Murray. 2007. *The will to improve: Governmentality, development and the practice of politics.* Durham: Duke University Press.

Liang, Lawrence. 2005. "Porous legalities and avenues of participation." *SARAI Reader 05: Bare Acts,* 6–16.

Livelaw Research Team. 2017. "You have no absolute control over your body, Attorney-General answers Aadhaar's critics in SC." May 2, 2017. https://www.livelaw.in/no-absolute-control-body-attorney-general-answers-aadhaars-critics-sc/

Lowe, Lisa. 2015. *The intimacy of four continents.* Durham: Duke University Press.

Lui, Xiao. 2019. *Information fantasies: Precarious mediation in postsocialist China.* Minneapolis: Minnesota University Press.

Lyall, J. B. 1874. *Settlement Report of the Kangra District.* Simla: Civil and Military Press.

Maitland, Frederic William. 1888. *Why the history of English law is not written.* Inaugural lecture pamphlet.

Major, Andrea. 2012. *Slavery, abolitionism and empire in India, 1772–1843.* Liverpool: Liverpool University Press.

Majumdar, Rochana. 2009. *Marriage and modernity: Family values in colonial Bengal.* New Delhi: Oxford University Press.

Malamoud, Charles, ed. 1983. *Debt and debtors.* Delhi: Vikas.

Malinowski, Bronislaw. 1926. *Crime and custom in a savage society.* London: Kegan Paul, Trench, Trubner, and co. Ltd.

Mamdani, Mahmood. 2012. *Define and rule: Native as political identity.* Cambridge, MA.: Harvard University Press.

Mani, Lata. 1998. *Contentious traditions: The debate on sati in colonial India.* Berkeley: University of California Press.

Manzar, Ozama. 2017. "Privacy and the Indian culture." *Livemint,* September 27, 2017 https://www.livemint.com/Opinion/rM3vgXErD5o-Wiv12IeaKcK/Privacy-and-the-Indian-culture.html//.

Mathur, Nayanika. 2016. *Paper tiger: Law, bureaucracy, and the developmental state in Himalayan India.* Cambridge: Cambridge University Press.

Mathur, Saloni. 2007. *India by design: Colonial history and cultural display.* Berkeley: University of California Press.

Maurer, Bill. 2004. "Cyberspatial properties: Taxing questions about proprietary regimes." In *Property in question: Value transformation in the global economy,* edited by C. Humphrey and K. Verdery, 297–318. Oxford: Berg.

———. 2013. "Jurisdiction in dialect: Sovereignty games in the British Virgin Islands." In *European integration and postcolonial sovereignty games,* edited by R. Adler-Nissen and U. P. Gadd, 130–144. New York: Routledge.

Mbembe, Achille. 2003. "Necropolitics." *Public Culture* 15 (1): 11–40.

McNally, David. 2011. *Monsters of the market: Zombies, vampires, and global capitalism.* Leiden: Brill.

Mehta, Uday Singh. 1999. *Liberalism and empire: A study in nineteenth-century British liberal thought.* Chicago: Chicago University Press.

———. 2010. "Constitutionalism." In *The Oxford handbook of politics in India*, edited by Niraja Jayal and Pratap B. Mehta, 15–27. Delhi: Oxford University Press.

———. 2016. "Indian constitutionalism: Crisis, unity, and history." In *The Oxford handbook of the Indian constitution*, edited by Sujit Choudhry, Madhav Khosla, and Pratap Banu Mehta, 38–54. Delhi: Oxford University Press.

Menon, Nivedita. 2011. "The Ayodhya judgement: What next?" *Economic and Political Weekly* 46 (31): 81–89.

Merlan, Francesca. 2009. "Indigeneity: Global and local." *Current Anthropology* 50 (3): 303–333.

Merry, Sally Engle. 1989. "Legal pluralism." *Law and Society Review* 22 (5): 869–896.

———. 1990. *Getting justice and getting even: Legal consciousness amongst working-class Americans.* Chicago: Chicago University Press.

———. 2006. *Human rights and gender violence: Translating international law into local justice.* Chicago: Chicago University Press.

Mezey, Naomi. 2001. "Law as culture." *Yale Journal of Law and Humanities* 13: 35–67.

———. 2007. "The paradoxes of cultural property." *Columbia Law Review* 7: 2004–2046.

Mezzadri, Alessandra. 2017. *The sweatshop regime: Labouring bodies, exploitation, and garments made in India.* Cambridge: Cambridge University Press.

Michelutti, Lucia. 2019. "Circuits of protection and extortion: Sovereignty in a provincial north Indian town." In *South Asian sovereignty: The conundrum of worldly power*, edited by D. Gilmartin, P. Price, and A. E. Ruud, 150–171. New Delhi: Routledge India.

Middleton, Leonard. 1919. *Manual of customary law of the Kangra district. (Punjab Customary Law, vol. 28).* Simla: Civil and Military Press.

Mir-Hosseini, Ziba. 2000 [1993]. *Marriage on trial: A study of Islamic family law— Iran and Morocco compared.* London: I. B. Tauris.

Mody, Perveez. 2008. *The intimate state: Love-marriage and the law in Delhi.* New Delhi: Routledge.

Mookherjee, Nayanika. 2015. *The spectral wound: Sexual violence, public memories, and the Bangladesh War of 1971*. Durham, NC: Duke University Press.

Moore, Sally Falk. 2002. "Certainties undone: Fifty turbulent years of legal anthropology, 1949–1999." *Journal of the Royal Anthropological Institute* 7 (1): 95–116.

Motha, Stewart. 2018. *Archiving sovereignty: Law, violence, empire*. Ann Arbor: University of Michigan Press.

Moumtaz, Nada. 2020. *God's property: Islam, charity, and the modern state*. Berkeley: University of California Press.

Mukherjee, Mithi. 2010. *India in the shadows of empire: A legal and political history (1774–1950)*. Delhi: Oxford University Press.

Mullally, Siobhan. 2004. "Feminism and multicultural dilemmas in India: Revisiting the Shah Bano case." *Oxford Journal of Legal Studies* 24 (4): 671–692.

Naipaul, V. S. 1989 [1961]. *A house for Mr. Biswas*. New York: Vintage.

Nair, Savithri Preetha. 2002. *The museum in colonial India (1770–1936): A history of collecting, exhibiting, and disciplining knowledge*. Unpublished doctoral dissertation. SOAS, University of London.

Nair, Vijayanka. 2018. "An eye for an I: Recording biometrics and reconsidering identity in postcolonial India." *Contemporary South Asia* 26 (2): 143–156.

Nancy, Jean-Luc. 2007. "Church, state, resistance." *Journal of Law and Society* 34 (1): 3–13.

Nandy, Ashis. 1981. "From outside the imperium: Gandhi's cultural critique of the 'West'." *Alternatives* 7 (2): 171–194.

Navaro, Yael. 2020. "The aftermath of violence: A negative methodology." *Annual Review of Anthropology* 49: 161–173.

Naziruddin, Ahmad. 1949. *Fallacy of the Hindu code bill exposed*. New Delhi: Pearson Press.

Newell, Alexander. 2019. "On the hospitality of hoarders: Accumulations and relations in US domestic space." *L'Homme* 231/232: 111–134.

Ocko, Jonathan K., and David Gilmartin. 2009. "State, sovereignty, and the people: A comparison of the 'rule of law' in China and India." *The Journal of Asian Studies* 68 (1): 55–100.

O'Flaherty, Wendy Doniger. 1973. *Siva: The erotic ascetic*. New York: Oxford University Press.

———. 1984. *Dreams, illusion, and other realities.* Chicago: Chicago University Press.

Orlove, Daniel J. 2004. *The digital person: Technology and privacy in the information age.* New York: New York University Press.

Orwell, George. 1944. "As I please". *Tribune,* January 28, 1944. Accessed September 4, 2020. http://www.telelib.com/authors/O/OrwellGeorge/essay/tribune/AsIPlease19440128.html.

Ostrom, Elinor. 1990. *Governing the commons: The evolution of institutions for collective action.* Cambridge: Cambridge University Press.

Pande, Amrita. 2014. *Wombs in labour: Commercial surrogacy in India.* New York: Columbia University Press.

Pandya, Vishwajit. 1993. *Above the forest: A study of Andamanese ethnoanemology, cosmology, and the power of ritual.* Delhi: Oxford University Press.

———. 2013. "In terra nullius: The legacies of science and colonialism in the Andaman Islands." Lecture presented at the Nehru Memorial Library and Museum, Teen Murti, New Delhi, May 22, 2013.

Parashar, Archana. 1992. *Women and family law reform in India.* New Delhi: Sage.

Parker, Kunal M. 2005. "The historiography of difference." *Law and History Review* 23 (3): 685–695.

Parry, Jonathan. 1979. *Caste and kinship in Kangra.* London: Routledge.

———. 1986. "The gift, the Indian gift, and the 'Indian gift'." *Man* 21 (3): 453–473.

———. 1994. *Death in Benaras.* Cambridge: Cambridge University Press.

Pathak, Zakia, and Rajeshwari Sunder Rajan. 1989. "Shahbano." *Signs* 14 (3): 558–582.

Peletz, Michael G. 2002. *Islamic modern: Religious courts and cultural politics in Malaysia.* Princeton, NJ: Princeton University Press.

Peluso, Nancy. 1992. *Rich forests, poor people: Resource control and resistance in Java.* Berkeley: University of California Press.

Phillimore, Peter. 2014. "'That used to be a famous village': Shedding the past in rural north India." *Modern Asian Studies* 48 (1): 159–187.

Pillai, Sarath. 2016. "Fragmenting the nation: Divisible sovereignty and Travancore's quest for federal independence." *Law and History Review* 34 (3): 743–782.

Pinch, William R. 2013. "Prostituting the mutiny: Sex-slavery and crime in the making of 1857." In *Mutiny at the margins: New perspectives on the*

Indian uprising of 1857, Vol. 1 (Anticipations and experiences in the locality), edited by Crispin Bates, 61–87. New Delhi: Sage.

Pinney, Christopher. 2011. *Photography and anthropology*. London: Reaktion Books.

Pistor, Katherine. 2019. *The code of capital: How the law creates wealth and inequality*. New Jersey: Princeton University Press.

Pitroda, Sam. 2015. *Dreaming big: My journey to connect India*. New Delhi: Penguin.

Pitt-Rivers, Julian. 2017. "The law of hospitality." In *From hospitality to grace: The Julian Pitt-Rivers Omnibus*, edited by Giovanni da Col and A. Shryock, 163–184. Chicago: Hau Books.

Pottage, Alain. 2001. "Persons and things: An ethnographic analogy." *Economy and Society* 30 (1): 112–138.

———. 2007. "The socio-legal implications of the new biotechnologies." *Annual Review of Law and Social Science* 3 (1): 321–344.

Pottage, Alain, and Martha Mundy, eds. 2004. *Law, anthropology, and the constitution of the social: Making persons and things*. Cambridge: Cambridge University Press.

Povinelli, Elizabeth A. 2002. *The cunning of recognition: Indigenous alterities and the making of Australian multiculturalism*. Durham, NC: Duke University Press.

———. 2006. *The empire of love: Toward a theory of intimacy, genealogy, and carnality*. Durham, NC: Duke University Press.

Prakash, Gyan. 1990. *Bonded histories: Genealogies of labour servitude in colonial India*. Cambridge: Cambridge University Press.

———. 2019. *Emergency chronicles: Indira Gandhi and democracy's turning point*. Princeton, NJ: Princeton University Press.

Prasad, Archana. 2003. *Against ecological romanticism: Verrier Elwin and the making of an anti-modern tribal identity*. New Delhi: Three Essays Collective.

Precarity Lab. 2020. *Technoprecarious*. London: Goldsmiths Press.

Puccio-Den, Deborah. 2019. "Mafiacraft: how to do things with silence." *Hau: Journal of Ethnographic Theory* 9 (3): 599–618.

Purushotham, Sunil. 2021. *From Raj to republic: Sovereignty, violence, and democracy in India*. Stanford: Stanford University Press.

Quigley, Muireann. 2018. *Self-ownership, property rights, and the human body: A legal and philosophical analysis.* Cambridge: Cambridge University Press.

Radcliffe-Brown, Alfred. 1948 [1922]. *The Andaman Islanders: A study in social anthropology.* Cambridge: Cambridge University Press.

Radin, Joanna. 2017. "Digital natives: How medical and indigenous histories matter for Big Data." *Osiris* 32: 43–64.

Raheja, Gloria Goodwin. 1988. *The poison in the gift: Ritual, prestation, and the dominant caste in a north Indian village.* Chicago: Chicago University Press.

Rai, Mridu. 2004. *Hindu rulers, Muslim subjects: Islam, rights, and the history of Kashmir.* London: Hurst.

Ramanathan, Usha. 2010. "On eminent domain and sovereignty." *Seminar* 613, September 2010. http://www.indiaseminar.com/2010/613/613_usha_ramanathan.htm.

Ramnath, N. S., and Charles Assisi. 2018. *The Aadhaar effect: Why the world's largest identity project matters.* Delhi: Oxford University Press.

Ramusack, Barbara. 2003. *The Indian princes and their states.* The New Cambridge History of India. Cambridge: Cambridge University Press.

Ranasinha, Ruvani. 2020. "Establishing material platforms in literary culture in the 1930s and 1940s." *The Cambridge history of Black and Asian British writing*, edited by Susheila Nasta and Mark U. Stein, 132–147. Cambridge: Cambridge University Press.

Ranganathan, Surabhi. 2019. "Ocean floor-grab: International law and the making of an extractive imaginary." *European Journal of International Law* 30 (2): 573–600.

Rangnekar, Dwijen. 2010. "The law and economics of geographical indications: Introduction to special issue of the Journal of World Intellectual Property." *Journal of World Intellectual Property* 13 (2): 77–80.

Rangnekar, Dwijen, and Sanjay Kumar. 2010. "Another look at Basmati: Genericity and the problems of a transborder geographical indication." *Journal of World Intellectual Property* 13 (2): 202–230.

Rao, Ursula, and Vijayanka Nair. 2019. "Aadhaar: Governing with biometrics." *South Asia: Journal of South Asian Studies* 42 (3): 469–481.

Rau, B.N. 1960. *India's constitution in the making.* Bombay: Orient Longmans.

Reddy, Sheela 2010 Interview: *"Khaps* have to reform." *Outlook*, July 10, 2010. Accessed October 28, 2010. http://www.outlookindia.com/article. aspx?266072.

Roe, Charles A., and H. A. B. Rattigan. 1895. *Tribal law in the Punjab: So far as it relates to right in ancestral land.* Lahore: Civil and Military Gazette Press.

Saberwal, Vasant K. 1999. *Pastoral politics: Shepherds, bureaucrats, and conservation in the western Himalayas.* Delhi: Oxford University Press.

Sahlins, Marshall. 2011. "What kinship is (part one)." *Journal of the Royal Anthropological Institute* 17 (1): 2–19.

Sanchez, Andrew, James Carrier, Christopher Gregory, James Laidlaw, Marilyn Strathern, Yunxiang Yan, and Jonathan Parry. 2017. "'The Indian gift': A critical debate." *History and Anthropology* 28 (5): 553–583.

Sangwan, Jagmati 2010 "Khap panchayat: signs of desperation?" *The Hindu*, May 7, 2010. Accessed November 1, 2010. http://beta.thehindu.com/ opinion/lead/article424506.ece.

Santos-Granero, Fernando. 2009. *Vital enemies: Slavery, predation, and the American political economy of life.* Austin: University of Texas Press.

Sanyal, Kalyan. 2007. *Rethinking capitalist development: Primitive accumulation, governmentality, and post-colonial capitalism.* New Delhi: Routledge.

Sarat, Austin, and Jonathan Simon, eds. 2003. *Cultural analysis, cultural studies, and the law: Moving beyond legal realism.* Durham, NC: Duke University Press.

Sarkar, Tanika. 2001. *Hindu wife, Hindu nation: Community, religion, and cultural nationalism.* New Delhi: Permanent Black.

Saumarez-Smith. 1996. *Rule by records: Land registration and village custom in early British India.* Delhi: Oxford University Press.

Schmitt, Carl. 2008. *The concept of the political.* Chicago: Chicago University Press.

Scott, James C., James Tehranian, and Jeremy Matthias. 2002. "The production of legal identities proper to the state: The case of permanent family surnames." *Comparative Studies of Societies and History* 44 (1): 4–44.

Scott, Joan Wallach. 2008. *The politics of the veil.* Princeton, NJ: Princeton University Press.

Sen, Satadru. 2009. *Savagery and colonialism in the Indian Ocean: Power, pleasure, and the Andaman Islands.* New York: Routledge.

Sen, Suhit. 2017. "The politics of bank nationalisation in India." In *Accumulation in postcolonial capitalism*, edited by Iman Kumar Mitra, Ranabir Samaddar, and Samita Sen, 125–145. London: Springer.

Sen, Uditi. 2017. "Developing *terra nullius*: Colonialism, nationalism, and indigeneity in the Andaman Islands." *Comparative Studies of Society and History* 59 (4): 944–973.

Sengoopta, Chandak. 2003. *Imprint of the Raj: How fingerprinting was born in colonial India*. London: Macmillan.

Serres, Michel. 2007 [1982]. *Parasite*. Minneapolis: University of Minnesota Press.

Sharma, Daamini. 2018. "Madhumala Chattopadhyay: The Indian woman who first established friendly contact with the Sentinelese." Blogpost at *Republic World*. Accessed February 2020. https://www.republicworld. com/india-news/general-news/madhumala-chattopadhyay-indian-woman-who-established-first-friendly-contact-with-sentinelese-tribe. html.

Sharma, K. L. 1976. "Jharkhand movement in Bihar." *Economic and Political Weekly* 11 (1/2): 37–43.

Sharma, Vrinda 2010. "'Khap panchayat' leaders condemn court ruling." *The Hindu*, April 13, 2010. Accessed November 1, 2010. http://www.the-hindu.com/news/national/article396373.ece.

Silbey, Susan S. 2005. "After legal consciousness." *Annual Review of Law and the Social Sciences* 1: 323–368.

Simpson, Nikita. 2021. *Tension: An ethnographic study of women's mental distress in rural north India*. PhD Thesis submitted to the Department of Anthropology, London School of Economics.

Singh, Bhrigupati. 2015. *Poverty and the quest for life: Spiritual and material staving in rural India*. Chicago: Chicago University Press.

Singh, Bhrigupati and Jane I. Guyer. 2016. "A joyful history of anthropology." *HAU: Journal of Ethnographic Theory* 6 (2): 197–211.

Singh, Ranjit. 2020. *Seeing like an infrastructure: Mapping uneven state-citizen relations in Aadhaar-enabled digital India*. Unpublished PhD dissertation. Department of Science and Technology Studies, Cornell University.

Singh, Tripudaman. 2020. *Sixteen stormy days: The story of the first amendment to the Constitution of India*. New Delhi: Penguin Viking.

Singha, Radhika. 1998. *A despotism of law: Crime and justice in early colonial India*. Delhi: Oxford University Press.

Sinha, Surajit and Baidyanath Saraswati. 1978. *The ascetics of Kashi: An anthropological exploration.* Varanasi: N. K. Bose Memorial Society.

Sivaramakrishnan, K. 2000. *Modern forests: Statemaking and environmental change in colonial eastern India.* Stanford: Stanford University Press.

Siwach, Sukhbir 2010. "In Jatland, child marriages to prevent girls eloping." *Times of India,* June 26, 2010. Accessed July 8, 2010. http://timesofindia.indiatimes.com/india/In-Jatland-child-marriages-to-prevent-girls-from-eloping/articleshow/6093087.cms.

Skaria, Ajay. 1997. "Shade of wildness: Tribe, caste, and gender in western India." *Journal of Asian Studies* 56 (3): 726–745.

———. 2002. "Gandhi's politics: Liberalism and the question of the *ashram*." *South Atlantic Quarterly* 101 (4): 955–986.

Solanki, Aakash. 2019. "Management of performance and performance of management: Getting to work on time in the Indian bureaucracy." *South Asia: Journal of South Asian Studies* 42 (3): 588–605.

Srivatsan, R. 2005. "Native noses and nationalist zoos: Debates in colonial and early nationalist anthropology of castes and tribes." *Economic and Political Weekly* 40 (19): 1986–1998.

Srnicek, Nick. 2016. *Platform capitalism.* Cambridge: Polity.

Ssorin-Chaikov, Nikolai. 2006. "On heterochrony: Birthday gifts to Stalin." *Journal of the Royal Anthropological Institute* 12 (2): 355–375.

Strathern, Marilyn. 1981. "Culture in a netbag: The manufacture of a sub-discipline in anthropology." *Man* 16 (4): 665–688.

———. 1988a. *The gender of the gift: Problems with women and problems with society in Melanesia.* Berkeley: University of California Press.

———. 1988b. "Commentary: Concrete topographies." *Cultural Anthropology* 3 (1): 88–96.

———. 1989. "Out of context: The persuasive fictions of anthropology." *Current Anthropology* 28 (3): 251–281.

———. 1992a. *Reproducing the future: Essays on anthropology, kinship, and the new reproductive technologies.* London: Routledge.

———. 1992b. "The decomposition of an event." *Cultural Anthropology* 7 (2): 244–254.

———. 1999. *Property, substance, and effect: Anthropological essays on persons and things.* London: Athlone Press.

———. 2004. "Losing (out on) intellectual resources." In *Law, anthropology, and the constitution of the social: Making persons and things,* edited by

Alain Pottage and Martha Mundy, 201–233. Cambridge: Cambridge University Press.

———. 2005. "The patent and the Malanggan." In *Kinship, law, and the unexpected: Relatives are always a surprise*, 92–110. Cambridge: Cambridge University Press.

———. 2014. "Anthropological reasoning: Some threads of thought." *HAU: Journal of Ethnographic Theory* 4 (3): 23–37.

Stuart, E. M. 1911. "East Indian art handicraft." *Fine Arts Journal* 35 (6): 402–414.

Sundar, Nandini. 2014. "Mimetic sovereignties, precarious citizenship: State effects in looking-glass world." *The Journal of Peasant Studies* 41 (4): 469–490.

Sundaram, Ravi. 2011. *Pirate modernity: Delhi's media urbanism*. New Delhi: Routledge.

———. 2017. "The postcolonial city: From planning to information?" *Techniques and Culture* 67 (Supplement): 1–5.

Sunder, Madhavi. 2003. "Piercing the veil." *The Yale Law Journal* 112 (6): 1399–1474.

Sunder Rajan, Kaushik, ed. 2012. *Lively capital: Biotechnologies, ethics, and governance in global markets*. Durham, NC: Duke University Press.

Supiot, Alain. 2007. *Homo juridicus: On the anthropological function of the law*. London: Verso.

Tarlo, Emma. 2003. *Unsettling memories: Narratives of the emergency in Delhi*. Berkeley: University of California Press.

Taussig, Michael. 2013. *The magic of the state*. New York: Routledge.

Taylor, Anne-Christine. 2001. "Wives, pets, and affines: Marriage among the Jivaro." In *Beyond the visible and the material: The Amerindianisation of society in Peter Rivière's work*, edited by Laura Rival and Neil Whitehead, 45–55. Oxford: Oxford University Press.

———. 2015. "Amazonian friendships: Two against one?" *Terrain* 65: 138–157.

Torpey, John. 2000. *The invention of the passport: Surveillance, citizenship, and the state*. Cambridge: Cambridge University Press.

Trawick, Margaret. 1990. *Notes on love in a Tamil family*. Berkeley: University of California Press.

Tully, James. 2002. "The unfreedom of the moderns in comparison to their ideals of constitutional democracy." *Modern Law Review* 65 (2): 204–228.

Tupper, Charles Lewis. 1881. *Punjab customary law*. 3 vols. Calcutta: Government Printing.

Turner, Terence. 1993. "Anthropology and multiculturalism: What is anthropology that multiculturalists should be mindful of it." *Cultural Anthropology* 8 (4): 411–429.

Uberoi, Patricia. 2002. "Enlightenment eugenics, Hindu orthodoxy, and north Indian prejudice: Legislating the family in post-independence India." *Occasional Papers in Sociology*, 8. Delhi: Institute of Economic Growth.

———, ed. 1996. *Social reform, sexuality, and the state*. New Delhi: Sage.

Vaidik, Aparna. 2010. *Imperial Andamans: Colonial encounter and island history*. New York: Palgrave Macmillan.

Vaidya, Suresh. 1953. *An English prison*. Madras: Teacher's Publishing House.

———. 1960. *Islands of the marigold sun*. London: The Travel Book Club.

Vatuk, Sylvia. 2009. "A rallying cry for Muslim Personal Law: The Shah Bano case and its aftermath." In *Islam in South Asia in practice*, edited by Barbara Metcalfe, 352–368. New Jersey: Princeton University Press.

Verdery, Katherine. 2003. *The vanishing hectare: property and value in postsocialist Transylvania*. Ithaca, NY: Cornell University Press.

Vivieros de Castro, Eduardo. 2009. "The gift and the given: Three nano-essays on kinship and magic." In *Beyond kinship: The genealogical model reconsidered*, edited by Sandra Bamford and James Leach, 237–268. New York: Berghahn Books.

———. 2014. *Cannibal metaphysics: For a poststructural anthropology*. Minneapolis: University of Minnesota Press.

Von Benda-Beckmann, Franz, Keebet von Benda-Beckmann, and Melanie G. Wiber, eds. 2009. *Changing properties of property*. New York: Bergahn Books.

Von Benda-Beckmann, Keebet. 1981. "Forum shopping and shopping forums: Dispute processing in a Minangkabau village in West Sumatra." *The Journal of Legal Pluralism and Unofficial Law* 13 (19): 117–159.

Wagner, Anja. 2013. *The Gaddis beyond pastoralism: Making place in the Indian Himalayas*. London: Bergahn Books.

Wagner, Roy. 1981. *The invention of culture.* Chicago: Chicago University Press.

———. 2001. *An anthropology of the subject: Holographic worldview in New Guinea and its meaning and significance for the world of anthropology.* Berkeley: University of California Press.

Wahi, Namita. 2014. "The tension between property rights and social and economic rights: A case study of India." In *Social and economic rights in theory and practice: Critical inquiries,* edited by Helena Alvia Garcia, Karl Klare, and Lucy A. Williams, 138–157. New York: Routledge.

———. 2015. "The fundamental right to property in the Indian Constitution." Available at SSRN: https://papers.ssrn.com/sol3/papers.cfm?abstract_id=2661212

Weiner, Annette. 1992. *Inalienable possessions: The paradox of keeping-while-giving.* Berkeley: University of California Press.

Wiebe, Andreas. 2017. "Protection of industrial data: A new property right for the digital economy?" *Journal of Intellectual Property Law and Practice* 12 (1): 62–71.

Wilder, Gary. 2015. *Freedom time: Negritude, decolonisation, and the future of the world.* Durham: Duke University Press.

Wilson, Jon. 2010. *The domination of strangers: Modern governance in Eastern India 1780–1835.* New York: Palgrave Macmillan.

Yudice, George. 2003. *The expediency of culture: Uses of culture in the global era.* Durham, NC: Duke University Press.

Zickgraf, Jens M. 2017. "Becoming like money: Proximity and the social aesthetics of 'moneyness'." *HAU: Journal of Ethnographic Theory* 7 (1): 301–326.

Zuboff, Shoshana. 2019. *The age of surveillance capitalism: The fight for a human future at the new frontier of power.* London: Profile Books.

Index

A

Aadhaar (biometric identification card), 20, 133-154; context of, 22, 138; making, 134, 139, 142, 154; mandatory status of, 132, 133, 141. *See also* Puttuswamy, K. S. (Justice)

Aboriginal, 85, 86, 88, 89, 90, 92, 99, 101, 102, 104, 105

accumulation, 5, 10, 1, 17, 50, 57, 59, 60, 61, 62, 68, 76, 144, 150, 157; logic of, 70

Adibasi Mahasabha, 99, 100, 101, 102, 103, 104

Agamben, Giorgio, 6, 12, 13, 155

age, marriageable, 42

agenda, reformist, 29, 39

agnatic, 40, 70, 71

alliance, matrimonial, 27

Amazonian, 6, 80

Andaman Islands, 20, 21, 77, 79-83, 88, 89, 106; Prowlers, 85; refugees, 78. *See also* indigeneity

Andamanese (Jarawas and Senti-nelese), 83, 86, 87, 88, 90, 92, 93, 96, 104, 106. *See also* Anda-man Islands; hospitality; Port Blair.

Anglo Indians, 103

animals, 3, 21, 51, 53, 59, 70; do-mestic, 55-56, 60, 64, 66-67, 146

anthropology: legal, 19, 26; reverse, 92; structural, 6, 155

Anthropological Survey of India, viii, 88, 89, 90, 91

anti-accumulation, 11, 12, 17, 144; coercive, 12

Appadurai, Arjun, 12, 62, 72, 75, 93, 94, 111, 131, 139

architecture, 110, 133, 140, 149

Arendt, Hannah, 147, 153

art, 107, 110, 111, 113, 116, 120, 122, 124

assimilationists, 96, 99

attachment, full, 85, 92, 93

Attorney General. *See under* Rohatgi, Mukul (Attorney General)

ATR (Andaman Trunk Road), 90, 91

Australia, 31, 48, 59

B

bandhua (bonded labor), 144-145
Bangladesh, 43, 85
Bataille, Georges, 12, 13, 19
belief, 38-39, 95, 100
Bengal, Government of, 114, 116n9, 122n17
Beteille, Andre, 95
*Bhagwad Gita,*11
biogenetic substances, 21, 69, 108, 110
body: enslaved, 149; individual, 139, 142; representative, 28
Bombay, 124
Brahminical worldview, 24
Britain, post-war, 130n2
British Government, 100, 117, 125
British India, 34, 83n11, 84, 108, 112; princely states, 58, 83n11, 84, 100

C

Callon, Michel, 22, 110, 122, 123, 124
capacity: judicial, 34; legal, 65, 110; state's, 114
capital, private, 132, 141, 143, 150
capitalism, 131, 148; platform, 141n13; surveillance, 141, 144
caste, 29, 37, 40, 47n21, 53, 93, 94-95, 104, 105, 140; as social character, 97; councils, 27, 28, 41; *dalit* (untouchables), 27, 28, 97; elders, 28; *gotra* (lineal subcaste), 28; groups, 29; hierarchy, 41, 49, 94; patriarchs,

30; *savarna* (twice-born), 28, 97; Scheduled, 97. *See also* violence
categories, stable, 8, 35, 124
census, 58, 98, 110; decennial, 94, 139
Chattopadhyay, Madhumala, 91n22
Chatterjee, Partha, 35n11, 36, 39, 136, 147, 148
child marriages. *See under* marriage
children, 2-3, 21, 43, 56, 60, 61, 68, 69, 70, 145; categories of, 72
Chowdhry, Prem, 2, 9, 30, 41n14, 42, 46
Christians, 46, 103
citizen, 12, 18, 22, 45, 46, 90, 100, 129, 131, 133-36, 141, 142, 149, 150, 152; biometric, 133; possessive, 16, 72
citizen's body, sovereignty of, 136, 137, 138, 150
citizenship, 15, 45, 86, 149
civil code, 37
Civil Judicature, 34
claims: aboriginal property, 104; competing, 69, 117; contested, 65; disputed, 127; political, 104; reciprocity, 115; sustainable, 134; temporal, 104; titular, 115, 126
clan god (*kul-debta*), 56. *See also* Gaddi men
clan goddess (*kulajs*), 3, 21, 56, 57, 61. *See also* Gaddis: women; *jaidaad* (wealth/property)
class, 61, 95, 105, 118, 121; landowning, 125; rural, 34
codification, 31, 34; legal, 68
Cohen, Lawrence, 108, 132

Cohn, Bernard, 49n1, 94, 106, 110, 111, 139

colonial, 5, 7, 13n6, 22, 32-35, 49, 57, 63, 71, 73, 82, 86, 106-09, 111, 118, 125, 130, 147-49, 151; administration, 67; conceptualization of India, 110, 123; expansion, 19; imaginary, 122; India, 49n1; rule, 33; transition to postmodern, 77, 78, 80, 83, 86, 87, 90, 93

colony, 82, 110; penal, 79, 89, 91n21

commodities, 109, 141, 143, 149

community, 3, 34, 44; national, 37, 99; pastoral, 3; tribal, 105

compensation, 15, 103, 118, 146

conjugal unit, 38-39, 66

consent, age of, 38

consequences, 4, 33, 46, 48; long-term, 15; triggering, 40

Constituent Assembly, 97-99

Constitution, 13, 14-16, 20, 27, 32n5, 35, 37, 41, 45-47, 73, 98, 100, 109, 134, 156

contexts: historical, 111; recent, 109

control, dispositional, 22

councils, 30, 33-34, 41, 113, 117; local, 28, 33; specialist, 33; tribal, 33

courts, 25, 35

cultural: category, 48, 95; commodification, 127; consumerism, 110; history, 127; norms, 31; prevailing, 34; practices, 31, 44, 48

culture, 20, 26, 27, 29, 30-32, 33, 35, 37, 39, 40, 41, 44-48, 80, 96, 103, 107-127; material, 109;

position, 45. *See also* Aboriginal; theft

cultures of consumption, 111

D

Da Col, Giovanni, 11n5, 19, 62, 79, 80, 93

data: aggregate, 140; emergence of, 143, 150; individuate, 140; ownership, 132; servitude, 149; -work, 143

databases, 141-42; searchable, 139; universal, 141

daughters, 3, 38, 43, 46, 65, 67

death penalty, 28

debt, 6, 13, 15n11, 22, 52, 103, 147-149, 152, 154; permanent, 150; unpaid, 103, 145

demographics, 134

Derrida, Jacques, 31, 47, 48, 80

Descola, Philippe, 21, 80, 87, 88, 97

dhan (flock), 53, 54, 55, 59, 60, 67. *See also* wealth

Dhauladhar mountain range, 3, 146

difference: aesthetic, 118; heteronomous, 102, 104; normative, 31; religious, 99; scalar, 95, 96; social, 96

difference-as-inequality, 98-99

digital, 137, 138, 141, 142, 143, 144; dossier, 139, 140, 142; identification, 132, 134. *See also* Aadhaar; biometric; liberty; surveillance

discourse, 148; legal, 97; post-Enlightenment, 148; public, 96

discrimination, 37, 47n21, 87, 94, 97, 98, 99, 102, 105

dispossession, 1, 4-7, 8, 12, 19, 20, 21, 49-76, 108, 130
disputes: adjudicating, 35; domestic, 28; local, 33; settled, 113
dividual. *See* personhood
divine, 10, 12, 23, 156
divorce, 147; legal, 38
doctrine of corpus nullius, 7, 8, 13, 18, 20, 22, 129-154. *See also* servitude
doctrine of res nullius, 7, 8, 13, 18, 20, 22, 107-127
doctrine of terra nullius, 7, 8, 13, 15, 18, 19, 20, 21, 77-106, 108, 118, 126
Dolgin, Janet, 69, 135
Dowleans, A. M., 116, 117, 120, 122, 125
dowry 29, 66, 70
Dowry Prohibition Act of 1961, 65
Dumont, Louis, 40, 94

E

Eastern Europe, 108
East India Company, 116-17
economy: modern market, 147; new, 132, 144; political, 42, 74, 104, 150, 151, 154; rural, 42
elopement, 2, 4, 50
empire, 82, 92, 107, 110-111, 114
employment, right to, 17
entitlement, 67; presumed, 136
equality, 14, 32, 38, 40, 44, 46-48, 95-96, 99, 102; domestic, 44; formal, 105; guaranteed, 103
equity, 14, 38, 44, 96
erasure, 7, 131, 144, 150
ethnicity, 95
Euro-America, 31

Europe, 31, 121, 123
exception, notion of, 6
exchange, 4, 40, 45, 108-10, 113-14, 116-18, 123, 126, 142, 148; colonial strategies, 22; commodity, 109; discrete, 142; isogamous, 146; monetary, 148; symbolic, 45
Exhibitions, Great, 22, 107, 110, 11, 112, 118; circulation of scientific knowledge and objects, 111; expropriation, 114-115; manufacturing potential, 121. *See also* colonial
extraction: revenue, 63, 100; extractive fear, 62

F

fabrics, valuable, 121-22
facial scans, 137, 139
family, 38, 40, 66-68, 114, 136, 145; natal, 65-66
fingerprints, 134, 136, 137, 139, 142, 153
First Nations theory, 31
flock: large, 146; pastoral, 66
freedom, 7, 8, 13, 14, 15, 16, 18, 44, 50, 130, 132, 137, 149, 150, 152
freedom-unfreedom paradigm, 148
friendship, 88, 89, 111
friendly contact, 83, 90, 91
forum shopping, 20, 47n20, 156
Frazer, Sir James, 151

G

Gaddis: 3, 4, 21, 50-76, 144, 145, 148, 149; marriage, 57; men, 59,

146; relation to divine, 21, 55, 56, 58, 76; women, 3, 55, 56, 65, 66, 68, 146
Gandhi, Indira, 17
Gandhi, Mahatma, 25, 49, 75, 152, 153, 154
gender, 38, 44, 47, 95, 109, 134, 140; dynamics, 29; imbalance, 65
Ghurye-Elwin debate, 96
gifts, 22, 45, 47, 109, 118, 125
goats, 66-67, 146
gold, 120-21
goods: artisanal, 123; consumer, 123; industrial, 117; market, 123; primitive, 122; surplus, 114, 118; worldly, 11
Grey, W. (British Secretary to the Government of India), 112, 116, 117
groups: affluent, 29; backward, 99; sublineal exogamous, 28; tribal, 104
Guha, B. S., 88
Guha, Ranajit, 125
Gupta, Akhil, 5
Gupta, Dipankar, 93

H

handicrafts, 123-124
hau (excess produced in giving), 1, 8, 45n18, 155. *See also* gifts; dispossession; erasure
Hegel, Georg Wilhelm Friedrich, 7, 8, 16
herding, 3, 54, 56, 58, 59, 61, 67, 68, 145, 146
herds, 60, 145, 146

heirs, 38, 70, 71; categories of, 70; equal, 38, 43; female, 65, 67; male, 43; new, 40; order of, 65; primary, 41; producing, 42
heritability, 147
heritage, 126-27
heterogeneity, 37; normative, 32
hierarchies: competing, 94; new, 104; traditional, 32
hierarchy, 14, 40, 47, 94, 96; distinction between difference and, 93; logic of, 96; ritual, 95, 97
Hindu, 10, 34, 38, 40, 46
Hindu Code Bill, 36-37, 39-40, 44
Hindu Marriage Act (HMA), 20, 30, 35, 36, 38, 39, 41, 43, 46
Hindu Succession Act (HSA), 20, 35, 36, 38, 40, 41, 43, 46, 65, 67, 68, 70
homosexuality, criminalized, 46
hospitality, 6, 11n5, 79, 80, 93, 103, 104; anthropology of, 79, 80; hostility and friendship, 88
households, 40, 43, 67, 126, 147; joint, 38; large herd-owning, 146
husband, 65-67

I

identification, 56, 80, 82, 87, 93, 121, 136, 138; biometric, 19, 20, 22, 132, 133, 134, 135, 140, 151; digital, 132, 134; originary, 102; photo, 153; social, 96
identity, 101, 141, 142, 152, 153. *See also* Aboriginal
identity politics, 30, 93, 94

illusion, 9, 10, 12, 23, 155, 156. *See also maya*

Independence, 16, 18, 35, 81, 84, 93, 97, 106, 126; post-, 27, 29, 35, 79, 83, 86, 87

India: contemporary, 3, 5, 32, 37, 94-95, 144; eastern, 43; independent, 15, 37, 39, 149; law in, 18, 31, 46, 48, 138, 144; modern, 18; tribal, 98

Indian Constitution: *See under* Constitution

Indian Penal Code, 46

Indian society: contemporary, 7, 95; north, 36, 40, 42

Indian state: contemporary, 10; paternalistic, 44

indigeneity, 21, 81, 93, 105, 106

individuals, private, 107, 115, 117, 125

inequality, 99, 105

information: financial, 140; statistical, 138

inheritance, 35, 68

injury, historical, 97

institutions: local juridical, 33; new legal, 37; social, 42

integrationists, 99

Islam, 31, 33, 101

Islanders. *See under* Andaman Islands

isogamy (*atta-satta*), 57, 146. *See also* Gaddis: marriage

isolationists, 99

J

jaidaad (wealth/property), 3, 21, 60, 61, 63, 68, 69. *See also* Gaddis; property; wealth

Jarawa: *See under* Andamanese

jewelry, women use, 68. *See also dhan, jaidaad, streedhan*, wealth

justice, 14, 27-28; blood, 27; popular, 29, 32; redistributive, 14, 105; runaway, 28

K

Karnal court, 28

khap panchayats (caste councils/caste elders), 27, 28, 29, 41, 42, 43, 45, 48. *See also* caste

killings, 28; honor, 28, 30, 41. *See also* caste

kinship, 4, 10, 11, 20, 27, 36, 38, 40, 47, 51, 56, 59, 63, 64, 68, 71, 145, 146, 147; Hindu, 37; north Indian, 41-42

kinship rules, Dravidian, 36n13

L

labor, 13, 19, 45, 54, 55, 56, 59, 130-154, 155; bride-service (*mundai*), 145, 146, 147; manual, 121; migrant, 146; misappropriation of, 131; non-waged, 148; uncompensated, 8, 131, 147; wage, 54, 61, 146, 147. *See also* personhood

laborers, indentured, 152, 153

labor relations, 148

land, 15, 33-34, 65, 67-68, 102-5, 109, 125, 144, 146, 156-57; agricultural, 65; dispossession of, 130; foreign, 32; reforms, 125; usury rights, 21; value of, 33, 42. *See also* Aboriginal

Land Alienation Act, 70, 71

law, 7, 14, 19, 31-33, 35, 37-39, 41, 44-48, 66, 99-100, 102; all-India, 35, 37; and culture, 20, 26, 30, 31, 32, 35, 37, 44, 45, 47, 48, 155; and popular justice, 32; anthropology of, 7, 27; colonial, 30, 71; Constitutional, 30, 37; customary, 34-35; doctrinal, 18; Euro-American, 31; force of, 48; gender-blind, 65; Indian state, 44; liberal, 125; modern, 14, 148-49; modern India, 11; modern liberal, 26; monadic calculus, 46, 48; new, 25, 33, 39, 40, 42, 70; personal, 34; postcolonial, 39; private, 108; promissory, 27; public, 108; regional case, 35; state, 30. *See* Civil Judicature; theft

legal: framework, 14, 32, 47, 65, 98, 116; norms, 30-32, 37, 39; pluralism, 20, 26, 32, 156

Lévy-Bruhl, Lucien, 151, 152.

liberty, 14, 45, 124, 130, 135-36, 152; personal, 32

life: mechanical, 153; *mokshic* (ascetic) 10, 11, 12; national, 97; political, 45; religious, 11; *samsaric* (worldly), 11; social, 14, 40, 44, 95

litigation, 33

logic, 45, 96; compensatory, 97; enumerative, 138-39; proprietorial, 144; singular, 103

M

male-child preference, 42

Malinowski, Bronislaw, 25, 26

manufactures: indigenous, 118; textile, 120

manufacturing, 121

marginality, 94

market forces, 123

marriage, 29-30, 33, 35, 40-43, 66; bad, 41; by abduction, 43; child, 43; payments, 33, 43, 44; re-marriage, 33, 38

Marx, Karl, 129, 147

material extravagance, 3

maya, doctrine of, 9-10. *See also moh-maya*

Melanesian, 45

members, tribal, 96, 99, 101

Merlan, Francesca, 104

methodology, negative, 5

military service, 130

Milner, Alfred, 153

minorities, 99-100; legal, 46; religious, 100; sexual, 46; statistical, 99, 101

misrecognize, 108, 113, 126

mobility, upward, 29, 41, 144

moh-maya, 10. *See also* anti-accumulation; life: *samsaric*

modernity, 30, 37, 41, 96-97

morality, conservative sexual, 4

Muhammadan Laws, 34

multicultural states, 31, 98-99

multinationalists, 99

Munda. *See under* Singh, Jaipal

murders, 28, 30, 77

Museum, Victoria and Albert, 20, 22, 125, 127

museums, 110, 116, 120. *See also* objects

Muslim Personal Code, 48

mythical thinking, 9-10

N

nationalism, 36, 87
nation-state, 37, 83, 87, 88, 91, 95, 96, 97, 98, 99, 104, 111, 149
New Zealand, 54, 59
nonrecognition, 33, 35, 37, 39, 92, 99, 100, 118
norms, prevailing, 36
North America, 31
North India, 28-30, 32, 40-41

O

objects: as raw material, 117, 119, 122, 123; assessment of, 120, 121; collected, 120; domestic, 11; museum, 5; nineteenth-century, 109; scientific, 122; showcased, 118
Orwell, George, 130
owners, 67, 114, 117-18, 123, 142, 146, 153; absolute, 65; original, 22, 100, 115, 125-26
ownership, 3-5, 18-19, 22, 102-4, 108, 115, 117, 125, 127, 141, 143-44, 146, 149-50; contested, 107; corporeal, 138; illusion of, 23; inalienable, 104; language of, 64; legal, 44-45; native, 126; new, 108; proprietary, 156; self, 149

P

Pandit, T. N., 91
Partition of India (1948), 78, 83n11, 84, 85
pastoralism, Gaddi, 53, 58, 59, 72, 145; transhumant, 55, 57

Patel, Sardar, 79, 86, 99
permanence, marital, 2
Personal Codes, 46, 100; religion-based, 37
personhood, 22, 36, 130; di-vidual, 46; legal, 125. *See also* dispossession
photography, 119, 134, 151, 152
PIL (public interest litigation), 133-34
pishach, vampiric, 156, 157
Pitt-Rivers, Julian, 80, 93,
politics, 48, 94, 98, 104-5, 26; anti-modern, 153; democratic, 94; indigenous, 105
polygamy, 39; outlawing, 38
Poona Pact of 1935, 99
Port Blair, 82, 87, 88, 89, 90, 91
possessions, 3-5, 1-12, 66, 112-13
postcolonial era, 5-6, 7, 18, 29, 36-37, 80, 88, 95-96, 102, 104, 126
Povinelli, Elizabeth, 48
power, 4, 9, 16, 110; agentive, 109; artistic, 9; colonizing, 112, 148; growing political, 42; sovereign, 108-9, 123, 126, 154; state, 5, 7, 31, 108-10
Prasad, Rajendra, 36, 110
predation, 6, 19, 81, 88, 90, 106
principles, 40, 94, 98; bedrock, 41; compensatory, 97; liberal, 99; structuring, 36; upholding, 14
privacy, 18, 22, 132, 134-36, 143; Indic notions of, 135. *See also* surveillance
products: handwoven, 120; infe-rior, 121; natural, 121
property, 3, 5, 11, 14-15, 17-18, 34, 36, 38, 65-68, 102-4, 107-10, 112, 116, 18, 125-27, 149-50;

ancestral, 65, 68; anthropology of, 50n2; codification, 63, 68; commons, 55, 57-58; cultural, 127; Gaddi woman's, 66; immovable, 65-66; intellectual, 108, 126; joint family, 68; matrilineal, 61; place of, 4, 109; private, 108. 125; question, 3, 8, 15, 18, 32, 93, 126, 157; registered, 66; relations, 18, 19, 21, 27, 63, 108, 109, 110, 12, 126; rights, 38, 65, 71, 103, 110; women's, 21, 51, 55, 56, 64, 68

Property Act of 1937, 36

property forms, 108, 110, 126-27, 132-33, 143, 150; emergent, 132; new, 131, 143, 150

proprietor, male, 65

puhaal (apprentice), 59, 145, 146, 147

Punjab, 25, 32-35, 147

Puttuswamy, K. S. (Justice), 22, 133-35

R

reciprocity, 115, 117-18

recognition: legal, 33, 48; nominal, 100; partial, 104; political, 100; tribal, 101

reform, 29, 36, 38-40, 44 95; anthropology of, 38; prison, 130; radical, 38; social, 29, 44, 95-96; welfare, 99. *See also* Hindu Marriage Act; Hindu Succession Act

regimes, 131; circulatory, 127; classificatory, 107, 110; new, 33; new revenue, 127; state juridical, 34

relation: affective, 66; debt, 22, 145, 147; gender, 36, 45; horizontal, 42; husband-wife, 46; important personal, 34; local, 4; prior, 118; proprietary, 3; social, 47, 110; state-citizen, 22, 135, 152; state-data, 132, 133, 150; state-labor, 133; wage, 148

relativism, cultural, 6

religion, 37, 40, 46-47, 95, 99, 101-3, 136; tribal, 100

religious codes, 34

Report on Minority Rights of 1947, 101

repression, 153

resources, 48, 66, 104, 125-26; expedient, 48; joint, 67

revenant, 156-57. *See also pishach*

rights, 14, 17, 32, 36, 43-46, 48, 101, 103, 149, 157; aborigine, 31; absolute, 22, 129, 134; equal dispositional, 41; fundamental, 15; group, 98; human, 31; inalienable, 103; prescriptive, 100; qualified, 104; retained, 136; theft of, 44-45; usury, 21

ritual, 2, 20, 40, 41, 54, 57, 60, 61, 62, 64, 82, 85, 95, 97, 105, 146; discrimination, 97; mortuary, 156; practices, 95

Rohatgi, Mukul (Attorney General), 129, 134, 136, 137, 149

rules, 3, 26, 32, 34, 35, 37, 63, 71

Rushdie, Salman, 31

S

Santos-Granero, Fernando, 150, 151

scalar. *See under* difference

Second World War, 129
secularism, 95-96
Sentinelese. *See under* Andamanese.
services: accessing state, 134, 140;
    compulsory military, 129-130
servitude, 22, 133, 144-48; data-,
    149; eternal, 145; marked debt-
    derived, 147
sex ratio, 42, 47; declining, 43; un-
    balanced, 42
sheep, 67, 146
Schmitt, Carl, 12
Sikhs, 103
silver, 66, 124; real, 120; solid, 124
Singh, Jaipal, 101-3, 105
slavery, 22, 129, 147-49; abolition
    of, 131; colonial anxiety of, 147;
    modern-day, 129, 131, 147
Smuts, J. C., 153
social abuses, worst, 29
social practices, isolated, 38
social values, 31, 42
sons, 40, 43, 65-67, 145
South Africa, 152-53
South Asia, 110, 154
sovereign. *See under* state
sovereignty, 5-6, 11-12, 19, 22,
    100, 108-9, 118, 125, 135-36;
    anthropology of, 6, 22, 155;
    -making, 4.
state: anthropology of, 5; as pro-
    prietor, 109; courts, 33-34; set-
    tler-colonialism, 19; sovereign,
    4-5, 7, 12, 19, 22, 39, 126, 130-
    31, 133, 144, 150; policy, 17,
    95; welfare, 97, 106. *See also* bi-
    ometrics; colonial; ownership;
    postcolonial era; possessions;
    power; sovereignty

status, 29, 36-37, 47, 66, 98-99,
    105, 107-8, 110, 116-17, 122-
    23, 146; fragile, 108; indistinct,
    109; industrial, 123; propri-
    etary, 116; salaried, 144
Strathern, Marilyn, 5, 6, 8, 32, 44,
    46, 47, 63, 64, 109, 110, 132,
    143
stratification, social, 94
streedhan (women's wealth), 64, 65,
    66,
subject: colonized, 130; legal, 65
Supreme Court, 17, 47, 133, 137.
Suresh, Vaidya, 129
surveillance, 18, 22, 132, 134, 138,
    141, 150, 153. *See also* capital-
    ism; Aadhaar
survey, anthropometric, 139

T

technologies, 28, 43, 95, 109, 137,
    154; biocultural, 108; corporeal,
    137; elicitory, 136; governmen-
    tal, 94; invasive, 137; reproduc-
    tive, 43
territory. *See under* land
textiles, 117, 120
theft, 45, 107, 109, 114-15, 126
things, anthropology of, 22, 109.
    See also objects
title: absolute, 21; indigenous, 5,
    126; prior, 15, 126; proprietary,
    115, 126
tradition, 30; bad, 97
transactions, 108, 111, 114, 118,
    140-42; financial, 140
transfers, 68, 152
transformation, 2, 9, 38, 41, 110,
    121, 123, 133, 142-43

transformative labor, Gaddi notions of, 133 *See also* Aadhaar; relation; servitude
transhumance/transhumant pastoralism. *See under* pastoralism
tribal: interests, 98, 100-101, 104; selfhood, 104; uprisings, 101
tribes, 95-100; category, 96, 98; heteronomous, 103; hill, 99; integration, 87, 99, 100; positioning, 103; Scheduled, 73, 92, 104, 105n32; the question of, 98. *See also* Andaman Islands; Aboriginal

U

Union of India, 21, 22, 83n11, 84, 88
unfreedom, 148

V

value, 44, 107, 114, 120-23, 132-33, 140-43; little, 123; low, 124; political, 132; potential, 141; surplus, 123

Victoria and Albert Museum. *See under* Museum, Victoria and Albert. *See also* exchange
vitality, 148, 151, 152, 154. *See also* life
violence, 27, 41, 99, 127; efficacious, 30; khap-inspired, 48

W

Wagner, Roy, 92
war, 44, 130. *See also* Second World War
wealth, 3, 10-11, 21, 38, 44, 53, 55, 56, 60, 61, 62, 63, 68, 133; items of, 66; new, 42; personal, 61, 62, 63, 68, 133; women's, 64, 65, 66. *See also dhan; jaidaad; streedhan*
weddings, 2-3, 29, 65. *See also dhan*
wives, 4, 9, 38, 40, 46, 66-67, 146
women's labor. *See under* labor
women's property. *See under* animals; heirs; jewelry; property, women's; wealth
Women's Rights to Property Act of 1937, 36
work, manual, 122, 145